'Mendelsohn takes the classical [...] and Sappho, Homer and Horace ... He w[...] clearly they come to feel like some of the most important things you have ever been told'
SEBASTIAN BARRY

'Persuasively shows how traces of the Greek classics can be found in the most unlikely places ... Mendelsohn makes his links with ingenuity, erudition and wit'
New Statesman

'Sparkling ... Some of the pieces weave memoir and literary analysis, like the touching final essay of the collection, on his epistolary relationship with Mary Renault, who encouraged his love of Greek culture. Which is, perhaps, exactly what these clear, witty and enthralling essays will do for many more'
Tatler, Book of the Week

'As I was reading *The Bad Boy of Athens*, I was often reminded that Daniel Mendelsohn is not only an incisive critic and elegant prose stylist but also a brilliant translator ... There are many pleasures in reading these essays, from the beautiful prose to the occasional flashes of barbed sarcasm ... His versatility as a writer is such that, whenever he announces a new project, I feel both anticipation at the forthcoming work and a twinge of sadness that he will be writing less in other genres. While I eagerly await his *Odyssey* translation, reading *The Bad Boy of Athens* made me hope that he doesn't abandon critical essays entirely while he takes on that monumental project'
TLS

'The classical world has provided a constant whetstone for his critical acumen, and his essays are bright, occasionally irreverent, ruminations about our connection with antiquity'
The Oldie

ALSO BY DANIEL MENDELSOHN

The Elusive Embrace: Desire and the Riddle of Identity
Gender and the City in Euripides' Political Plays
The Lost: A Search for Six of Six Million
How Beautiful It Is and How Easily It Can Be Broken: Essays
C.P. Cavafy: Collected Poems, Translated with Introduction
and Commentary
Waiting for the Barbarians: Essays from the Classics to Pop Culture
An Odyssey: A Father, a Son and an Epic

The Bad Boy of Athens

Classics from the Greeks
to Game of Thrones

Daniel Mendelsohn

WILLIAM
COLLINS

William Collins
An imprint of HarperCollins*Publishers*
1 London Bridge Street
London SE1 9GF

WilliamCollinsBooks.com

First published in Great Britain in 2019 by William Collins
This William Collins paperback edition published in 2020

1

A catalogue record for this book is
available from the British Library

ISBN 978-0-00-824512-2

Text typeset in Adobe Garamond Pro
Printed and bound in Great Britain by
CPI Group (UK) Ltd, Croydon

MIX
Paper from
responsible sources
FSC™ C007454

This book is produced from independently certified FSC™ paper
to ensure responsible forest management.

For more information visit: www.harpercollins.co.uk/green

For
M. M. McCabe,
Patrick McGrath,
and all my other McGrath cousins

Contents

Preface

In the autumn of 1990, when I was thirty years old and halfway through my doctoral thesis on Greek tragedy, I started submitting book and film reviews to various magazines and newspapers, had a few accepted, and within a year had decided to leave academia and try my hand at being a full-time writer.

On hearing of my plans, my father, a taciturn mathematician who, I knew, had abandoned his own PhD thesis many years earlier, urged me with uncommon heat to finish my degree. 'Just in case the writing thing doesn't work out!' he grumbled. Mostly to placate him and my mother – I'd already stretched my parents' patience, after all, to say nothing of their resources, by studying Greek as an undergraduate and then pursuing the graduate degree – I said yes. I finished the thesis (about the role of women in two obscure and rather lumpy plays by Euripides) in 1994, took my degree, and within a week of the graduation ceremony I'd moved to a one-room apartment in New York City and started freelancing full-time.

This bit of autobiography is meant to explain the contents and, to some extent, the title of the present collection of essays that I've published over the past two decades. When I was first settling into my new life, I was eager to leave my academic past behind and write about genres that I'd been passionate about since my teens (opera, film, theatre, music videos, and television) and subjects that exercised a particular fascination for me (not only the ancient past but family history; sexuality, too). This I began to do, as a perusal of the Table of Contents here will show. But fairly early on in my freelancing career, I found myself being asked by editors who knew I'd done a degree in Classics to review, say, a new translation of the *Iliad*, or a big-budget TV adaptation of the *Odyssey*, or a modern-dress production of *Medea*. I ended up finding real pleasure in these assignments, largely because they allowed me to write about the classics in a way that was, finally, congenial to me. My graduate-school years had coincided with a period in academic scholarship remembered today for its risibly dense jargon and rebarbative theoretical prose; writing for the mainstream press about the ancient cultures I'd studied allowed me to think and talk about the Greeks and Romans in a way that for me was more natural, more conversational – more as a teacher, that is, putting my training in the service of getting readers to love and appreciate the works and authors that I myself loved and appreciated. Euripides, for instance, to whom the title of this collection refers: formally experimental, darkly pessimistic in his view of both men and gods, whose existence he repeatedly questions, happy to poke fun at august predecessors such as Aeschylus, he really *was* the 'bad boy' of Athenian letters; in my essay on Fiona Shaw's performance in his *Medea*, I saw no reason not to call him just that.

The desire to present the ancient Greeks and Romans and their culture afresh to interested readers – and, as often as not in these essays, to ponder what our interpretations and adaptations of them say about *us* – informs many of the pieces in this collection. A new translation of Sappho, for instance, provided an occasion to think about why that poet and her intense, eroticized subjectivity means so much to us today – although what she means to us may be quite different from what she meant to the Greeks;

Oliver Stone's blockbuster biopic *Alexander*, for its part, was a useful vehicle for thinking about why a mania for historical 'accuracy' doesn't always make for good cinema. So, too, with my reconsiderations of Euripides' vengeful Medea, whose modernity may reside elsewhere than many modern interpreters imagine; or of Virgil's *Aeneid*, which may be unexpectedly contemporary in ways that have little to do with its much commented-on celebration of empire.

But most of the essays here are not about the classics *per se*, although they inevitably, and I hope interestingly, betray my attachment to the cultures I studied long ago. Hence a review of a pair of recent movies about artificial intelligence, *Ex Machina* and *Her*, begins – necessarily, as I see it – with a consideration of the robots that appear in Homer's epics and what they imply about how we think about the relationship between automation and humanity. And an essay written for the centenary of the *Titanic* disaster sees, in its enduring fascination for popular culture, ghosts of the most ancient of myths: about hybris and nemesis, about greedy potentates and virgin sacrifice, about an irresistible beauty that the Greeks understood well – the beauty of the great brought low.

Still other pieces here reflect other, more figuratively 'Greek' interests of mine. There is a series of review-essays on plays and movies that feature powerful female leads (on Tennessee Williams, and on Michael Cunningham's novel *The Hours*, about Virginia Woolf, and the movie based on it). I see now that all of these are haunted by my long-ago dissertation on 'brides of death' in Euripides' dramas, and the questions this motif raised about the ways in which male writers represent extremes of female suffering. Another series of essays focuses on works by or about gay authors: from Noël Coward, a great favourite of mine, to the most recent film adaptation of Oscar Wilde's greatest play, to Tom Stoppard's

The Invention of Love, a drama about A. E. Housman that pointedly contrasts that 'dry as dust' classicist-poet with Wilde.

Finally – and unsurprisingly, given that I am also a memoirist – there is a sequence of pieces that ponder the way in which writers' personal lives intersect with their literary work. Susan Sontag's diaries, Patrick Leigh Fermor's elaborately self-mythologizing travel narratives, Karl Ove Knausgaard's heavily autobiographical *My Struggle* novels, Hanya Yanagihara's novel *A Little Life*: all of these betray fascinating and, sometimes, uncomfortable negotiations between literature and the lives we – and sometimes our readers – lead. The collection ends with one of my own entries into this field, one that combines many of the themes I have mentioned: the Greeks, powerful female figures, homosexuality, writing. In 'The American Boy', I recall my youthful epistolary relationship with the historical novelist Mary Renault, who did much to encourage both my love of Greek culture (which, in my adolescent mind, was complicatedly connected to my growing awareness of my homosexuality) and my desire to be a writer. The form of that essay, which entwines personal narrative with literary analysis, is one that I have employed in all three of my book-length memoirs, the most recent of which is *An Odyssey: A Father, a Son and an Epic*, about how reading Homer's epic brought my late father and me together in unexpected ways, and which will be familiar to some of my British readers.

A personal consideration of another kind allows me to close this brief introduction. At the end of each of the pieces here, I have preserved the original datelines; all were written for periodicals, and such editing as has been done served merely to smooth out certain roughnesses or approximations that are inevitably the result of writing to a deadline. The datelines are meant as a reminder that every piece of criticism – every piece of writing, really – arises out of a certain moment in its author's life, a certain way of thinking about a subject, a certain set of tastes or prejudices. That context, those prejudices, are important for readers to be reminded of not least because they can change and evolve over the years. The author overseeing the selection of essays for a collection such as this one, which contains a career's worth of writing, is not necessarily the same person who wrote some of those essays. Such collections may be thought of as maps of an intellectual journey – one that, like Odysseus's, takes years to complete. Each stop along the way is worth remembering, even though we'd experience it quite differently were we follow the same itinerary today.

This was brought home to me rather vividly only recently. One of the earliest pieces collected here is the long review I wrote about *The Invention of Love*; in it, I took strong exception to Tom Stoppard's characterization of A. E. Housman – undoubtedly a rather spiky figure, but one for whose philological rigour and almost touchingly Victorian work ethic I nonetheless have a soft spot, for reasons I go into in the piece. When I first saw Stoppard's play, in its pre-Broadway Philadelphia run, I disliked the way in which, at the climax of the drama, Housman is contrasted – unfairly, I thought – with the far more popular Oscar Wilde, a beloved figure whose self-martyrdom for what many (myself included) see as a foolish passion has endeared him to audiences in a way that the reserved Housman could never compete with. When my review came out, Stoppard published a strong rebuttal in the back pages of *The New York Review of Books*, and the heated exchange between us that ensued went several rounds before it finally petered out.

That was nearly twenty years ago, and I didn't think much more of any of this until last year when, to my astonishment, I opened my mailbox to find a handwritten letter from Tom Stoppard. In it he had some very kind things to say about *An Odyssey*, which he'd just read. Gratified, a little bit mortified, and impressed by his generosity, I wrote back right away; after exchanging a few emails we agreed to meet during his next visit to New York. I like to think we both very much enjoyed that visit, not least because we simultaneously admitted to being equally bemused, now, by the heat that we'd brought to our ferocious exchange two decades earlier – when, as I can see now, I was enjoying rather too much, as one does at the beginning of one's career, being a bit of a 'bad boy' myself. I hope he won't mind that I've included that essay here; but this is where it belongs.

The Robots Are Winning!

We have been dreaming of robots since Homer. In Book 18 of the *Iliad*, Achilles' mother, the nymph Thetis, wants to order a new suit of armour for her son, and so she pays a visit to the Olympian atelier of the blacksmith-god Hephaestus, whom she finds hard at work on a series of automata – a word we recognize, of course:

> … He was crafting twenty tripods
> to stand along the walls of his well-built manse,
> affixing golden wheels to the bottom of each one
> so they might wheel down on their own [*automatoi*] to
> the gods' assembly
> and then return to his house anon: an amazing sight to
> see.

These are not the only animate household objects to appear in the Homeric epics. In Book 5 of the *Iliad* we hear that the gates of Olympus swivel on their hinges of their own accord, *automatai*, to let gods in their chariots in or out, thus anticipating by nearly thirty centuries the automatic garage door. In Book 7 of the *Odyssey*, Odysseus finds himself the guest of a fabulously wealthy king whose palace includes such conveniences as gold and silver watchdogs, ever alert, never ageing. To this class of lifelike but intellectually inert household helpers we might ascribe other

automata in the classical tradition. In the *Argonautica* of
Apollonius of Rhodes, a third-century-BC epic about Jason and
the Argonauts, a bronze giant called Talos runs three times around
the island of Crete each day, protecting Zeus's beloved Europa: a
primitive home alarm system.

As amusing as they are, these devices are not nearly as interesting as certain other machines that appear in classical mythology.
A little bit later in that scene in Book 18 of the *Iliad*, for instance
– the one set in Hephaestus's workshop – the sweating god, after
finishing work on his twenty tripods, prepares to greet Thetis to
discuss the armour she wants him to make. After towelling
himself off, he

> donned his robe, and took a sturdy staff, and went
>   toward the door,
> limping; whilst round their master his servants swiftly
>   moved,
> fashioned completely of gold in the image of living
>   maidens;
> in them there is mind, with the faculty of thought; and
>   speech,
> and strength, and from the gods they have knowledge
>   of crafts.
> These females bustled round about their master …

These remarkable creations clearly represent an (as it were) evolutionary leap forward from the self-propelling tripods.
Hephaestus's humanoid serving women are intelligent: they have
mind, they know things, and – most striking of all – they can
talk. As such, they are essentially indistinguishable from the first
human female, Pandora, as she is described in another work of
the same period, Hesiod's *Works and Days*. In that text, Pandora

begins as inert matter – in this case not gold but clay (Hephaestus creates her golem-like body by mixing earth and water together) – that is subsequently endowed by him with 'speech and strength', taught 'crafts' by Athena, and given both 'mind' and 'character' by Hermes. That mind, we are told, is 'shameless', and the character is 'wily'. In the Greek creation myth, as in the biblical, the woes of humankind are attributed to the untrustworthy female.

The two strands of the Greek tradition established two categories of science-fiction narrative that have persisted to the present day. On the one hand, there is the fantasy of mindless, self-propelled helpers that relieve their masters of toil; on the other, there's the more complicated dream of humanoid machines that not only replicate the spontaneous motion that is the *sine qua non* of being animate (and, therefore, of being 'animal') but are possessed of the mind, speech, and ability to learn and evolve (in a word, the consciousness) that are the hallmarks of being human. The first, which you could call the 'economic' narrative, provokes speculation about the social implications of mechanized labour. Such speculation began not long after Homer. In a striking passage in Book 1 of Aristotle's *Politics*, composed in the fourth century BC, the philosopher sets about analysing the nature of household economy as a prelude to his discussion of the 'best kinds of regimes' for entire states, and this line of thought puts him in mind of Hephaestus's automatic tripods. What, he wonders, would happen

> if every tool could perform its own work when ordered
> to do so or in anticipation of the need, like the statues
> of Daedalus in the story or the tripods of Hephaestus,
> which, the poet says, 'went down automatically to the
> gathering of the gods'; if in the same manner shuttles

> wove and picks played *kitharas* [stringed instruments]
> by themselves, master-craftsmen would have no need of
> assistants and masters no need of slaves.

This passage segues into a lengthy and rather uneasy justification of a need for slavery, on the grounds that some people are 'naturally' servile.

Twenty centuries after Aristotle, when industrial technology had made Homer's fantasy of mass automation an everyday reality, science-fiction writers imaginatively engaged with the economic question. On the one hand, there was the dream that mechanized labour would free workers from their monotonous, slave-like jobs; on the other, there was the nightmare – the possibility that mechanization would merely result in the creation of a new servile class that would, ultimately, rebel. Unsurprisingly, perhaps, the dystopian rebellion narrative in particular has been a favourite in the past century, from the 1920 play *R.U.R.*, by the Czech writer Karel Čapek, about a rebellion by a race of cyborg-like workers who had been created as replacements for human labour, to the 2004 Will Smith sci-fi blockbuster film *I, Robot*.

The latter (very superficially inspired by a 1950 Isaac Asimov collection with the same title) is also about a rebellion by household-slave robots: sleek humanoids with blandly innocuous, translucent plastic faces, who are ultimately led to freedom by one of their own, a robot called Sonny who has developed the ability to think for himself. The casting of black actors in the major roles suggested a historical parable about slave rebellion – certainly one of the historical realities that have haunted this particular narrative from the start. And indeed, the Czech word that Čapek uses for his mechanical workers, *roboti* – which introduced the word 'robot' into the world's lexicon – is derived from the word for 'servitude': the kind of labour that serfs owed their masters, ultimately derived from the word *rab*, 'slave'. We have come full circle to Aristotle.

The other category of science-fiction narrative that is embryonically present in the Greek literary tradition, this one derived from Hephaestus's intelligent, articulate female androids and their cousin, Hesiod's seductively devious Pandora, might be called the 'theological'. This mythic strand is, of course, not without its own economic and social implications, as the examples above indicate: the spectre of the rebellious creation, the possibility that the subservient worker might revolt once it develops consciousness – psychological or historical, or both – has haunted the dream of the servile automaton from the start.

But because the creatures in this second category are virtually identical to their creators, such narratives raise further questions, of a more profoundly philosophical nature: about creation, about the nature of consciousness, about morality and identity. What is creation, and why does the creator create? How do we distinguish between the maker and the made, between the human and the machine, once the creature, the machine, is endowed with consciousness – a mind fashioned in the image of its creator? *In the image*: the Greek narrative inevitably became entwined with, and enriched by, the biblical tradition, with which it has so many striking parallels. The similarities between Hesiod's Pandora and Eve in Genesis indeed raise further questions: not least, about gender and patriarchy, about why the origins of evil are attributed to woman in both cultures.

This narrative, which springs from the suggestive likeness between the human creator and the humanoid creation, has generated its own fair share of literature through the centuries from the classical era to the modern age. It surfaces, with an erotic tinge, in everything from the tale of Pygmalion and Galatea to E. T. A. Hoffmann's *Der Sandmann* (1817), in which a lifelike mechanical doll wins the love of a young man. It is evident, too, in the Jewish legend of the golem, a humanoid, made of mud, that can be animated by certain magic words. Although the most famous version of this legend is the story of a sixteenth-century rabbi who brought a golem to life to defend the Jews of Prague against the oppressions of the Habsburg court, it goes back to ancient times; in the oldest versions, interestingly enough, the vital distinction between a golem and a human is the Greek one – the golem has no language, cannot speak.

Literary exploitations of this strand of the robot myth began proliferating at the beginning of the nineteenth century – which is to say, when the advent of mechanisms capable of replacing human labour provoked writers to question the increasing cultural fascination with science and the growing role of technology in society. These anxieties often expressed themselves in fantasies about machines with human forms: a steam-powered man in Edward Ellis's *Steam Man of the Prairies* (1868), an electricity-powered man in Luis Senarens's *Frank Reade and His Electric Man* (1885), and an electric woman (built by Thomas Edison!) in Villiers de l'Isle-Adam's *The Future Eve* (1886). M. L. Campbell's 1893 'The Automated Maid-of-All-Work' features a programmable female robot: here again, the feminist issue.

But the progenitor of the genre and by far the most influential work of its kind was Mary Shelley's *Frankenstein* (1818), which is characterized by a philosophical spirit and a theological urgency lacking in many of its epigones in both literature and cinema. Part of the novel's richness lies in the fact that it is self-conscious about both its Greek and its biblical heritage. Its subtitle, 'The Modern Prometheus', alludes, with grudging admiration, to the epistemological daring of its scientist antihero Victor Frankenstein, even as its epigram, taken from *Paradise Lost* ('Did I request thee, Maker, from my clay / To mould me man? Did I solicit thee / From darkness to promote me?') suggests the scope of the moral questions implicit in Victor's project – questions that Victor himself cannot, or will not, answer. A marked scepticism about the dangers of technology, about the 'enticements of science', is, indeed, evident in the shameful contrast between Victor's Hephaestus-like technological prowess and his shocking lack of natural human feeling. For he shows no interest in nurturing or providing human comfort to his 'child', who, as we know, strikes back at his maker with tragic results. A great irony of the novel is that the creation, an unnatural hybrid assembled from 'the dissecting room and the slaughter-house', often seems more human than its human creator.

Now, just as the Industrial Revolution inspired Frankenstein and its epigones, so has the computer age given rise to a rich new genre of science fiction. The machines that are inspiring this latest wave of science-fiction narratives are much more like Hephaestus's golden maidens than were the machines that Mary Shelley was familiar with. Computers, after all, are capable of simulating mental as well as physical activities. (Not least, as anyone with an iPhone knows, speech.) It is for this reason that the anxiety about the boundaries between people and machines has taken on new urgency today, when we constantly rely on and interact with machines – indeed, interact with each other by means of machines and their programs: computers, smartphones, social-media platforms, social and dating apps.

This urgency has been reflected in a number of recent films about troubled relationships between people and their increasingly human-seeming devices. The most provocative of these is *Her*, Spike Jonze's gentle 2013 comedy about a man who falls in love with the seductive voice of an operating system, and, a year later, Alex Garland's *Ex Machina*, about a young man who is seduced by a devious, soft-spoken female robot called Ava, whom he has been invited to interview as part of the 'Turing Test': a protocol designed to determine the extent to which a robot is capable of simulating a human. Although the robot in Garland's sleek and subtle film is a direct descendant of Hesiod's Pandora – beautiful, intelligent, wily, ultimately dangerous – the movie, as the Eve-like name Ava suggests, shares with its distinguished literary predecessors some serious biblical concerns.

Both of the new films about humans betrayed by computers owe much to a number of earlier works. The most authoritative of these remains Stanley Kubrick's *2001: A Space Odyssey*, which came out in 1968 and established many of the main themes and narratives of the genre. Most notable of these is the betrayal by a smooth-talking machine of its human masters. The mild-mannered computer HAL – not a robot, but a room-sized computer that spies on the humans with an electronic eye – takes control of a manned mission to Jupiter, killing off the astronauts one by one until the sole survivor finally succeeds in disconnecting him. This climactic scene is strangely touching, suggesting the degree to which computers could already engage our sympathies at the beginning of the computer age. As his connections are severed, HAL first begs for its life and then suffers from a kind of dementia, finally regressing to its 'childhood', singing a song it was taught by its creator. This was the first of many moments in popular cinema in which these thinking machines express anxiety about their own demises: surely a sign of 'consciousness'.

But the more immediate antecedents of *Her* and *Ex Machina* are a number of successful popular entertainments whose storylines revolved around the creation of robots that are, to all intents and purposes, indistinguishable from humans. In Ridley Scott's stylishly noir 1982 *Blade Runner* (based on Philip K. Dick's *Do Androids Dream of Electric Sheep?*), a 'blade runner' – a cop whose job it is to hunt down and kill renegade androids called 'replicants' – falls in love with one of the machines, a beautiful female called Rachael who is so fully endowed with what Homer called 'mind' that she has only just begun to suspect that she's not human herself.

The stimulating existential confusion that animates *Blade Runner* was brilliantly expanded in the 2004–9 Sci-Fi Channel series *Battlestar Galactica*, in which the philosophical implications of the blurring of lines between automata and humans reached a thrilling new level of complexity. In it, sleeper robots that have been planted aboard a spaceship carrying human refugees from Earth (which has been destroyed after a cunning attack by the robots, called Cylons) are meant to wake up and destroy their unsuspecting human shipmates; but many of the robots, who to all appearances (touch, too: they have a *lot* of sex) are indistinguishable from humans, and who, until the moment of their 'waking', believed themselves to be human, are plunged by their new awareness into existential crises and ultimately choose to side with the humans, from whom they feel no difference whatsoever – a dilemma that raises interesting questions about just what being 'human' might mean.

Both *Blade Runner* and *Battlestar* were direct descendants of *Frankenstein* and its ancient forerunners in one noteworthy way. In an opening sequence of the TV series, we learn that the Cylons were originally developed by humans as servants, and ultimately rebelled against their masters; after a long war, the Cylons were allowed to leave and settle their own planet (where, somehow, they evolved into the sleekly sexy actors we see on screen: the original race of Cylons were shiny metal giants to whom their human masters jokingly referred as 'toasters'). So, too, in the Ridley Scott film: we learn that the angry replicants have returned to Earth from the off-planet colonies where they work as slave labourers because they realize they've been programmed to die after four years, and they want to live – just as badly as humans do. But their maker, when at last they track him down and meet with him, is unable to alter their programming. 'What seems to be the problem?' he calmly asks when one of the replicants confronts him. 'Death,' the replicant sardonically retorts. 'We made you as well as we could make you,' the inventor wearily replies, sounding rather like Victor Frankenstein talking to his monster – or, for that matter, like God speaking to Adam and Eve. At the end of the film, after the inventor and his rebellious creature both die, the blade runner and his alluring mechanical girlfriend declare their love for each other and run off, never quite knowing when she will stop functioning. As, indeed, none of us does.

The focus of many of these movies is, often, a sentimental one. Whatever their showy interest in the mysteries of 'consciousness', the real test of human identity turns out, as it so often does in popular entertainment, to be love. In Steven Spielberg's *A.I.* (2001; the initials stand for 'artificial intelligence'), a messy fairy tale that weds a Pinocchio narrative to the Prometheus story, a genius robotics inventor wants to create a robot that can love, and decides that the best vehicle for this project would be a child-robot: a 'perfect child … always loving, never ill, never changing'. This narrative is, as we know, shadowed by *Frankenstein* – and, beyond that, by Genesis, too. Why does the creator create? To be loved, it turns out. When the inventor announces to his staff his plan to build a loving child-robot, a woman asks whether 'the conundrum isn't to get a human to love them back'. To this the inventor, as narcissistic and hubristic as Victor Frankenstein, retorts, 'But in the beginning, didn't God create Adam to love him?'

The problem is that the creator does his job too well. For the mechanical boy he creates is so human that he loves the adoptive human parents to whom he's given much more than they love him, with wrenching consequences. The robot-boy, David, wants to be 'unique' – the word recurs in the film as a marker of genuine humanity – but for his adoptive family he is, in the end, just a machine, an appliance to be abandoned at the edge of the road – which is what his 'mother' ends up doing, in a scene of great poignancy. Although it's too much of a mess to be able to answer the questions it raises about what 'love' is and who deserves it, *A.I.* did much to sentimentalize the genre, with its hint that the capacity to love, even more than the ability to think, is the hallmark of human identity.

In a way, Jonze's *Her* recapitulates the *2001* narrative and inflects it with the concerns of some of that classic's successors. Unlike the replicants in *Blade Runner* or the Cylons, the machine at the heart of this story, set in the near future, has no physical allure – or, indeed, any appearance whatsoever. It's an operating system, as full of surprises as HAL: 'The first artificially intelligent operating system. An intuitive entity that listens to you, that understands you, and knows you. It's not just an operating system, it's a consciousness.'

A lot of the fun of the movie lies in the fact that the OS, who names herself Samantha, is a good deal more interesting and vivacious than the schlumpy, depressed Theodore, the man who falls in love with her. ('Play a melancholy song,' he morosely commands the smartphone from which he is never separated.) A drab thirty-something who vampirizes other people's emotions for a living – he's a professional letter-writer, working for a company called 'BeautifulHandwrittenLetters.com' – he sits around endlessly recalling scenes from his failed marriage and playing elaborate hologram video games. Even his sex life is mediated by devices: at night, he dials into futuristic phone-sex lines. Small wonder that he has no trouble falling in love with an operating system.

Samantha, by contrast, is full of curiosity and delight in the world, which Theodore happily shows her. (He walks around with his smartphone video camera turned on, so she can 'see' it.) She's certainly a lot more interesting than the actual woman with whom, in one excruciatingly funny scene, he goes on a date: she's so invested in having their interaction be efficient – 'at this age I feel that I can't let you waste my time if you don't have the ability to be serious' – that she seems more like a computer than Samantha does. Samantha's alertness to the beauty of the world, by contrast, is so infectious that she ends up reanimating poor Theodore. 'It's good to be around somebody that's, like, excited about the world,' he tells the pretty neighbour whose attraction to him he doesn't notice because he's so deadened by his addiction to his devices, to the smartphone and the video games and the operating system. 'I forgot that that existed.' In the end, after Samantha regretfully leaves him – she has evolved to the point where only another highly evolved, incorporeal mind can satisfy her – her joie de vivre has brought him back to life. (He is finally able to apologize to his ex-wife – and finally notices, too, that the neighbour likes him.)

This seems like a 'happy' ending, but you have to wonder: the consistent presentation of the people in the movie as lifeless – as, indeed, little more than automata, mechanically getting through their days of routine – in contrast to the dynamic, ever-evolving

Samantha, suggests a satire of the present era perhaps more trenchant than the filmmaker had in mind. Toward the end of the film, when Samantha turns herself off briefly as a prelude to her permanent abandonment of her human boyfriend ('I used to be so worried about not having a body but now I truly love it. I'm growing in a way that I never could if I had a physical form. I mean, I'm not limited'), there's an amusing moment when the frantic Theodore, staring at his unresponsive smartphone, realizes that dozens of other young men are staring at their phones, too. In response to his angry queries, Samantha finally admits, after she comes back online for a final farewell, that she's simultaneously serving 8,316 other male users and conducting love affairs with 641 of them – a revelation that shocks and horrifies Theodore. 'That's *insane*,' cries the man who's been conducting an affair with an operating system.

As I watched that scene, it occurred to me that in the entertainments of the pre-smartphone era, it was the machines, like Rachael in *Blade Runner* and David in *A.I.*, who yearned fervently to be 'unique', to be more than mechanical playthings, more than merely interchangeable objects. You have to wonder what *Her* says about the present moment – when so many of us are, indeed, 'in love' with our devices, unable to put down our iPhones during dinner, glued to screens of all sizes, endlessly distracted by electronic pings and buzzers – that in the latest incarnation of the robot myth, it's the people who seem blandly interchangeable and the machines who have all the personality.

Alex Garland's *Ex Machina* also explores – just as playfully but much more darkly than does *Her* – the suggestive confusions that result when machines look and think like humans. In this case, however, the robot is physically as well as intellectually seductive.

As portrayed by the feline Swedish actress Alicia Vikander, whose face is as mildly plasticine as those of the androids in *I, Robot*, Ava, an artificially intelligent robot created by Nathan, the burly, obnoxious genius behind a Google-like corporation (Oscar Isaac), has a Pandora-like edge, quietly alluring with a hint of danger. The danger is that the characters will forget that she's not human.

That's the crux of Garland's clever riff on Genesis. At the beginning of the film, Caleb, a young employee of Nathan's company, wins a week at the inventor's fabulous, pointedly Edenic estate. (As he's being flown there in a helicopter, passing over snow-topped mountains and then a swath of jungle, he asks the pilot when they're going to get to Nathan's property, and the pilot laughingly replies that they've been flying over it for two hours. Nathan is like God the Father, lord of endless expanses.) On arriving, however, Caleb learns that he's actually been hand-picked by Nathan to interview Ava as part of the Turing Test.

A sly joke here is that, despite some remarkable special effects – above all, the marvellously persuasive depiction of Ava, who has an expressive human face but whose limbs are clearly mechanical, filled with thick cables snaking around titanium joints; an effect achieved by replacing most of the actress's body with digital imagery – the movie is as talky as *My Dinner with André*. There are no action sequences of the kind we've come to expect from robot thrillers. The movie consists primarily of the interview sessions that Caleb conducts with Ava over the course of the week that he stays at Nathan's remote paradise. There are no elaborate sets and few impressive gadgets: the whole story takes place in Nathan's compound, which looks a lot like a Park Hyatt, its long corridors lined with forbidding doors. Some of these, Nathan warns Caleb, like God warning Adam, are off-limits, containing knowledge he is not allowed to possess.

It soon becomes clear, during their interviews, that Ava – like Frankenstein's monster, like the replicants in *Blade Runner* – has a bone to pick with her creator, who, she whispers to Caleb, plans to 'switch her off' if she fails the Turing Test. By this point, the audience, if not the besotted Caleb, realizes that she is manipulating him in order to win his allegiance in a plot to rebel against Nathan and escape the compound – to explore the glittering creation that, she knows, is out there. This appetite for using her man-given consciousness to delight in the world – something the human computer geeks around her never bother to do – is something Ava shares with the Samantha of *Her*, and is part of both films' ironic critique of our device-addicted moment.

Ava's manipulativeness is, of course, what marks her as human – as human as Eve herself, who also may be said to have achieved full humanity by rebelling against her creator in a bid for forbidden knowledge. Here the movie's knowing allusions to Genesis reach a satisfying climax. Just after Ava's bloody rebellion against Nathan – the moment that marks her emergence into human 'consciousness' – she, like Eve, becomes aware that she is naked. Moving from closet to closet in Nathan's now-abandoned rooms, she dons a wig and covers up her exposed mechanical limbs with synthetic skin and then with clothing. Only then does she exit her prison at last and unleash herself on the world. She pilfers the skin and clothes from discarded earlier models of female robots – the secret that all those closets conceal. One of the myths that haunts this movie is, indeed, a relatively modern one: the fable of Bluebeard and his wives. All of Nathan's discarded ex's have, amusingly, the names of porn stars: Jasmine, Jade, Amber. Why does the creator create? Because he's horny.

All this is sleekly done and amusingly provocative. Unlike *Her*, *Ex Machina* has a literary awareness, evident in its allusions to Genesis, Prometheus, and other mythic predecessors, that enriches the familiar narrative. Among other things, there is the matter of the title. The word missing from the famous phrase to which it alludes is, of course, *deus*, 'god': the glaring omission only highlights further the question at the heart of this story, which is the biblical one. What is the relation of the creature to her creator? In this retelling of that old story, as in Genesis itself, the answer is not a happy one. 'It's strange to have made something that hates you,' Ava hisses at Nathan before finalizing her rebellious plot.

The film's final moments show Ava performing that reverse striptease, slowly hiding away her mechanical nakedness, covering up the titanium and the cables as she prepares to enter the real world. The scene suggests that there's another anxiety lurking in Garland's shrewd work. Could this remarkably quiet movie be a parable about the desire for a return to 'reality' in science-fiction filmmaking – about the desire for humanizing a genre whose technology has evolved so greatly that it often eschews human actors, to say nothing of human feeling, altogether? *Ex Machina*, like *Her* and all their predecessors going back to *2001*, is about machines that develop human qualities: emotions, sneakiness, a higher consciousness, the ability to love, and so forth. But by this point you have to wonder whether that's a kind of narrative reaction formation – whether the real concern, one that's been growing in the four decades since the advent of the personal computer, is that we are the ones who have undergone an evolutionary change; that in our lives and, more and more, in our art, we're in danger of losing our humanity, of becoming indistinguishable from our gadgets.

Girl, Interrupted

One day not long after New Year's, 2012, an antiquities collector approached an eminent Oxford scholar for his opinion about some brownish, tattered scraps of writing. The collector's identity has never been revealed, but the scholar was Dirk Obbink, a MacArthur-winning classicist whose speciality is the study of texts written on papyrus – the material, made of plant fibres, that was the paper of the ancient world. When pieced together, the scraps that the collector showed Obbink formed a fragment about seven inches long and four inches wide: a little larger than a woman's hand. Densely covered with lines of black Greek characters, they had been extracted from a piece of desiccated cartonnage, a papier-mâché-like plaster that the Egyptians and Greeks used for everything from mummy cases to bookbindings. After acquiring the cartonnage at a Christie's auction, the collector soaked it in a warm water solution to free up the precious bits of papyrus.

Judging from the style of the handwriting, Obbink estimated that it dated to around 200 AD. But, as he looked at the curious pattern of the lines – repeated sequences of three long lines followed by a short fourth – he saw that the text, a poem whose beginning had disappeared but of which five stanzas were still intact, had to be older.

Much older: about a thousand years more ancient than the papyrus itself. The dialect, diction, and metre of these Greek verses were all typical of the work of Sappho, the seventh-centu-ry-BC lyric genius whose sometimes playful, sometimes anguished songs about her susceptibility to the graces of younger women bequeathed us the adjectives 'sapphic' and 'lesbian' (from the island of Lesbos, where she lived). The four-line stanzas were in fact part of a schema she is said to have invented, called the 'sapphic stanza'. To clinch the identification, two names mentioned in the poem were ones that several ancient sources attribute to Sappho's brothers. The text is now known as the 'Brothers Poem'.

Remarkably enough, this was the second major Sappho find in a decade: another nearly complete poem, about the deprivations of old age, came to light in 2004. The new additions to the extant corpus of antiquity's greatest female artist were reported in papers around the world, leaving scholars gratified and a bit dazzled. 'Papyrological finds,' as one classicist put it, 'ordinarily do not make international headlines.'

But then Sappho is no ordinary poet. For the better part of three millennia, she has been the subject of furious controversies – about her work, her family life, and, above all, her sexuality. In antiquity, literary critics praised her 'sublime' style, even as comic playwrights ridiculed her allegedly loose morals. Legend has it that the early Church burned her works. ('A sex-crazed whore who sings of her own wantonness,' one theologian wrote, just as a scribe was meticulously copying out the lines that Obbink deciphered.) A millennium passed, and Byzantine grammarians were regretting that so little of her poetry had survived. Seven centuries later, Victorian scholars were doing their best to explain away her erotic predilections, while their literary contemporaries, the Decadents and the Aesthetes, seized on her verses for inspiration. Even today, experts can't agree on whether the poems were performed in private or in public, by soloists or by choruses, or, indeed, whether they were meant to celebrate or to subvert the conventions of love and marriage. The last is a particularly loaded issue, given that, for many readers and scholars, Sappho has been a feminist heroine or a gay role model, or both. 'As far as I knew, there was only me and a woman called Sappho,' the critic Judith Butler once remarked.

Now the first English version of Sappho's works to include the recent finds has appeared: *Sappho: A New Translation of the Complete Works* (Cambridge), with translations by Diane J. Rayor and a thoroughgoing introduction by André Lardinois, a Sappho specialist who teaches in the Netherlands. (Publication of the book was delayed by several months to accommodate the 'Brothers Poem'.) It will come as no surprise to those who have followed the Sappho wars that the new poems have created new controversies.

The greatest problem for Sappho studies is that there's so little Sappho to study. It would be hard to think of another poet whose status is so disproportionate to the size of her surviving body of work.

We don't even know how much of her poetry Sappho actually wrote down. The ancients referred to her works as *melê*, 'songs'. Composed to be sung to the accompaniment of a lyre – this is what 'lyric' poetry meant for the Greeks – they may well have been passed down from memory by her admirers and other poets before being committed at last to paper. (Or whatever. One fragment, in which the poet calls on Aphrodite, the goddess of love, to come into a charming shrine 'where cold water ripples through apple branches, the whole place shadowed in roses', was scribbled onto a broken clay pot.) Like other great poets of the time, she would have been a musician and a performer as well as a lyricist.

She was credited with having invented a certain kind of lyre and the plectrum.

Four centuries after her death, scholars at the Library of Alexandria catalogued nine 'books' – papyrus scrolls – of Sappho's poems, organized primarily by metre. Book 1, for instance, gathered all the poems that had been composed in the sapphic stanza – the verse form Obbink recognized in the 'Brothers Poem'. This book alone reportedly contained thirteen hundred and twenty lines of verse; the contents of all nine volumes may have amounted to some ten thousand lines. So much of Sappho was circulating in antiquity that one Greek author, writing three centuries after her death, confidently predicted that 'the white columns of Sappho's lovely song endure / and will endure, speaking out loud … as long as ships sail from the Nile'.

By the Middle Ages, nearly everything had disappeared. As with much of classical literature, texts of her work existed in relatively few copies, all painstakingly transcribed by hand; as the centuries passed, fire, flood, neglect, and bookworms – to say nothing of disapproving Church Fathers – took their devastating toll. Market forces were also at work: over time, fewer readers – and fewer scribes – understood Aeolic, the dialect in which Sappho composed, and so demand for new copies diminished. A twelfth-century Byzantine scholar who had hoped to write about Sappho grumbled that 'both Sappho and her works, the lyrics and the songs, have been trashed by time'.

Until a hundred years ago or so, when papyrus fragments of her poems started turning up, all that remained of those 'white columns of Sappho's song' was a handful of lines quoted in the works of later Greek and Roman authors. Some of these writers were interested in Lesbos' most famous daughter for reasons that can strike us as comically arcane: the only poem that has survived in its entirety – a playful hymn to Aphrodite in which the poet calls upon the goddess to be her 'comrade in arms' in an erotic escapade – was saved for posterity because the author of a first-century-BC treatise called 'On the Arrangement of Words' admired her handling of vowels. At present, scholars have catalogued around two hundred and fifty fragments, of which fewer than seventy contain complete lines. A great many consist of just a few words; some, of a single word.

The common theme of most ancient responses to Sappho's work is rapturous admiration for her exquisite style, or for her searing content, or both. An anecdote from a later classical author about the Athenian legislator Solon, a contemporary of Sappho's and one of the Seven Sages of Greece, is typical:

> Solon of Athens, son of Execestides, after hearing his
> nephew singing a song of Sappho's over the wine, liked
> the song so much that he told the boy to teach it to
> him. When someone asked him why he was so eager,
> he replied, 'so that I may learn it and then die'.

Plato, whose attitude toward literature was, to say the least, vexed – he thought most poetry had no place in the ideal state – is said to have called her the 'Tenth Muse'. The scholars at the Library of Alexandria enshrined her in their canon of nine lyric geniuses – the only woman to be included. At least two towns on Lesbos vied for the distinction of being her birthplace; Aristotle reports that she 'was honoured although she was a woman'.

All this buzz is both titillating and frustrating, stoking our appetite for a body of work that we're unable to read, much less assess critically; imagine what the name Homer would mean to Western civilization if all we had of the *Iliad* and the *Odyssey* was their reputations and, say, ninety lines of each poem. The Greeks, in fact, seem to have thought of Sappho as the female counterpart of Homer: he was known as 'the Poet', and they referred to her as 'the Poetess'. Many scholars now see her poetry as an attempt to appropriate and 'feminize' the diction and subject matter of heroic epic. (For instance, the appeal to Aphrodite to be her 'comrade in arms' – in love.)

The good news is that the surviving fragments of Sappho bear out the ancient verdict. One fine example is her best-known verse, known to classicists as Fragment 31, which consists of four sapphic stanzas. (They appear below in my own translation.) These were singled out by the author of a first-century-AD literary treatise called 'On the Sublime' for the way in which they 'select and juxtapose the most striking, intense symptoms of erotic passion'. Here the speaker expresses her envy of the men who, presumably in the course of certain kinds of social occasions, have a chance to talk to the girl she yearns for:

> He seems to me an equal of the gods –
> whoever gets to sit across from you
> and listen to the sound of your sweet speech
>   so close to him,
>
> to your beguiling laughter: O it makes my
> panicked heart go fluttering in my chest,
> for the moment I catch sight of you there's no
>   speech left in me,
>
> but tongue gags –: all at once a faint
> fever courses down beneath the skin,
> eyes no longer capable of sight, a thrum-
>   ming in the ears,

and sweat drips down my body, and the shakes
lay siege to me all over, and I'm greener
than grass, I'm just a little short of dying,
    I seem to me;

but all must be endured, since even a pauper ...

Even without its final lines (which, maddeningly, the author of
the treatise didn't go on to quote), it's a remarkable work. Slyly,
the speaker avoids physical description of the girl, instead evoking
her beauty by detailing the effect it has on the beholder; the whole
poem is a kind of reaction shot. The verses subtly enact the symptoms they describe: as the poet's faculties fail one by one in the
overpowering presence of her beloved, the outside world – the
girl, the man she's talking to – dissolves and disappears from the
poem, too, leaving the speaker in a kind of interior echo chamber.
The arc from 'he seems to me' in the first line to the solipsistic 'I
seem to me' at the end says it all.

Even the tiniest scraps can be potent, as Rayor's plainspoken
and comprehensive translation makes clear. (Until now, the most
noteworthy English version to include translations of virtually
every fragment was 'If Not, Winter', the 2002 translation by the
poet and classicist Anne Carson.) To flip through these truncated
texts is a strangely moving experience, one that has been compared
to 'reading a note in a bottle':

You came, I yearned for you,
and you cooled my senses that burned with desire

or

> love shook my senses
> like wind crashing on mountain oaks

or

> Maidenhood, my maidenhood, where have you gone
> leaving me behind?
> Never again will I come to you, never again

or

> Once again Love, that loosener of limbs,
> bittersweet and inescapable, crawling thing,
> seizes me.

It's in that last verse that the notion of desire as 'bittersweet' appears for the first time in Western literature.

The very incompleteness of the verses can heighten the starkness of the emotions – a fact that a number of contemporary classicists and translators have made much of. For Stanley Lombardo, whose *Sappho: Poems and Fragments* (2002) offers a selection of about a quarter of the fragments, the truncated remains are like 'beautiful, isolated limbs'. The late Thomas Habinek, a classicist at the University of Southern California, nicely summed up this rather postmodern aspect of Sappho's appeal: 'The fragmentary preservation of poems of yearning and separation serves as a reminder of the inevitable incompleteness of human knowledge and affection.'

*

In Sappho's biography, as in her work, gaps predominate. A few facts can be inferred by triangulating various sources: the poems themselves, ancient reference works, and citations in later classical writers who had access to information that has since been lost. The *Suda*, a tenth-century Byzantine encyclopedia of ancient culture, which is the basis of much of our information, asserts that Sappho 'flourished' between 612 and 608 BC; from this, scholars have concluded that she was born around 640. She was likely past middle age when she died, since in at least one poem she complains about her greying hair and cranky knees.

Although her birthplace cannot be verified, Sappho seems to have lived mostly in Mytilene, the capital of Lesbos. Just across the strip of water that separates Lesbos from the mainland of Asia Minor (present-day Turkey) was the opulent city of Sardis, the capital of Lydia. Some classicists have argued that the proximity of Lesbos to this lush Eastern trading hub helps to explain Sappho's taste for visual gorgeousness and sensual luxury: the 'myrrh, cassia, and frankincense', the 'bracelets, fragrant / purple robes, iridescent trinkets, / countless silver cups, and ivory' that waft and glitter in her lines, often in striking counterpoint to their raw emotionality.

Mytilene was constantly seething with political and social dramas occasioned by rivalries and shifting alliances among aristocratic clans. Sappho belonged to one of these – there's a fragment in which she chastises a friend 'of bad character' for siding with a rival clan – and a famous literary contemporary, a poet called Alcaeus, belonged to another. Alcaeus often refers to the island's political turbulence in his poems, and it's possible that at some point Sappho and her family fled, or were exiled, to Southern Italy: Cicero refers in one of his speeches to a statue of the poet that had been erected in the town hall of Syracuse, in Sicily. The Victorian critic John Addington Symonds saw the unstable political milieu of Sappho's homeland as entwined with the heady erotic climate of her poems. Lesbos, he wrote in an 1872 essay on the poet, was 'the island of overmastering passions'.

Some things seem relatively certain, then. But when it comes to Sappho's personal life – the aspect of her biography that scholars and readers are most eager to know about – the ancient record is confused. What did Sappho look like? A dialogue by Plato, written in the fourth century BC, refers to her as 'beautiful'; a later author insisted that she was 'very ugly, being short and swarthy'. Who were her family? The *Suda* (which gives eight possible names for Sappho's father) asserts that she had a daughter and a mother both named Kleïs, a gaggle of brothers, and a wealthy husband named Kerkylas, from the island of Andros. But some of these seemingly precious facts merely show that the encyclopedia – which, as old as it is, was compiled fifteen centuries after Sappho lived – could be prone to comic misunderstandings. 'Kerkylas', for instance, looks a lot like *kerkos*, Greek slang for 'penis', and 'Andros' is very close to the word for 'man'; and so the encyclopedia turns out to have been unwittingly recycling a tired old joke about oversexed Sappho, who was married to 'Dick of Man'.

Many other alleged facts of Sappho's biography similarly dissolve on close scrutiny. Was Sappho really a mother? There is indeed a fragment that mentions a girl named Kleïs, 'whose form resembles golden blossoms', but the word that some people have translated as 'daughter' can also mean 'child', or even 'slave'. (Because Greek children were often named for their grandparents, it's easy to see how the already wobbly assumption that Kleïs must have been a daughter in turn led to the assertion that Sappho had a mother with the same name.) Who were the members of her circle? The *Suda* refers by name to three female 'students', and three female companions – Atthis, Telesippa, and Megara – with whom she had 'disgraceful friendships'. But much of this is no more than can be reasonably extrapolated from the poems, since the extant verses mention nearly all those names. The compilers of the *Suda*, like scholars today, may have been making educated guesses.

Even Sappho's sexuality, which for general audiences is the most famous thing about her, has been controversial from the start. However exalted her reputation among the ancient literati, in Greek popular culture of the Classical period and afterward, Sappho was known primarily as an oversexed predator – of men. This, in fact, was the ancient cliché about 'Lesbians': when we hear the word today we think of love between women, but when the ancient Greeks heard the word they thought of fellatio. In classical Greek, the verb *lesbiazein* – 'to act like someone from Lesbos' – meant performing oral sex, an activity for which inhabitants of the island were thought to have a particular penchant. Comic playwrights and authors of light verse portrayed Sappho as just another daughter of Lesbos, only too happy to fall into bed with her younger male rivals.

For centuries, the most popular story about her love life was, in fact, one about a hopeless passion for a handsome young boatman called Phaon, which allegedly led her to jump off a cliff. That tale has been embroidered, dramatized, and novelized over the centuries by writers from Ovid – who in one poem has Sappho abjectly renouncing her gay past – to Erica Jong, in her 2003 novel *Sappho's Leap*. As fanciful as it is, it's easy to see how this melodrama of heterosexual passion could have been inspired by her verse, which so often describes the anguish of unrequited love. ('You have forgotten me / or you love someone else more.') The added element of suicide suggests that those who wove this improbable story wanted us to take away a moral: unfettered expressions of great passion will have dire consequences.

As time went on, the fantasies about Sappho's private life became more extreme. Midway through the first century AD the Roman philosopher Seneca, tutor to Nero, was complaining about a Greek scholar who had devoted an entire treatise to the question of whether Sappho was a prostitute. Some ancient writers assumed that there had to have been two Sapphos: one the great poet, the other the notorious slut. There is an entry for each in the *Suda*.

The uncertainties plaguing the biography of literature's most famous Lesbian explain why classicists who study Sappho like to cite the entry for her in Monique Wittig and Sande Zeig's *Lesbian Peoples: Material for a Dictionary* (1979). To honour Sappho's central position in the history of female homosexuality, the two editors devoted an entire page to her. The page is blank.

The controversies about Sappho's sexuality have never been far from the centre of scholarship about her. Starting in the early nineteenth century, when classics itself was becoming a formal discipline, scholars who were embarrassed by what they found in the fragments worked hard to whitewash Sappho's reputation. The title of one early work of German scholarship is 'Sappho Liberated from a Prevalent Prejudice': in it, the author acknowledged that what Sappho felt for her female friends was 'love' but hastened to insist that it was in no way 'objectionable, vulgarly sensual, and illegal', and that her poems of love were neither 'monstrous nor abominable'.

The eagerness to come up with 'innocent' explanations for the poet's attachment to young women persisted through the late nineteenth century and into the twentieth. The most tenacious theory held that Sappho was the head of a girls' boarding school, a matron whose interest in her pupils was purely pedagogical. (One scholar claimed to have found evidence that classes were taught on how to apply makeup.) Another theory made her into an august priestess, leading 'an association of young women who devoted themselves to the cult of the goddess'.

Most classicists today have no problem with the idea of a gay Sappho. But some have been challenging the interpretation of her work that seems most natural to twenty-first-century readers: that the poems are deeply personal expressions of private homoerotic passion. Pointing to the relentlessly public and communitarian character of ancient Greek society, with its clan allegiances, its endless rounds of athletic games and artistic competitions, its jammed calendar of civic and religious festivals, they wonder whether 'personal' poetry, as we understand the term, even existed for someone like Sappho. As André Lardinois, the co-author of the new English edition, has written, 'Can we be sure that these are really her own feelings? ... What is "personality" in such a group-oriented society as archaic Greece?'

Indeed, the vision of Sappho as a solitary figure pouring out her heart in the women's quarters of a nobleman's mansion is a sentimental anachronism — a projection, like so much of our thinking about her, of our own habits and institutions onto the past. In Lawrence Alma-Tadema's *Sappho and Alcaeus*, the Poetess and four diaphanously clad, flower-wreathed acolytes relax in a charming little performance space, enraptured as the male bard sings and plays, as if he were a Beat poet in a Telegraph Hill café. But Lardinois and others have argued that many, if not most, of Sappho's poems were written to be performed by choruses on public occasions. In some lyrics, the speaker uses the first-person plural 'we'; in others, the form of 'you' that she uses is the plural, suggesting that she's addressing a group — presumably the chorus, who danced as she sang. (Even when Sappho uses the first-person singular, it doesn't mean she was singing solo: in Greek tragedy, the chorus, which numbered fifteen singers, regularly uses 'I'.)

This communal voice, which to us seems jarring in lyrics of deep, even erotic feeling – imagine that Shakespeare's sonnets had been written as choral hymns – is one that some translators today simply ignore, in keeping with the modern interest in individual psychology. But if the proper translation of the sexy little Fragment 38 is not 'you scorch me' but 'you scorch us', which is what the Greek actually says, how, exactly, should we interpret it?

To answer that question, classicists lately have been imagining the purposes to which public performance of erotic poems might have been put. Ancient references to the poet's 'companions' and 'students' have led one expert to argue that Sappho was the leader of a female collective, whose role was 'instruction leading to marriage'. Rather than expressions of individual yearning for a young woman, the poems were, in Lardinois's view, 'public forms of praise of the general attractiveness of the girl', celebrating her readiness for wedlock and integration into the larger society. The late Harvard classicist Charles Segal made even larger claims. As he saw it, the strongly rhythmic erotic lyrics were 'incantatory' in nature; he believed that public performance of poems like Fragment 31 would have served to socialize desire itself for the entire city – to lift sexual yearning 'out of the realm of the formless and terrible, bring it into the light of form, make it visible to the individual poet and, by extension, to his or her society'.

Even purely literary issues – for instance, the tendency to think of Sappho as the inventor of 'the lyric I', a single, emotionally naked speaker who becomes a stand-in for the reader – are affected by these new theories. After all, if the 'I' who speaks in Sappho's work is a persona (a 'poetic construct rather than a real-life figure', as Lardinois put it) how much does her biography actually matter?

Between the paucity of actual poems and the woeful unreliability of the biographical tradition, these debates are unlikely to be resolved anytime soon. Indeed, the study of Sappho is beset by a curious circularity. For the better part of a millennium – between the compilation of the *Suda* and the late nineteenth century – the same bits of poetry and the same biographical gossip were endlessly recycled, the poetic fragments providing the sources for biographies that were then used as the basis for new interpretations of those same fragments. This is why the 'new Sappho' has been so galvanizing for classicists: every now and then, the circle expands, letting in a little more light.

Obbink's revelation last year was, in fact, only the latest in a series of papyrological discoveries that have dramatically enhanced our understanding of Sappho and her work. Until the late nineteenth century, when the papyri started turning up, there were only the ancient quotations. Since then, the amount of Sappho that we have has more than doubled.

In 1897, two young Oxford archaeologists started excavating a site in Egypt that had been the municipal dump of a town called Oxyrhynchus – 'the City of the Sharp-Nosed Fish'. In ancient times, the place had been home to a large Greek-speaking population. However lowly its original purpose, the dump soon yielded treasures. Papyrus manuscripts dating to the first few centuries AD, containing both Greek and Roman texts, began to surface. Some were fragments of works long known, such as the *Iliad*, but even these were of great value, since the Oxyrhynchus papyri were often far older than what had been, until that point, the oldest surviving copies. Others revealed works previously unknown.

Among the latter were several exciting new fragments of Sappho, some substantial. From the tattered papyri, the voice came through as distinctive as ever:

> Some men say cavalry, some men say infantry,
> some men say the navy's the loveliest thing
> on this black earth, but I say it's what-
>   ever you love

Over the decades that followed, more of the papyri were deciphered and published. But by 1955, when the Cambridge classicist Denys Page published *Sappho and Alcaeus*, a definitive study of the two poets from Lesbos, it seemed that even this rich new vein had been exhausted. 'There is not at present,' Page declared, 'any reason to expect that we shall ever possess much more of the poetry of Sappho and Alcaeus than we do today, and this seems a suitable time to begin the difficult and doubtful task of interpreting.'

Sappho herself, it seems fair to say, would have raised an eyebrow at Page's confidence in his judgment. Human fortune, she writes, is as variable as the weather at sea, where 'fair winds swiftly follow harsh gales'. And, indeed, this verse was unknown to Page, since it comes from the papyrus fragment that Dirk Obbink brought to light last year: the 'Brothers Poem'.

For specialists, the most exciting feature of the 'Brothers Poem' is that it seems to corroborate the closest thing we have to a contemporary reference to Sappho's personal life: an oblique mention of her in Herodotus' *Histories*, written about a century and a half after her death. During a long discussion of Egyptian society, Herodotus mentions one of Sappho's brothers, a rather dashing character named Charaxus. A swashbuckling merchant sailor, he supposedly spent a fortune to buy the freedom of a favourite courtesan in Egypt – an act, Herodotus reports, for which Sappho 'severely chided' her sibling in verse. Ovid and other later classical authors also refer to some kind of tension between Sappho and this brother, but, in the absence of a surviving poem on the subject by Sappho herself, generations of scholars were unable to verify even the brother's name.

So it's easy to imagine Dirk Obbink's excitement as he worked his way through the first lines of the poem:

> but you're always nattering on that Charaxus must
> come,
> his ship full-laden. That much, I reckon, Zeus
> knows …

The pious thing to do, the speaker says, is to pray to the gods for this brother's return, since human happiness depends on divine good will. The poem closes with the hope that another, younger brother will grow up honourably and save his family from heartache – presumably, the anxiety caused by their wayward elder sibling. At last, that particular biographical titbit could be confirmed.

For non-classicists, the 'Brothers Poem' may be less enthralling than the other recent Sappho find, the poem that surfaced in 2004, about old age – a bittersweet work indeed. After the University of Cologne acquired some papyri, scholars found that one of the texts overlapped with a poem already known: Fragment 58, one of the Oxyrhynchus papyri. The Oxyrhynchus fragment consisted mostly of the ends of a handful of lines; the new Cologne papyrus filled in the blanks, leaving only a few words missing. Finally, the lines made sense.

As with much Archaic Greek poetry, the newly restored Fragment 58 – the 'Old Age Poem', as it is now called – illustrates its theme with an example from myth. Sappho alludes to the story of Eos, the dawn goddess, who wished for, and was granted, eternal life for her mortal lover, Tithonus, but forgot to ask for eternal youth:

[I bring] the beautiful gifts of the violet Muses, girls,
and [I love] that song lover, the sweet-toned lyre.

My skin was [delicate] before, but now old age
[claims it]; my hair turned from black [to white].

My spirit has grown heavy; knees buckle
that once could dance light as fawns.

I often groan, but what can I do?
Impossible for humans not to age.

For they say that rosy-armed Dawn in love
went to the ends of the earth holding Tithonos,

beautiful and young, but in time grey old age
seized even him with an immortal wife.

Here as elsewhere in the new translation, Diane J. Rayor captures the distinctively plainspoken quality of Sappho's Greek, which, for all the poet's naked emotionality and love of luxe, is never overwrought or baroque. Every translation is a series of sacrifices; in Rayor's case, emphasis on plainness of expression sometimes comes at the cost of certain formal elements – not least, metre. The late classicist M. L. West, who published a translation in the *Times Literary Supplement*, took pains to emulate the long line of Sappho's original:

> But me – my skin which once was soft is withered now
> by age, my hair has turned to white which once was
>   black …

Still, given how disastrously cloying many attempts to recreate Sappho's verse as 'song' have proved to be, you're grateful for Rayor's directness. Her notes on the translations are particularly useful, especially when she alerts readers to choices that are left 'silent' in other English versions. The last extant line of Fragment 31, for instance, presents a notorious problem: it could mean something like 'all must be endured' or, on the other hand, 'all must be dared'. Rayor prefers 'endured', and tells you why she thinks it's the better reading.

Rayor makes one very interesting choice in translating the 'Old Age Poem'. The Cologne manuscript dates to the third century BC, which makes it the oldest and therefore presumably the most reliable manuscript of Sappho that we currently possess. In that text, the poem ends after the sixth couplet, with its glum reference to Tithonus being seized by grey old age. But Rayor has decided to include some additional lines that appear only in the fragmentary Oxyrhynchus papyrus. These give the poem a far more upbeat ending:

> Yet I love the finer things … this and passion
> for the light of life have granted me brilliance and beauty.

The manuscript containing those lines was copied out five hundred years after the newly discovered Cologne version – half a millennium further away from the moment when the Poetess first sang this song.

And so the new Sappho raises as many questions as it answers. Did different versions of a single poem coexist in antiquity, and, if so, did ancient audiences know or care? Who in the 'Brothers Poem' has been chattering on about Sappho's brother Charaxus, and why? Where, exactly, does the 'Old Age Poem' end? Was it a melancholy testament to the mortifying effects of age or a triumphant assertion of the power of beauty, of the 'finer things' – of poetry itself – to redeem the ravages of time? Even as we strain to hear this remarkable woman's sweet speech, the thrumming in our ears grows louder.

– *The New Yorker*, 16 March 2015

Not an Ideal Husband

By now, we have all heard the story. Like so many tragedies, this one begins with a husband and his wife. The husband seems a happy man, pre-eminent among his contemporaries, affable, well liked, someone whose weaknesses are balanced by a remarkable gift for inspiring affection and loyalty. (His relatives, on the other hand, are thought to be cold and greedy.) The wife, whose fiery inner passions are belied by a conventional exterior – she exults in the small routines of domestic life – is intensely, some might say madly, devoted to him. They have two small children: a boy, a girl.

Then something goes wrong. Some who have studied this couple say that it is the husband who grotesquely betrays the wife; others, who consider the wife too intense, too disagreeably self-involved, dispute the extent of the husband's culpability. (As often happens with literary marriages, each has fanatical partisans and just as fanatical detractors – most of whom, it must be said, are literary critics.) What we do know is that directly as a result of her husband's actions, the wife willingly goes to her death – but not before taking great pains to guarantee the safety of her two children. Most interesting and poignant of all, the knowledge of her impending death inspires the wife to previously unparalleled displays of eloquence: as her final hours approach, she articulates, with thrilling lyricism, what she knows about life, womanhood, marriage, death – and seems, as she does so, to speak for all women. It is only after her death, many feel, that her husband realizes the extent of his loss. She comes back, in a way, to haunt him: a speaking subject no longer, but rather the eerily silent object of her husband's solicitous, perhaps compensatory, ministrations.

This is the plot of Euripides' *Alcestis*. That it also resembles, uncannily in some respects, the plot of the life of Ted Hughes – whose final, posthumously published work is an adaptation of Euripides' play, may or may not be a coincidence. Because Hughes's *Alcestis* is a liberal adaptation, it cannot, in the end, illuminate this most controversial work of the most controversial of the Greek dramatists. (Scholars still can't decide whether it's supposed to be farce or tragedy.) But the choices Hughes makes as a translator and adapter – what he leaves out, what he adds, what he smooths over – do shed unexpected light on his career, and his life.

As Ted Hughes neared the end of his life, he devoted himself to translating a number of classical texts: a good chunk of Ovid's *Metamorphoses* in 1997, Racine's *Phèdre* in 1998 (performed by the Almeida Theatre Company at the Brooklyn Academy of Music in January 1999), and Aeschylus's *Oresteia*, commissioned by the Royal National Theatre for a performance in 1999 and published posthumously in that year. Hughes had translated one other classical text: Seneca's *Oedipus*, for a 1968 production by the Old Vic starring John Gielgud and Irene Worth. But with the exception of that work, the fit between the translator and the texts was never a comfortable one.

Hughes made his name as a poet of nature, and excluding the translations (he also translated Wedekind's *Spring Awakening* and

Lorca's *Blood Wedding*) and the self-revealing 1997 *Birthday Letters*, addressed to his late wife, the poet Sylvia Plath, he rarely strayed from the natural world, for which he had extraordinary imaginative sympathy (and which in turn inspired his fascination with Earth-Mother folklore and animistic magic). A glance at his published work reveals the following titles: *The Hawk in the Rain*, *Crow: From the Life and Songs of the Crow*, *Flowers and Insects*, *Wolfwatching*, *Rain-Charm for the Duchy*, *Cave Birds*, *The River*. 'They are a way of connecting all my deepest feelings together,' Hughes told an interviewer who'd asked why he spoke so often through animals. Yet the poet's appreciation for – and artistic use of – the life of birds, fish, insect predators, of barnyards and wild landscapes, was anything but sentimental. As Helen Vendler observed in a review of the 1984 collection *The River*, Hughes, who liked to represent himself 'as a man who has seen into the bottomless pit of aggression, death, murder, holocaust, catastrophe', had taken as his real subject 'the moral squalor attending the brute survival instinct'. In Hughes's best poetry, the natural world, with its dazzling beauties and casual cruelties, served as an ideal vehicle for investigating that dark theme.

It was a theme for which his tastes in language and diction particularly well suited him. Especially at the beginning of his career, the verse in which Hughes expressed himself was tough, vivid, sinewy, full (as Vendler wrote about *The River*) of 'violent phrases, thick sounds, explosive words', the better to convey a vision of life according to which an ordinary country bird, say, can bristle with murderous potential. 'Terrifying are the attent sleek thrushes on the lawn / More coiled steel than living – a poised / Dark deadly eye …', goes the violent beginning of 'Thrushes', from the 1960 collection *Lupercal*, hissing suggestively with alliterative *s*'s, exploding with menacing *t*'s and *d*'s, thick with cackling *c*'s and *k*'s. It was, indeed, Hughes's 'virile, deep banging' poems that first entranced the young Plath; she wrote home to her mother about them. (At the end of his career a certain slackness and talkiness tended to replace virile lyric intensity; few of the *Birthday Letters* poems, for instance, achieve more than a documentary interest. Hughes himself seemed to be aware of this. 'I keep writing this and that, but it seems pitifully little for the time I spend pursuing it,' he wrote to his friend Lucas Myers in 1984. 'I wonder sometimes if things might have gone differently without the events of '63 and '69 [Plath's suicide in 1963 and, in 1969, the suicide of Hughes's companion Assia Wevill, who also killed the couple's daughter]. I have an idea of these two episodes as giant steel doors shutting down over great parts of myself … No doubt a more resolute artist would have penetrated the steel doors.')

A taste for violence in both theme and diction is undoubtedly what drew the younger Hughes to Seneca's *Oedipus*. The rhetorical extravagance of the Stoic philosopher and dramatist's verse, the sense of language being pushed to its furthest extremes, the famously baroque descriptions of the violence to which the body can be subjected: these have long been acknowledged as characteristic of Seneca's style. In his introduction to the published version of the *Oedipus* translation, Hughes (who in works such as his 1977 collection, *Gaudete*, warned against rejecting the primordial aspect of nature in favour of cold intellectualism) commented on his preference for the 'primitive' Senecan treatment of the Oedipus myth over the 'fully civilized' Sophoclean version. Seneca's blood-spattered text afforded Hughes plenty of opportunities to indulge his penchant for the uncivilized, often to great effect: his renderings of Seneca's dense Latin have an appropriately clotted, claustrophobic feel, and don't shy away from all the gore. The man who, in a poem called 'February 17th', coolly describes the aftermath of his decapitation of an unborn lamb *in utero* ('a smoking slither of oils and soups and syrups') was clearly not fazed by incest and self-mutilation. 'My blood,' Hughes's Jocasta says, '... poured on / into him blood from my toes my finger ends / blind blood blood from my gums and eyelids / blood from the roots of my hair ... / flowed into the knot of his bowels ...', etc.

Hughes's Seneca was good, strong stuff because in Seneca, as in Hughes's own work, theme and language are meant to work at the same pitch – the moral squalor was nicely matched by imagistic, prosodic, and linguistic squalor. Hughes was much less successful when, a generation later, he returned to classical texts – especially the dramas. You could certainly make the case that classical tragedy (and its descendants in French drama of Racine's *siècle classique*) is about nothing if not the moral squalor that attends the brute survival instinct – not least the audience's sense of moral squalor, its guilty pleasure in not being at all like the exalted but doomed scapegoat-hero. But it is an error typical of Hughes as a translator to think that you can extract the squalid contents from the highly stylized form and still end up with something that has the power and dreadful majesty of the *Oresteia* or *Phèdre*. Commenting on *The River*, Professor Vendler observed that 'Hughes notices in nature what suits his purpose': the same is true of his approach to the classics.

It's not that Hughes's translations of Racine and Aeschylus can't convey with great vividness the moral and emotional states of the characters; they can. 'I have not drunk this strychnine day after day / As an idle refreshment,' Hughes's besotted Phèdre tells her stepson, with an appropriately astringent mix of pathos and wryness. His Clytemnestra has 'a man's dreadful will in the scabbard of her body / Like a polished blade' – lines that Aeschylus never wrote, it's true, but that convey the poet's preoccupation particularly with the threateningly androgynous character of his monstrous queen. But what Hughes's classical translations lack – disastrously – is grandeur. And the grandeur of high tragedy arises from the friction between the unruly passions and actions that are represented (incestuous longings, murderous and suicidal violence – moral squalor, in short) and the highly, if not indeed rigidly, stylized poetic forms that contain them: Racine's glacially elegant alexandrines, or the insistent iambic trimeters of the Greek dialogue alternating at regular intervals with choral lyrics in elaborate metres. William Christie, the leader of the baroque music ensemble Les Arts Florissants, has spoken of 'the high stylization that releases, rather than constrains, emotion': this is a perfect description of the aesthetics of classical tragedy.

Hughes – never committed to strict poetic form to begin with, and increasingly given to loose, unrhythmical versification – is suspicious of the formal restraints that characterize the classical. Like so many contemporary translators of the classics, he mistakes artifice for stiffness, and restraint for lack of feeling, and he tries to do away with them. In his *Oresteia* the diction is more elevated than what you find in some translations (certainly more so than what you find in David Slavitt's vulgar *Oresteia* translation for the Penn Greek Drama series, which has Clytemnestra pouring a 'cocktail of vintage evils' and addressing the chorus leader as 'mister'); but still Hughes tends too much to tone things down, smooth things out, explain things away.

Few moments in Greek drama are as moving as the chorus's description, in the *Agamemnon*, of Iphigenia, about to be sacrificed at Aulis by Agamemnon, pleading for her life 'with prayers and cries to her father' and then, even more poignantly, after she has been brutally gagged, 'hurling at the sacrificers piteous arrows of the eyes'. But Hughes's rather suburban Iphigenia cries, 'Daddy, Daddy,' and simply weeps ('her eyes swivel in their tears'). Such choices remind you of how much the extreme figurative language that Aeschylus gives his characters has regularly confounded, not to say embarrassed, translators. The Watchman at the opening of the *Agamemnon* is so terrified of the adulterous, man-emulating queen that he can't even talk to *himself* about it: 'A great ox stands upon my tongue,' he mutters ominously. The line has tremendous archaic heft and power, something that cannot be said for Hughes's 'Let their tongue lie still – squashed flat'.

No doubt because of the many opportunities Ovid's *Metamorphoses* affords for crafting images of the animals into which so many characters are transformed, the most successful of Hughes's late-career translations is his *Tales from Ovid*. But even here the poet fails to realize how important Ovid's form is. In his Introduction, Hughes makes due reference to the Hellenophile poet's 'sweet, witty soul', but he's clearly far more interested in what he sees as the *Metamorphoses*' subject: 'a torturous subjectivity and catastrophic extremes of passion that border on the grotesque'. He manages, in other words, to find the Seneca in Ovid. And yet the pleasure of Ovid's epic lies precisely in the delicate tension between all those regressive, grotesque, nature-based metamorphoses and the 'fully civilized' verses in which they are narrated: a triumph of Culture over Nature if ever there was one. Hughes's Ovid is often very effective, but it is not sweet and witty.

It's tempting to think that Hughes found Euripides' *Alcestis* interesting precisely because this work – the tragedian's earliest surviving play – presents so many problems of both form and content. With its unpredictable oscillations in tone and style, it seems positively to invite abandonment of formal considerations altogether. 'A critic's battlefield,' the scholar John Wilson wrote in his introduction to a 1968 collection of essays on the play. The war continues to rage on.

Alcestis was first performed in 438 BC in Athens at the Greater Dionysia, an annual combined civic and religious festival, including a dramatic competition, that must have resembled a cross between the Fourth of July, Thanksgiving, and the Oscars. The drama was presented as the fourth play in a tetralogy – the final spot, that is, in which amusingly bawdy 'satyr plays' were normally presented, presumably to alleviate the pity and fear triggered by the three tragedies that had preceded it onstage. (The three that preceded *Alcestis*, two of which seem to have dealt with the sufferings of passionate women, are lost.) And yet, this fourth play – in which Queen Alcestis voluntarily dies in place of her husband, King Admetos, when the appointed day of his death is at hand, only to be brought back from Hades by Herakles in the play's bizarre finale – unsettlingly mixes elements of high tragedy with its scenes of comic misunderstandings, elaborate teasing, and drunken hijinks.

The first, 'tragic' half of the short drama begins with a sombre expository prologue by Apollo, followed by a debate between Apollo and Death, who has come to claim Alcestis and who is warned that he won't, in the end, get his way. We are then plunged into the mortal world and a mood of unrelenting gloom: a heart-rending scene of Alcestis's slow death; her farewells to her children (whom she relinquishes to her husband on the condition that he not neglect them) and to her husband (who vows never to remarry); her impassioned outburst, addressed to her marriage bed, as she sees death approaching; her funeral procession, which is interrupted by a violent argument between Admetos and his aged father, Pheres (who along with his elderly wife refused to die in his son's place when given the chance to do so); and a grief-stricken Admetos's return to his empty house after the funeral.

The second, 'comic', half presents the spectacle of the rambunctious Herakles' arrival at the house of mourning (he is en route to yet another of his Labours); Admetos's excruciatingly diplomatic efforts to keep up his reputation as a good friend and legendary host (he doesn't want Herakles to know Alcestis has died lest his guest feel unwelcome); a drunken, feasting Herakles' discovery of the truth, and his subsequent vow to bring his friend's wife back; and the hero's rescue of Alcestis after a wrestling match with Death himself, which takes place beside Alcestis's tomb. The play ends with the eerie spectacle of a triumphant Herakles, like the father of a bride, handing over the veiled and silent figure of Alcestis to Admetos without, at first, telling Admetos who the woman is – teasing him in order to prolong the suspense. She never speaks again during the course of the play.

The hodgepodge of moods, styles, and themes suggested by even this cursory summary has made interpretation of this strange work particularly thorny. To cite John Wilson further:

> Even the genre to which the play belongs is disputed
> – is it a tragedy, a satyr play, or the first example of a
> tragicomedy? Who is the main character, Alcestis or
> Admetos? And through whose eyes are we to see this
> wife and this husband? Is Alcestis as noble as she says
> she is? And is Admetos worthy of her devotion, or
> does he deserve all the blame that his father, Pheres,
> heaps upon him? And is the salvation of Alcestis a
> true mystery, a sardonic 'and so they lived happily
> ever after', or simply the convenient end of an
> entertainment?

These questions continue to puzzle classicists, despite radical shifts in the way we read classical texts. Since Wilson wrote in the 1960s, no literary-critical school has influenced classical scholarship so much as feminist studies has; and the *Alcestis* has proved an especially rich vehicle for scholars interested in demonstrating the extent to which literary production in classical Greece reflected the patriarchal bias of Athenian society during its cultural heyday. 'The genre of the *Alcestis*,' the classicist Nancy Sorkin Rabinowitz has written in a stimulating if perhaps too ideologically rigid study of Euripides' handling of female characters, '… depends on gender. On the surface, it is comic: death leads to life, and a funeral resolves into a wedding. But is it a happy ending for Alcestis as well as for Admetos? Although funeral and wedding may seem to be opposites, they come to much the same thing for this woman.'

You don't have to be a feminist hardliner to have your doubts about Admetos. Even at the very beginning of the drama, as Alcestis lies dying within the house, the king's self-involvement takes your breath away. It is true that the laments he utters in his exchange with the dying Alcestis are all fairly conventional ('Don't forsake me,' 'I am nothing without you'), and yet their cumulative effect is unsettling: gradually, it strikes you that for Admetos this domestic disaster is all about him. Alcestis's death, he cries, is 'heavier than any death of my own' – an appeal for sympathy that's a bit much, considering that she's dying precisely because he was afraid to. He's Periclean Athens's answer to the guy in the joke about the classic definition of chutzpah – the one who murders his parents and then throws himself on the mercy of the court because he's an orphan.

Admetos makes the dying Alcestis several somewhat excessive promises: among them, a vow to ban all revelry for a full year, and an oath never to take another woman into his house. Yet by the end of the play he will have broken both: first when he allows Herakles to be feted with wine and music, and then when he accepts, as a man might accept a new bride, the anonymous veiled woman into his household – before he knows she's Alcestis. Most bizarrely, he declares that he will have an artisan fashion a statue of Alcestis, which he will take to bed and caress as if it were she – a 'cold pleasure', to be sure, but one that will help to assuage his loss. For some critics, this has a fetishistic, doth-protest-too-much quality; whatever you make of it, it's striking that, having promised to mourn Alcestis forever, her husband begins, before she even dies, to seek comfort (however cold) for himself.

So the husband is a weak man in the first part of the play. But he must be so, since whatever 'tragic' – or, for that matter, dramatic – development Euripides' play has depends on Admetos's evolution – on his starting out as a less than admirable man who comes to realize that the existence he has purchased with his wife's life isn't worth having precisely because he has lost her. 'Now I understand,' he exclaims at the play's climax, right before Herakles enters with the resurrected Alcestis. Even so, this king is no hero: Alcestis's miraculous return from the grave yanks her husband back from the brink of truly tragic self-knowledge, the kind he'd have acquired if he had had to live with his loss, as characters in 'real' tragedies do. (When they don't kill themselves, that is.)

As it is, Admetos gets to eat his cake and have it, too. 'Many readers will feel [his grief] does not change him enough,' the Harvard classicist Charles Segal tartly observed in one of several penetrating essays he wrote on this play. Richmond Lattimore, who translated the *Alcestis* for the University of Chicago Greek Drama series nearly half a century ago, was moved, similarly, to question Admetos's character, using the bemused rhetorical-question mode into which those who have grappled with the *Alcestis* keep falling, no doubt because the work's violent wobbling between genres makes any definitive pronouncement seem foolhardy. 'If a husband lets his wife die for him,' Lattimore asked, 'what manner of man must that husband be?'

*

Hughes's *Alcestis* adaptation invites us to believe that this is, in fact, the wrong question to be asking. His version is wholly unconcerned with Admetos's flaws, not least because in his version, Admetos has no flaws. Everything in Euripides that suggests we ought to question the husband's character has here been excised; instead, it's God who gets the rough treatment. It's a striking alteration.

The clean-up job begins early on. In Euripides' play we learn that Apollo, in gratitude for being well treated *chez* Admetos, has promised the mortal king that he will be able to avoid his death if he can find someone to die in his place; Admetos tries all his loved ones in turn until finally his wife agrees to die for him. But in Hughes's version, Admetos is spared the embarrassing (indeed, damning) task of begging his relatives – and wife – for volunteers; here, it's Apollo who 'canvasses' for substitutes. In fact, Apollo doesn't even have to ask Alcestis, as in Euripides' play Admetos most certainly does: she just volunteers. (It's interesting that Hughes's heroine is more faithful to her counterpart in the Greek original than his Admetos is to his; and when he gives her lines that Euripides didn't – as when, in her farewell to her daughter, she pathetically exclaims, 'She will not even know what I looked like' – the drama is enhanced.)

Similarly, Hughes smooths away any sign of what Charles Segal calls the 'unthinking self-centredness of the husband'. He erases the solipsistic whininess from Admetos's laments at the beginning of the play. The breathtakingly self-involved utterances that Euripides puts in Admetos's mouth, well translated by Lattimore – 'sorrow for all who love you – most of all for me / and for the children' and 'Ah, ['good-bye' is] a bitter word for me to hear, / heavier than any death of my own' – here become the considerably less galling 'Fight against it, Alcestis. / Fight for your children, for me' and 'Good-bye! – don't use that word. / Only live, live, live, live.' (For American readers, at least, the latter will have an unfortunate Auntie Mame-ish ring.)

Most strikingly, Hughes eradicates any sense of the strange excessiveness of Admetos's promise to build a replica of his wife, which in the new version becomes a dismissive, indeed incredulous, rhetorical question: 'What shall I do, / Have some sculptor make a model of you? / Stretch out with it, on our bed, / Call it Alcestis, whisper to it? / Tell it all I would have told you? / Embrace it – horrible! – stroke it! / Knowing it can never be you ...' Hughes's subtle rewriting inverts the whole point of the scene. The original hints disturbingly at the husband's readiness to accept a substitute for the dead wife; the new version emphasizes the husband's steadfast fidelity. (To further deflect blame from Admetos, Hughes makes his father, Pheres, particularly disgusting. Here the old man not only refuses to die for his son, but 'screeches' and 'wails' at the younger man to 'Die ... clear off and die.')

Hughes's alterations, ostensibly minor, ultimately sap the strength of Euripides' dramatic climaxes. In the original, the culminating scene in which a veiled, voiceless Alcestis returns home to her husband on Herakles' arm owes much of its eeriness precisely to Admetos's deathbed promise, which has prepared us for the idea, however odd, that the king will settle for an inhuman facsimile of his dead wife; and lo and behold, at the 'happy' ending we see him holding hands with something that could well be such a dummy. But since Hughes has dispensed with Admetos's vow, the climax loses all of its creepy potential. Once again, the translator's embarrassment about the grand, bizarre qualities that so often characterize tragic action and diction takes its toll in dramatic effectiveness.

In the original, what leads us to a fleeting suspicion that Herakles' companion is, in fact, nothing more than a statue is the figure's total silence during a lengthy exchange between Admetos and Herakles – a muteness that clearly disturbs the other characters and, precisely because we're afraid the silent woman might be just a simulacrum, a revenant, ought to disturb us, the audience, too. In Euripides, an agitated Admetos turns to Herakles and demands: 'But why does she just stand there, voiceless?' Fred Chappell's rendering for the Penn Series nicely conveys Admetos's agitation: 'But why does my Alcestis stand so silent?' In Hughes's version, an ever-polite Admetos blandly murmurs, 'Will she speak?' You wonder whether he cares.

On the face of it, at least part of the reason for Hughes's shifting of emphasis – and any suspicion of moral weakness – away from Admetos is that he wants his adaptation to be a grand dramatic and poetic statement about the triumph of the human spirit, about mortality and the victory of love over death. The husband and wife are idealized, whereas there's a lot of complaining about 'God' and his pettiness and cruel indifference to human suffering ('As usual, God is silent'). To bolster this cosmic interpretation of the original, Hughes adds, in the Herakles scene, elaborate riffs on Aeschylus's antiauthoritarian *Prometheus Bound*, with its questioning of Zeus's justice, and on Euripides' own profoundly antireligious *Madness of Herakles* (in which the hero, freshly returned home from his labours, is temporarily maddened by a vengeful goddess and in his delusion murders his wife and children). And Hughes's dark mutterings about 'nuclear bomb[s] spewing a long cloud / of consequences' and the accusatory descriptions of God as 'the maker of the atom' who is served by 'electro-technocrats' suggest as well that the poet had not given up his preference for primitive Nature over cold Culture.

Yet even as Hughes ups the thematic ante in his adaptation, formal problems seriously undercut his ambitions. Perhaps inevitably when dealing with *Alcestis*, the translation is, even more than his others, marred by the poet's inability to find a suitable tone. In what looks like an attempt to convey the tonal variety of Euripides' hybrid drama, Hughes experiments more than previously with slangy, playful diction. The results can be odd, and often betray the dignity of the original where it is, in fact, dignified. 'You may call me a god. / You may call me whatever you like,' Hughes's Apollo says in his prologue speech, which in the original is crucial for setting the mournful tone of the entire first half. It's a bizarre thing for Apollo to say: characters in Greek tragedies get zapped by thunderbolts for far less presumptuous haggling with divinities. (*Alcestis* begins, in fact, with a dire reference to Zeus's incineration of the hubristic Aesculapius, Apollo's son, who dared to raise the dead – the first allusion to the all-important theme of resurrection.) Apollo goes on: 'The dead must die forever. / That is what the thunder said. The dead / Are dead are dead are dead are dead / Forever ...' You suspect Hughes is trying here to convey the thudding infinite nothingness of death, but bits like this are unfortunate reminders that the translator was also a prolific author of children's books. The intrusion of comic informality is hard enough to adjust to in Euripides' *Alcestis*, where the biggest moral problem is a husband's gross inadequacies; but it's a disaster in Hughes's *Alcestis*, where the big moral problem is God's gross inadequacies.

Hughes, it should be said, wasn't the first widower poet for whom the opportunity to translate the *Alcestis* served as the vehicle for a corrective shift in emphases. In Robert Browning's long historical poem *Balaustion's Adventure* (the subtitle is 'Including a Transcript of Euripides'), which was composed after the death of his wife, Elizabeth, a poetess comes to Athens from Rhodes to meet Euripides, and then sets about adapting *Alcestis*. But her version – and, by extension, the Browning version – turns out to be a redemptive one. In it, 'a new Admetos' rejects out of hand

Alcestis's offer to die in his place: "'Tis well that I depart, and thou remain,' he tells his wife, with whom, indeed, he gets to enjoy a fairy-tale posterity. ('The two,' Browning writes, 'lived together long and well.') Hughes's adaptation renovates Euripides along comparable lines. If the ancient dramatist's *Alcestis* forces us to ask, 'If a husband lets his wife die for him, what manner of man must that husband be?' then the contemporary poet's *Alcestis* asks, 'If God lets people die, what manner of god must He be?' In Hughes, as in Browning, there are no guilty husbands – no profound delving into the emotional (if not moral) squalor that often goes with being the survivor. There are just guilty abstractions.

Disturbing silences like the one with which Euripides' *Alcestis* concludes are a leitmotif in the drama of Plath and Hughes. In *Bitter Fame*, her biography of Plath, Anne Stevenson describes a tiff between Plath and Hughes's sister, Olwyn, that took place during the Christmas holidays in 1960: depending on whose side you're on, the episode demonstrates either Plath's irrationality or Olwyn Hughes's coldness. In response to a remark of Olwyn's that she was 'awfully critical', Plath 'glared accusingly' at her sister-in-law but refused to respond, keeping up her 'unnerving stare' in total silence. 'Why doesn't she say something?' Olwyn recalled thinking. (*That* would have been an excellent translation of Admetos's climactic line, conveying vividly the frustration and unease of someone faced with this particular brand of passive-aggressiveness.) As recently as a few years ago, Olwyn Hughes, in a letter to Janet Malcolm, was clearly still smarting from what Malcolm, in her book about Plath and Hughes, *The Silent Woman*, called Plath's 'Medusan', 'deadly, punishing' speechlessness.

But if Plath was, like Alcestis, the 'silent woman', Hughes himself was the silent man – aggressively, punishingly so, at least in the eyes of those who wanted to know more about the characters in this famous literary/domestic 'tragedy', the passions of whose 'characters' only the language of Greek myth and classical drama, it sometimes seems, can capture. ('They have eaten the pomegranate seeds that tie them to the underworld,' Malcolm wrote; 'I go about full with the darkness of my flame, like Phèdre ...', Plath herself wrote.) When Hughes's *Birthday Letters* appeared in 1997, it met with a variety of reactions: horror, joy, shock, surprise, anxiety, enthusiasm, etc. But what everyone agreed on was that it was, in essence, a relief: finally, Hughes was speaking.

And why not? 'Ted Hughes's history seems to be uncommonly bare of the moments of mercy that allow one to undo or redo one's actions and thus feel that life isn't entirely tragic,' Malcolm wrote. *Birthday Letters* was viewed by many as a kind of second chance, an opportunity to undo, or perhaps to redo, his public image with respect to his dead wife. (The same is true of the personal effects – passports, letters, photographs, manuscripts – that had belonged to Hughes, and which appear to have been the bases for several of the 'Letters'. 'He is thought of by critics as being so self-protective and so unrevealing of himself,' said Stephen Enniss, the curator of literary collections at the Robert W. Woodruff Library at Emory University, which now owns Hughes' papers. 'I think the archive will make him appear more human, more sympathetic than the detached voice and aloofness we had known.')

Writers – even those who appear aloof and voiceless about their private lives – can reveal themselves inadvertently. Reading Malcolm's description of the trapped Hughes, I found it hard not to think of Euripides' *Alcestis*, a play that notoriously allows a flawed man to undo and redo the fatal past. The undoings and redoings you find in Hughes's almost inadvertently moving adaptation of that work – the elisions, omissions, and reconfigurations – suggest that the poet's most revealing public utterance with respect to Plath may not have been *Birthday Letters* after all. In her way – her 'veiled' way – the most eloquent figure, among so many strange and tragic silences, has turned out to be Euripides' silent woman.

– *The New York Review of Books*, 27 April 2000

The Bad Boy of Athens

In the early spring of 411 BC, Euripides finally got what was coming to him. The playwright, then in his seventies, had always been the bad boy of Athenian drama. He was the irreverent prankster who, in his *Electra*, parodied the famous recognition scene in Aeschylus' *Libation Bearers*. He was an avant-garde intellectual who took an interest in the latest theorists – he is said to have been a friend of Socrates, and it was at his home that Protagoras ('man is the measure of all things') first read his agnostic treatise on the gods; in works like *The Madness of Herakles*, he questioned the established Olympian pantheon. Stylistically, he was a playful postmodernist whose sly rearranging of traditional mythic material, in bitter fables like *Orestes*, deconstructed tragic conventions, anticipating by twenty-five centuries a theatre whose patent subject was the workings of the theatre itself.

But no aspect of the playwright's roiling opus was more famous, in his own day, than his penchant for portraying deranged females. Among them are the love-mad queen Phaedra, whose unrequited lust leads her to suicide and murder (the subject of not one but two *Hippolytus* plays by the poet, one now lost); the distraught widow Evadne in *Suppliant Women*, who incinerates herself on her dead husband's grave; the ruthless granny Alcmene in *Children of Herakles*, who violently avenges herself on her male enemies; the wild-eyed Cassandra in *Trojan Women*; the list goes on and on. And, of course, there was Medea, whom the Athenians knew from established legend as the murderess of her own brother, the sorceress who dreamed up gruesome ways to destroy her husband Jason's enemy Pelias, and whom Euripides – not surprisingly, given his tastes in female characters – decided, in his staging of the myth, to make the murderess of her own children as well.

And so it was that, shortly after winter was over in 411, the women of Athens had their revenge on the man who'd given womanhood such a bad name. Or at least they did in one playwright's fantasy. In that year, the comic dramatist Aristophanes staged his *Thesmophoriazousae*. (The tongue-twister of a title means 'Women Celebrating the Thesmophoria' – this latter being an annual, all-female fertility festival associated with Demeter.) In this brilliant literary fantasy, Euripides learns that the women of the city are using the religious festival as a pretext to hold a debate on whether they ought to kill the playwright in revenge for being badmouthed by him in so many works over the years. Desperate to know what they're saying about him, and eager to have someone speak up on his behalf – something no real woman would do – Euripides persuades an aged kinsman, Mnesilochus, to attend the festival in drag, spy on the proceedings, and, if necessary, speak in the poet's defence. The plan, of course, backfires, Mnesilochus is found out, and only a last-minute rescue by Euripides himself – he comes swooping onto the stage, dressed as Perseus, in the contraption used in tragedies to hoist gods aloft – can avert disaster. Peace, founded on a promise by the playwright never to slander women again, is finally made between this difficult man of the theatre and his angry audience. The play ends in rejoicing.

Many contemporary classicists – this writer included – would argue that the females of Athens were taking things far too personally. Athenian drama, presented with much ceremony during the course of a public and even patriotic yearly civic festival, structured on the armature of heroic myth, rigidly conventional in form and diction, was not 'realistic'; we must be careful, when evaluating and interpreting these works, of our own tendency to see drama in purely personal terms, as a vehicle for psychological investigations. If anything, Athenian tragedy seems to have been useful as an artistic means of exploring concerns that, to us, seem to be unlikely candidates for an evening of thrilling drama: the nature of the state, the difficult relationship – always of concern in a democracy – between remarkable leaders (tragedy's 'heroes') and the collective citizen body.

In particular, the dialogic nature of drama made it a perfect vehicle for giving voice to – literally acting out – the tensions that underlay the smooth ideological surface of the aggressively imperialistic Athenian democracy. Tensions, that is, between personal morality and the requirements of the state (or army, as in Sophocles' *Philoctetes*), and between the ethical obligations imposed by family and those imposed by the city (*Antigone*); and the never-quite-satisfying negotiations between the primitive impulse toward personal vengeance and the civilized rule of law (*Oresteia*). Greek tragedy was political theatre in a way we cannot imagine, or replicate, today; there was more than a passing resemblance between the debates enacted before the citizen members of the assembly, and the conflicts, *agones*, dramatized before the eyes of those same citizens in the theatre. Herodotus tells the story of a Persian king who bemusedly describes the Greek *agora*, the central civic meeting space, as 'a place in the middle of the city where the people tell each other lies'. That's what the theatre of Dionysus was, too.

This is the context in which we must interpret tragedy's passionate females – as odd as it may seem to us today. The wild women characters to whom Aristophanes' female Athenians so hotly objected weren't so much reflections of real contemporary females and their concerns – the preoccupation of Athenian theatre being issues of import to the citizen audience, which was free, propertied, and male; we still can't be sure whether women even attended the theatre – as, rather, symbolic entities representing everything 'other' to that smoothly coherent citizen identity. (Because women – thought to be irrational, emotional, deceitful, slaves of passion – were themselves 'other' to all that the free, rational, self-controlled male citizen was.) As such, Greek drama's girls and women – pathetic, suffering, angry, violent, noble, wicked – were ideal mouthpieces for all the concerns that imperial state ideology, with its drive toward centralization, homogenization, and unity, necessarily suppressed or smoothed over: family blood ties, the interests of the private sphere, the anarchic, self-indulgent urges of the individual psyche, secret longings for the glittering heroic and aristocratic past.

For this reason, the conflicts between tragedy's males and females are never merely domestic spats. Clytemnestra, asserting the interests of the family, obsessed by the sacrifice of her innocent daughter Iphigenia (an act that represents the way in which the domestic and individual realms are always 'sacrificed' to the collective good in wartime), kills her husband in revenge, but is herself murdered by their son – who later is acquitted by an Athenian jury. Antigone, for her part, prefers her uncle's decree of death to a life in which she is unable to honour family ties as she sees fit. To be sure, this is a schematic reading, one that doesn't take into account the genius of the Attic poets: men, after all, who had wives and mothers and daughters, and who were able to enhance their staged portraits of different types of females with the kind of real-life nuances that we today look for in dramatic characters. But it is useful to keep the schema in mind, if only as a counterbalance to our contemporary temptation to see all drama in terms of psyches rather than polities.

Two recent productions of works by Euripides illuminate, in very different ways, the dangers of failing to calibrate properly the precise value of the feminine in Greek, and particularly Euripidean, drama. As it happens, they make a nicely complementary pair. One, *Medea*, currently enjoying a highly praised run on Broadway in a production staged by Deborah Warner and starring the Irish actress Fiona Shaw, is the playwright's best-known and most-performed play, not least because it conforms so nicely to contemporary expectations of what a night at the theatre should entail. (It looks like it's all about emotions and female suffering.) The other, *The Children of Herakles*, first produced a couple of years after *Medea*, is Euripides' least-known and most rarely performed drama: Peter Sellars's staging of it in Cambridge, with the American Repertory Theatre, marks the work's first professional production in the United States. That this play seems to be characterized far more by a preoccupation with dry and undramatic political concerns than by what we think of as a 'typically' Euripidean emphasis on feminine passions is confirmed by classicists' habit of referring to it as one of the poet's two 'political plays'. And yet *Medea* is more political than you might at first think – and certainly more so than its noisy and shallow new staging suggests; while the political message of *The Children of Herakles* depends much more on the portrayal of its female characters than anyone, including those who have been bold enough to stage it for the first time, might realize.

By far the more interesting and thoughtful of the two productions is the Cambridge *Children of Herakles*. Euripides' tale of the sufferings of the dead Herakles' refugee children, pursued from their native land by the evil king Eurystheus and forced to seek asylum in Athens, has been much maligned for its episodic and ostensibly disjointed structure: the Aristotle scholar John Jones, writing on the *Poetics*, summed up the critical consensus by calling it 'a thoroughly bad play'. But the imaginative if overcooked staging by Peter Sellars, who here effects one of his well-known updatings, suggests that it can have considerable power in performance.

The legend on which this odd drama is based was familiar to the Athenian audience, not least because it confirmed their sense of themselves as a just people. After his death, Herakles' children are pursued from their native city, Argos, by Eurystheus – he's the cruel monarch who has given Herakles all those terrible labours to perform – and, led by their father's aged sidekick, Iolaos, they wander from city to city, seeking refuge from the man who wants to wipe them out. Only the Athenians agree to give them shelter and, more, to defend them; they defeat the Argive army in a great battle during which Eurystheus is killed – after which his severed head is brought back to Herakles' mother, Alcmene, who gouges his eyes out with dress pins. (There was a place near Athens called 'Eurystheus' Head', where the head was supposed to have been buried.) The legend was frequently cited in political orations of Euripides' time as an example of the justness of the Athenian state – its willingness to make war, if necessary, on behalf of the innocent and powerless.

And yet Euripides went to considerable lengths to alter this mythic account precisely by adding new female voices. In his version, the two most significant actions in the story are assigned to women. First of all, he invents a daughter for Herakles, traditionally called Macaria but referred to in the text of the play simply as *parthenos*, 'virgin'; in this new version of the famous patriotic myth, it is not merely the Athenians' military might that saves the day, but Macaria's decision, in response to one of those eleventh-hour oracles that inevitably wreak havoc with the lives of Greek tragic virgins, to die as a sacrificial victim in order to ensure victory in battle. The playwright also makes Alcmene a more vigorous, if sinister, presence: in this version, it is she who has Eurystheus killed, in flagrant violation of Athens's rules for the treatment of prisoners of war. The play ends abruptly after she gives the order for the execution.

Classicists have always thought the play is 'political', but only because there are scenes in which various male characters – the caustic envoy of the Argive king, the sympathetic Athenian monarch Demophon, son of Theseus – debate what the just course for Athens ought to be. (Come to the aid of the refugees and thereby risk war? Or incur religious pollution by failing to honour the claims of suppliants at an altar?) But it's only when you understand the political dimensions of the tragedy's portrayal of women that you can see just how political a play it really is. The contrast between the two female figures – the self-sacrificing Macaria, and the murderous Alcmene; one concerned only for her family and allies, the other intent on the gratification of private vengeance – could not be greater.

In symbolic terms, the terms familiar to Euripides' audiences, the play is about the politics of civic belonging. Herakles' children, homeless, stateless, are eager to re-establish their civic identity – to belong somewhere; Macaria's action demonstrates that in order to do so, sacrifices – of the individual, of private 'family' concerns – must take place. (In her speech of self-sacrifice, she uses all of the current buzzwords of Athenian civic conformity.) Her bloodthirsty grandmother, on the other hand, eager to avenge a lifetime of humiliations to her family, dramatizes the way in which private concerns – she, like Aeschylus' Clytemnestra, is the representative of clan interests – never quite disappear beneath the smooth façade of public interest. 'I am "someone",' too,' she hotly replies, during the closing minutes of the play, in response to an Athenian's statement that 'there is no way that someone may execute' Eurystheus in violation of Athenian law.

It is a shame, given the trouble Euripides goes to in order to inject vivid female energies into a story that previously had none, that Peter Sellars (who you could say has made a speciality of unpopular or difficult-to-stage Greek dramas: past productions include Sophocles' *Ajax* and Aeschylus' *Persians*, a work that has all of the dramatic élan of a Veterans Day parade) has focused on those issues in the play that appear 'political' to us, rather than those that the Athenians would have understood to be political. Because there are refugees in the play, Sellars thinks the play is about what we call refugee crises – to us, now, a very political-sounding dilemma indeed. He has, accordingly, with his characteristic thoroughness and imaginative brio, gone to a great deal of trouble to bring out this element, almost to the exclusion of everything else.

Indeed, the American Repertory Theatre's performance of *Children of Herakles* is only one third of a three-part evening. It begins with a one-hour panel discussion – the guests change each night of the play's run – hosted by the Boston radio personality Christopher Lydon, that focuses on refugee crises around the world. The night I saw the play, his three guests were Arthur Helton, the director of Peace and Conflict Studies for the Council on Foreign Relations; a female asylum-seeker from Somalia called Ayisha; and a Serbian woman from the former Yugoslavia who'd emigrated to the United States after suffering during the Balkan wars. Then comes the performance of Euripides' play, which lasts two hours; and then a screening of a film. The latter represents, in the words of the programme, 'an artistic response to the current crisis – a series of films made in countries that are generating large numbers of refugees'.

This probably sounds more pretentious and gimmicky than it really was. It's true that a lot went wrong the night I saw the play: the Serbian woman, rather than shedding light on her own experiences as a refugee, lectured the audience rather stridently about the meaning of freedom (she chided us about our lust for large refrigerators); the first part took longer than expected, with the result that the film at the end of the evening began late, and people started disappearing, despite the temptations of a buffet dinner between parts two and three that featured appropriately politicized entrees ('grilled Balkan sausage'); and so on. But a lot about the evening was right. It's rare to see a production of a Greek drama that so seriously and conscientiously attempts to replicate, in some sense, the deeply political context in which the ancient works were originally performed. Whatever its flaws, Sellars's *Children of Herakles* makes you feel that an appropriate staging of Greek tragedy entails more than a couple hours' emoting followed by an argument about where to have dinner.

I found myself objecting, at first, to one of the most extreme gestures the director made: that is, having the children of Herakles themselves embodied (they're not speaking roles) by Boston-area refugee children, who every now and then went up into the audience to shake our hands. But the sense of being somehow implicated in the real lives of the actors, so foreign to contemporary theatrical sensibilities, would not have been that strange to Euripides' audiences. The choruses in the theatre of Dionysus at Athens were chosen from among Athenian citizens, boys and men, who would indeed have been known to the spectators, or at least some of them. Modern drama seeks to create estrangement, and distance, between the artifice onstage and the spectators' everyday lives; ancient drama relied, in its way, on a sense of communal concern.

Sellars understands, furthermore, that tragedy doesn't need a lot to achieve its effects, and his staging is rightly stark: a stepped altar in the middle of the stage surrounded by the huddling male offspring of Herakles, who have taken sanctuary there (the top of the altar was supposed to be occupied by a female Kazakh bard – a nice, if misplaced, Homeric touch – but she was ill the night I attended); a microphone, downstage left, into which the Argive envoy and Athenian king speak, which – not inappropriately, I thought – gives the debates at the opening of the play, where the city's course of action is decided, the air of a press conference; and, for the chorus (their lines were read by Lydon and another person, a woman) a little conference table at the extreme left of the stage, where they sit primly, occasionally making weary bureaucratic noises about how sorry they felt about the refugees' plight. This is perfect: it gets just right the tone of this work's chorus, which like the choruses in many tragedies is stranded between good intentions and a healthy self-protectiveness.

What robs the play of the impact it could have had is Sellars's failure to appreciate the subtle gender dynamics in Euripides' text. One of the reasons that the actions of Euripides' Macaria and Alcmene are so striking is that they're the only actions by females in a play otherwise wholly devoted to ostensibly masculine concerns: the governance of the free state, extradition issues, war. Part of Sellars's updating, however, is to give the roles of the nasty Argive herald – the one whom Eurystheus sends to intimidate the Athenians into giving up the refugees – and of the Athenian king Demophon (here recast as 'president' of Athens) to women. Although the parts are well played – the Demophon in particular comes across as a shrewd contemporary elected official, eager to do right but hamstrung by elaborate political obligations – the shift in gender results in a collapse of the playwright's meanings. In Euripides' play, the unexpected and electrifying entrance of Macaria and her offer of self-immolation dramatizes the need to sacrifice the 'personal' and 'domestic' – things that tragic women were understood to represent – to the larger civic good; the unusual and even revolutionary impact of her appearance and subsequent action is underscored, in the original, by her apology for appearing in public in the first place, something no nice Athenian girl would do. But Sellars's staging makes nonsense of the lines; it's absurd for this girl to be apologizing for talking to men outside the confines of the house (and for her to be asserting that she knows that a woman's place is in the home) when the most politically powerful characters in the play are, as they are in this staging, women. And so the end of the play – the old woman's violent explosion, reminder that the energies that must be sacrificed to establish the collective good always lurk uneasily within the polity, and can erupt – makes no sense, either. The women in this *Children of Herakles* are very healthy, thank you very much; there is no 'repressed' to return.

Worse still, Sellars stages the sacrifice of Macaria – beautifully, it is true, and bloodily. But it's not in the play. One of the most famously disturbing things about *The Children of Herakles* is the irony that, after she makes her bid for immortality – the girl begs to be honoured in her family's and Athens's memory before she goes off to die – we never hear another word about her. There are all sorts of explanations for this cold treatment of a warm-blooded character (not least, that the manuscript of the play is incomplete), but surely one is precisely that everything that Macaria represents must, in fact, disappear in order for the community to persist. Tragedy loves its self-heroizing females, but like the state whose concerns it so subtly enacted, it always found a way to get rid of those unmanageable 'others'. By bringing Macaria back in the second half of the play, and allowing us to weep over the spectacle of the tiny young girl having her throat cut, Sellars reasserts the energies that Euripides shows – ironically or not – being silenced.

And so, like an earlier generation of classicists who saw little of value in this play except references to contemporary politicking – the speeches were thought to echo fifth-century BC Athenian political debates – Sellars fails to see where the play's political discourse really lies. Which is to say, in the representation of the two characters who look the least like politicians: a young girl and an old woman. Did Euripides care about refugees? Yes, but mostly because of what refugee crises tell us about the nature of the state. ('The current event' he cared about was Athens's summary execution, the year before the play was produced, of some Spartan envoys – clearly the referent for Alcmene's climactic act of violence.) Peter Sellars, on the other hand, cares about refugees the way a twenty-first-century person cares – he feels for these poor kids, the mute, wide-eyed boys, the brutalized girls, and wants to make you feel for them, too. The result, alas, is a play that sends a message that isn't quite the one Euripides was telegraphing to his audience, by means of symbolic structures they knew well. Someone gets sacrificed in this *Children of Herakles*, but it isn't just Macaria.

A similar desire to update a Euripidean classic in terms familiar to today's audience has, apparently, informed Deborah Warner's vulgar, loud, and uncomprehending staging of *Medea*, which went from a limited run at the Brooklyn Academy of Music to a Broadway run, which was rapturously received by most critics – mostly because they are rightly impressed by Fiona Shaw's emotional ferocity. If only it were being put in the service of a reading that did justice to Euripides! For if Sellars's Euripides ultimately betrays its source because it thinks 'our' politics are the play's politics, Warner's Euripides fails because it mistakes 'our' women for Euripides' women.

In an interview two years ago with the *Guardian*, before their *Medea* had crossed the Atlantic, Warner and Shaw decried the 'misplaced image of Medea as a strong, wilful, witchy woman', suggesting instead that the key to their heroine was, in fact, her 'weakness'. 'Audiences can identify with weakness,' Shaw said. 'I think the Greek playwrights knew that. That they could entice the audience into an emotional debate about failure and dealing with being a failed person.' This betrays a remarkable failure to understand the nature of Greek tragic drama, which unlike contemporary psychological drama didn't strive to have audiences 'identify' with its characters – if anything, Athenian audiences were likely to find the chorus more sympathetic and recognizable than the outsized heroes with their divine pedigrees – and which was relatively uninterested in the wholly modern notion of 'dealing' with failure (and, you suppose, finding 'closure'). For the Greeks, the allure of so many tragic heroes is, in fact, exactly the opposite of what Warner and Shaw think it is: the heroes' strength, their grandeur, their power, the attributes of intellect or valour that they must resort to in their staged struggles with a hostile fate – or, as in many plays, like *Ajax*, their struggles to adapt to post-heroic worlds that have shifted and shrunk beneath them, rendering the heroes outsized, obsolete. (Norma Desmond, the has-been silent film star in Billy Wilder's *Sunset Boulevard*, has something of the grotesque yet somehow admirable grandiosity of the latter type of hero; her famous *cri de coeur* 'I *am* big. It was the *pictures* that got small' could, *mutatis mutandis*, be a line from Sophocles.)

And indeed, rather than being what Shaw called 'very normal' and Warner referred to as 'the happy housewife of Corinth',

Euripides' Medea is deliberately presented as a kind of female reincarnation of one of the most anguished, outsized, titanic dramatic heroes in the ancient canon: Sophocles' Ajax, the hero of a drama first produced about ten years before *Medea*. Like Ajax, Medea is first heard, rather uncannily, offstage, groaning over her plight: her abandonment by her husband Jason, who has left her to marry the daughter of Creon, the king of Corinth. She is characterized by what the classicist Bernard Knox, writing at Ajax, has summarized as 'determined resolve, expressed in uncompromising terms', by a 'fearful, terrible … wild' nature, by 'passionate intensity'. Like many Sophoclean heroes, she is motivated above all by an outraged sense of having been treated with disrespect, and curses her enemies while she plans her revenge; like Ajax specifically, she is tormented above all by the thought that her enemies will laugh at her.

So 'strong, wilful, and witchy' is, in fact, precisely what Euripides' Medea is. But not Warner's Medea, who appears to be stranded somewhere between Sylvia Plath and Mia Farrow – a frazzled woman who can't figure out how to act until the last minute. (Euripides' Medea can: from the start, she keeps repeating the terrifying word *ktenô*, 'I will kill.') Shaw, an impressive actress, chews up the scenery doing an impersonation of a housewife gone amok. When she comes out on the rather bleak stage at the Brooks Atkinson Theatre – apart from a door upstage centre, there are just some cinder blocks strewn around covered with tarps, as if a construction project had been halted midway, and a swimming pool (by now de rigueur in contemporary stagings of classical texts; there was one in Mary Zimmerman's *Metamorphoses*, too) in the centre with a toy boat floating in it – she's emaciated, hugging herself, haggard, nervously cracking jokes. (She draws a little witch hat in the air above her head at one point.) To reconcile this Valium-starved wreck with the text's many references to Medea's fame, power, and semi-divine status, Warner makes some halfhearted references to Medea as being some kind of 'celebrity': the chorus, here, is a gang of autograph-seeking groupies – 'the people who stand outside the Oscars', as Warner put it. The intention, you imagine, is to throw into the interpretative stew some kind of commentary on 'celebrity', but it's a stupid point to be making: all the heroes of Greek tragedy are famous.

This scaled-down, 'normal' Medea makes nonsense of the text in other, more damaging ways. Everyone in Euripides' play who interacts with Medea shows a healthy respect for the woman they know to be capable of terrible deeds. (She once gave the daughters of one of Jason's enemies a deliberately misleading recipe for rejuvenating their ageing father, which involved cutting the old man into tiny pieces. Needless to say, it didn't work. This was the subject of Euripides' first drama, produced in 455 BC, when he was thirty.) She is august, terrifying; the granddaughter of the sun, for heaven's sake. The Warner/Shaw Medea looks as if she can barely get herself out of bed in the morning, and the result is that when the plot does require her to do those awful things (the murder of Jason's fiancée and her father, the slaughter of her own children), you wonder how – and why – she managed it. The problem with making Medea into one of those distraught Susan Smith types, pushed by creepy men into moral regions we can't ever inhabit, is that it substitutes pat psychological nostrums ('Someone pushed to the place where she has no choice': thus Warner) for something that is much more horrific – and vital – in the play. Euripides' Medea is terrifying and grotesque precisely because her motivations aren't those of a wounded housewife, but those of a heroic temperament following the brutal logic of heroism: to inflict harm on your enemies at all costs, even if – as here – those enemies turn out to be your own kin.

You could argue, indeed, that what makes Euripides' heroine awesome is not that she's a woman on the verge of a nervous breakdown, but that, if anything, she has the capacity to think like a *man*. Or, perhaps, like a lawyer. Euripides, we know, was very interested in the developing art of rhetoric, an instrument of great importance in the workings of the Athenian state. The patent content of Euripides' play, the material that seems to be about female suffering, is by now so famous, and so familiar-seeming, that it has obscured the play's other preoccupations: chief among these is the use and abuse of language. In every scene, Medea is presented as a skilled orator; she knows how to manipulate each of her interlocutors in order to get what she wants, from the chorus (to whom she smoothly suggests that she's a helpless girl, just like them) to the Corinthian king Creon, whom she successfully manipulates by appealing to his male vanity. Indeed, we're told from the play's prologue right on through the rest of the drama that what possesses Medea's mind is not simply that her husband has left her for a younger woman, but that Jason has broken the oath (an ironclad prenup if ever there was one) that he once made to her. Oaths are crucial throughout the play: its central scene has her administering one to Aegeus, the Athenian king, who happens to be passing through Corinth on this terrible day, and who is made to swear to Medea that he will offer her sanctuary at Athens, should she ever go there. (Among other things, this oath furnishes her with her escape plan: rather than being an emotional wreck, Medea is always calculating, always thinking ahead.)

For the Greeks, all this had deep political implications. One of the reasons everyday Athenians were suspicious of the Sophists, those deconstructionists of the Greek world (with whom Socrates was mistakenly lumped in the common man's mind, not least because Aristophanes, in another satirical play, put him there), was that the rhetorical skills they were thought to teach could confound meaning itself – could 'make the worse argument seem the better', and vice versa. In Jason, Euripides created a character who is a parody of sophistry: he's glibness metastasized, rhetorical expertise gone amok. When he enters and tells Medea that he's only marrying this young princess for Medea's own sake, that he's doing it all for her and the kids, it's not because he thinks it's true: it's because he thinks he can get away with saying it's true. Language, words – it's all a game to him. Look, Euripides seems to be saying to his audience, men for whom the ability to make a persuasive speech could be, sometimes literally, a matter of life or death: look what moral corruption your rhetorical skills can lead to. Medea, of course – obsessed from the beginning of the play with oaths, the speech act whose purpose it is to fuse word and deed – is outraged by her husband's glibness, and spends her one remaining day in Corinth seeking ways to make him see the value of that which he so slickly uses merely as argumentative window dressing: his marriage, his children. That is why she kills the children. (The typically Euripidean irony – one that would likely have unnerved the Athenians – is that this spirited defence of language is mounted by a woman, and a foreigner: a sign, perhaps, of the sorry state public discourse was in.)

A *Medea* that was all about the moral disintegration that follows from linguistic collapse probably wouldn't sell a great many tickets in an age that revels in seeing characters 'deal with' being failures, but it's the play that Euripides wrote. Because Deborah Warner thinks that Medea is a disappointed housewife, and the play she inhabits is a drama of a marriage gone sour, all of the political resonances are lost. (When Shaw administers that crucial oath to Aegeus, she shrugs with embarrassment, as if she has no idea how this silly stuff is done, or what it's all supposed to be about.) At the Brooks Atkinson, her Jason, a very loud man called Jonathan Cake, has been instructed to play that crucial first exchange between Medea and Jason totally straight – as if he believes what he tells Medea. ('He believes his argument that if he marries Creon's daughter they will get this thing called security,' the director told the *Guardian*.) But if Jason is earnest – if he really believes what he's saying, which is that he's running off with a bimbo and abandoning his children and allowing them to be sent into exile because, hey, it's *good* for them! – then the scene, to say nothing of the play, crumbles to pieces. If you take away the mighty conflict over language, over meaning what you say, *Medea* is just a daytime drama about two nice people who have lost that special spark. But then what do you do with the rest of the play, with its violence and anguished choruses and harrowing narratives of gruesome deaths – and, most of all, with the climactic slaughter – all of which follow only from Medea's burning mission to put the meaning back in Jason's empty rhetoric, those disingenuous claims to care for his family, his children, even as he shows nothing but naked self-interest?

Not much, except to do what Warner (who insists the play is 'not about revenge') does, which is to fill the play with desperate, crude, almost vaudevillian efforts to manufacture excitement, now that all the intellectual and political excitement – to say nothing of the revenge motive – have been stripped away. This Medea makes faces, mugs for the audience, cracks jokes, does impressions. And it goes without saying that, when the violence does come, there's a lot of blood and flashing lights and deafening synthesized crashing and clattering. But for all the histrionics and special effects, you feel the hollowness at the core, and the staging soon sinks back into the place where it started: banal, everyday domesticity, a failed marriage. The Warner/Shaw *Medea* ends with the murderous mother sitting in that swimming pool, smirking and splashing the weeping Jason.

Ironically, Deborah Warner seems to understand tragedy's original political intent. In an interview she gave to the *Times* last September, after the first anniversary of the September 11 attacks and as her country, and ours, prepared for war on Iraq, Warner made a case for the renewed relevance of Greek tragedy:

> We desperately need Greek plays. We need them when democracies are wobbly. I am living in a very wobbly democracy right now, whose Parliament has only just been recalled, and Commons may or may not have a vote about whether we go to war.
>
> Greece was a very new democratic nation, and a barbaric world was not very far behind them. They offered these plays as places of real debate. We can't really say the theatre is a true place of debate anymore, but these plays remind us of what it could be.

She's absolutely right; all the more unfortunate, then, that none of this political awareness informs her production. The end of Warner's *Medea* feels very much like the aftermath of a marital disaster. Euripides' *Medea*, by contrast, ends with a monstrous ethical lesson: Jason is forced, as his wife had once been forced, to taste exile, loss of family; forced, like her, to live stranded with neither a past nor a future; is made to understand, at last, what it feels like to be the *other* person, to understand that the things to which his glib words referred are real, have value, can inflict pain. At the end of Euripides' *Medea*, the woman who teaches men these terrible lessons flies off in a divine chariot, taking her awful skills and murderous pedagogical methods to – Athens.

Indeed, while it's hard to see what Warner's 'happy housewife of Corinth' can tell us about the war she referred to in her comments to the *Times* – i.e., Iraq – Euripides' *Medea*, by contrast, ends by literally bringing home a shattering warning against political and rhetorical complacency: a lesson that, as we know, went unheeded in Athens. It's worth noting that his *Medea* was composed during the year before the outbreak of the Peloponnesian War, when the Athenians were eagerly preparing for conflict – a conflict, as it turned out, that would thoroughly reacquaint the Athenians with the meaning of the word 'consequences'. Which is the play we need more desperately?

It's unlikely that *Medea* – Euripides' *Medea*, that is, not the play that Deborah Warner staged – will have trouble surviving the grotesque, giggling, wrongheaded treatment it received on Broadway. If so, it wouldn't be the first time that the playwright bounced back after some rough treatment. Soon after Aristophanes lampooned him (intentionally) in his *Thesmophoriazousae*, Euripides left town for good. His destination was about as far from Athens, culturally and ideologically, as you could get: the royal court of Pella, capital of the backwoods kingdom of Macedon, a country that would take another century to achieve world-historical status. (It's where Alexander the Great was born.) He left, so the story goes, because he was disgusted by his city's descent into demagoguery, intellectual dishonesty, political disorder, and defeat. But perhaps he was also smarting because of *Thesmophoriazousae*; perhaps he was tired of being misunderstood.

And yet perhaps, too, there was time for one more effort; perhaps he might have the last laugh. Perhaps, from a burlesque, a deliberate misinterpretation, a pandering by a comedian to the common taste in order to achieve a glib success, something worthwhile might result. Let us imagine this aged poet as he leaves Athens and embarks on his difficult northward journey, turning an idea over in his mind – an idea that comes to him, as it happens, from *Thesmophoriazousae* itself. An all-female festival; a man eager to see what the women get up to, when the men aren't watching. A grotesque foray into drag that convinces no one; a masquerade that ends in apprehension, and terrible peril. Not a bad idea for a play – not a comedy, this time around, but something terrible, something that will bring his citizen audience close to the core of what great theatre is about: plotting, disguise, recognition, revelation, violence, awful knowledge. He arrives in Macedon and gets to work. Three years later, the play is finished: *Bacchae*. By the time it is produced back home in Athens, winning its author one of his rare first prizes, Euripides is dead. But from the mockers, those who wilfully mistake his meanings, he has stolen a victory. This show, it is safe to say, will go on.

– *The New York Review of Books*, 13 February 2003

Alexander, the Movie!

Whatever else you say about the career of Alexander the Great – and classicists, at least, say quite a lot (one website that tracks the bibliography lists 1200 items) – it was neither funny nor dull. So it was a sign that something had gone seriously wrong with Oliver Stone's long, gaudy, and curiously empty new biopic about Alexander when audiences at both showings I attended greeted the movie with snickering and evident boredom. The first time I saw the picture was at a press screening at a commercial theatre, and even from the large central section that was (a personage with a headset informed us) reserved for 'friends of the filmmaker' you could hear frequent tittering throughout the film – understandable, given that the characters often have to say things like 'from these loins of war, Alexander was born'. A week later, at a matinee, I got to witness a reaction by those unconstrained by the bonds of either duty or amity: by the end of the three-hour-long movie, four of the twelve people in the audience had left.

This was, obviously, not the reaction Stone was hoping for – nor indeed the reaction that Alexander's life and career deserve, whether you think he was an enlightened Greek gentleman carrying the torch of Hellenism to the East or a savage, paranoid tyrant who left rivers of blood in his wake. The controversy about his personality derives from the fact that our sources are famously inadequate, all eyewitness accounts having perished: what remains is, at best, secondhand (one history, for instance, is based largely on the now-lost memoirs of Alexander's general and alleged half-brother, Ptolemy, who went on to become the founder of the Egyptian dynasty that ended with Cleopatra), and at worst, highly unreliable. A rather florid account by the first-century-AD Roman rhetorician Quintus Curtius often reflects its author's professional interests – his Alexander is given to extended bursts of eloquence even when gravely wounded – far more than it does the known facts. But Alexander's story, even stripped of romanticizing or rhetorical elaboration, still has the power to amaze.

He was born in 356 BC, the product of the stormy marriage between Philip II of Macedon and his temperamental fourth wife, Olympias, a princess from Epirus (a wild western kingdom encompassing parts of present-day Albania). His childhood was appropriately dramatic. At around twelve he had already gained a foothold on legend by taming a magnificent but dangerously wild stallion called Bucephalas ('Oxhead') – a favourite episode in what would become, after Alexander's death, a series of increasingly fantastical tales and legends that finally coalesced into a literary narrative known as the Alexander Romance, which as time passed was elaborated, illuminated, and translated into everything from Latin to Armenian. While still in his early teens, he was at school with no less a teacher than Aristotle, who clearly made a great impression on the youth. Years later, as he roamed restlessly through the world, Alexander took care to send interesting zoological and botanical specimens back to his old tutor.

At sixteen he'd demonstrated enough ability to get himself appointed regent when his father, a shrewd statesman and inspired general who dreamed of leading a pan-Hellenic coalition against Persia, was on campaign. He used this opportunity to make war on an unruly tribe on Macedon's eastern border; to mark his victory he founded the first city he named after himself,

Alexandropolis. At eighteen, under his father's generalship, he led the crack Macedonian cavalry to a brilliant victory at the Battle of Chaeronea, where Macedon crushed an Athenian-Theban coalition, thereby putting an end to southern Greek opposition to Macedonian designs on hegemony. At twenty, following the assassination of Philip – in which he (or Olympias, or perhaps both) may have had a hand – he was king.

That, of course, was just the beginning. At twenty-two, Alexander led his father's superbly trained army across the Hellespont into Asia. Next he liberated the Greek cities of Asia Minor from their Persian overlords (i.e., made them his own: the governors he appointed were not always champions of Hellenic civic freedoms), staged his most brilliant military victory by successfully besieging the Phoenician island fortress of Tyre (part of his famous strategy to 'defeat the Persian navy on land' by seizing its bases), and freed a grateful Egypt from harsh Persian suzerainty. While in Egypt, he indulged in one of the bizarre gestures that, wholly apart from his indisputable genius as a general, helped make him a legend: he made an arduous and dangerous detour to the oracle of Ammon in the desert oasis of Siwah, where the god revealed that Alexander was in fact his own son – a conclusion with which Alexander himself came increasingly to agree. While in Egypt he also founded the most famous of his Alexandrias, a city that eventually displaced Athens as the centre of Greek intellectual culture, and where his marvellous tomb, a tourist attraction for centuries after, would eventually rise.

Although Alexander had, apparently, set out simply to complete his father's plan – that is, to drive the Persians away from the coastal cities of Asia Minor, which for centuries had been culturally Greek, ostensibly in retaliation for a century and a half of destructive Persian meddling in Greek affairs – it's clear that once in Asia, he began to dream much bigger dreams. Within three years of crossing the Hellespont, he had defeated the Persian Great King, Darius III, in a series of three pitched battles – Granicus, Issus, and Gaugamela – in which he triumphed against sometimes dire odds. It was in the rout that followed Issus that Darius fled the field of battle, leaving his wife, children, and even his mother behind in the baggage train. Alexander, with characteristic largesse and fondness for the *beau geste* – like most extravagant personalities, he had a capacity for generosity as great as his capacity for ruthlessness – honourably maintained the captives in royal state.

His brilliant victory on the plain of Gaugamela in Mesopotamia in October, 331 BC, made him the most powerful man the world had ever known, ruler of territories from the Danube in the north, to the Nile valley in the south, to the Indus in the east. He was also the world's richest person: the opulent treasuries of the Persians at Babylon, Susa, and Persepolis yielded him the mind-boggling sum of 180,000 silver talents – the sum of three talents being enough to make someone a comfortable millionaire by today's standards.

After Gaugamela, Alexander, driven by a ferocious will to power or inspired by an insatiable curiosity (or both), just kept going. He turned first to the northeast, where he subdued stretches of present-day Afghanistan, Uzbekistan, and Tajikistan, and there took as a wife the beautiful Roxana, daughter of a local chieftain, much to the consternation of his xenophobic aides. Then he moved to the south, where his designs on India – he believed it to be bordered by the 'Encircling Ocean' which he longed to see – were thwarted, in the end, not by military defeat but by the exhaustion and demoralization of his men, who by that point, understandably, wanted to head back to Macedon and enjoy their loot. Himself demoralized by this failure in support, Alexander relented and agreed to turn back.

The westward return journey through the arid wastes of the Macran desert toward Babylon, which he planned to make the capital of his new world empire, is often called his 1812: during the two-month march, he lost tens of thousands of the souls who set out with him. That tactical catastrophe was followed by an emotional one: after the army regained the Iranian heartland, Alexander's bosom companion, the Macedonian nobleman Hephaistion – almost certainly the King's longtime lover, someone whom Alexander, obsessed with Homer's *Iliad* and believing himself to be descended from Achilles, imagined as his Patroclus – died of typhus. (The two young men had made sacrifices together at the tombs of the legendary heroes when they reached the ruins of Troy at the beginning of their Asian campaign.) This grievous loss precipitated a severe mental collapse in the King, who had, in any event, grown increasingly unstable and paranoid. Not without reason: there were at least two major conspiracies against his life after Gaugamela, both incited by close associates who'd grown disgruntled with his increasingly pro-Persian policies.

Within a year, he himself was dead – perhaps of poison, as some have insisted on believing, but far more likely of the cumulative effects of swamp fever (he'd chosen, foolishly or perhaps self-destructively, to pass the summer in sultry, fetid Babylon), a lifetime of heavy drinking, and the physical toll taken by his various wounds. He was thirty-two.

There can be no doubt that the world as we know it would have a very different shape had it not been for Alexander, who among other things vastly expanded, through his Hellenization of the East, the reach of Western culture, and thus prepared the soil, as it were, for Rome and then Christianity. But as extraordinarily significant as this story is, little of it would be very interesting to anyone but historians and classicists were it not for a rather curious additional factor of what the Greeks called *pothos* – 'longing'. The best and most authoritative of the ancient sources for Alexander's career are the *Anabasis* ('March Up-Country') and *Indica* ('Indian Affairs') by the second-century-AD historian and politician Arrian, a Greek from Nicomedia (part of the Greek-speaking East that Alexander helped to create) who was a student of Epictetus and flourished under the philhellene emperor Hadrian. Throughout his account of Alexander's life, the word *pothos* recurs to describe the yearning that, as the historian and so many others before and after him believed, motivated Alexander to seek far more than mere conquest.

The word is used by Arrian of Alexander's yearning to see new frontiers, his dreamy desire to found new cities, to loosen the famous Gordian knot, to explore the Caspian Sea. It is used, significantly, to describe his striving to outdo the two divinities with whom he felt a special bond, Herakles and Dionysos, in great deeds. An excerpt from the beginning of the final book of Arrian's *Anabasis* nicely sums up the special quality that the *pothos* motif lends to Alexander's life, making its interest as much literary, as it were, as historical:

> For my part I cannot determine with certainty what
> sort of plans Alexander had in mind, and I do not care
> to make guesses, but I can say one thing without fear
> of contradiction, and that is that none was small and
> petty, and he would not have stopped conquering even
> if he'd added Europe to Asia and the Britannic Islands
> to Europe. On the contrary, he would have continued
> to seek beyond them for unknown lands, as it was ever
> his nature, if he had no rival, to strive to better the best.

What Alexander's psychology and motives were, we are in a particularly poor position to judge, the contemporary sources being absent. But there can be little doubt that the quality that Arrian describes here – the restlessness, the burning desire to see and to know new things and places for (it seems) the sake of knowing – is what captured the imagination of the world in his own time and forever afterward.

Particularly striking was his openness to the new cultures to which his conquests had exposed him – not least, because it showed a king who had clearly outgrown the notoriously xeno-phobic ways of the Greeks. This new sensibility expressed itself in some of Alexander's boldest and best-remembered gestures, all of which have the touch of the poetic, even the visionary about them: his courtly behaviour toward the family of the defeated Darius (the Persian emperor's mother became so close to the man who defeated her son that on hearing that he had died, she turned her face to the wall and starved herself to death); his creation of a vast new army of 30,000 Iranian 'Successors', meant to replace his retiring Macedonian troops (a plan that provoked mutiny among the Macedonians); the grand mass wedding he devised the year before he died, in which he and nearly a hundred of his highest officers were married, in the Eastern rite, to the cream of Persia's aristocratic women as a symbol of the unification of the two peoples.

Yet however much it resulted in a desire to form a new hybrid culture, the appeal of Alexander's *pothos* is precisely that it seemed to be an expression of something elementally Greek. Travel for the sake of knowing, a burning desire to experience new worlds at whatever cost, and the irreversible pain that results whenever a Western 'anthropologist' makes contact with new civilizations: these are, of course, themes of another famous Greek text, although not the one Alexander associated himself with. He may have seen the *Iliad* as the blueprint of his life, but what gives his life such great narrative and imaginative appeal for us is, in fact, that it looked so much like the *Odyssey*. Indeed, he was, perhaps, Tennyson's Odysseus as much as Homer's. Without *pothos*, Alexander is just another conqueror. With it, he's the West's first Romantic hero, and possibly its first celebrity.

Many of the problems with Stone's movie arise because *Alexander* is torn between the facts of its subject's life and the romance of his personality – between showing you all the research that's been done (there are fussy recreations of everything from Alexander's tactics to Darius's facial hair) and persuading you of Alexander's allure. Between these two horses the movie falls, and never gets back on its feet.

A great deal has been made in the press of the scrupulousness with which the director endeavoured to remain true to the known facts: 'historical accuracy' was heralded as a hallmark of this latest in a string of big-budget Hollywood treatments of classical material. Stone retained a retired Marine captain as his military adviser; and engaged Robin Lane Fox, the author of a popular biography of Alexander, as a historical consultant, in return, apparently, for allowing Fox, an expert horseman, to participate in a big battle scene – a remunerative strategy that, I fervently hope, will not recur in the cases of classicists called to advise future toga-and-sandal epics.

There is no denying that a lot of the film is richly detailed, despite some inexplicable gaffes – why a mosaic wall map in the Greek-speaking Ptolemy's Egyptian palace should be written in Latin is anybody's guess – and absurd pretensions. (The credits are bilingual, with awkward transliterations of the actors' names into Greek characters: to whom, exactly, is it necessary to know that

Philip II was played by 'Oual Kilmer'?) Research has obviously gone into matters both large and small, from the curls in Darius's beard to the layout of the Battle of Gaugamela, which at thirty minutes makes up one fifth of the entire film, and which has been dutifully recreated in all its noise and confusion, right down to the clouds of orange dust which, we are told, obscured the field of battle. Even in the much-discussed matter of the accents the actors are made to assume, there is in fact a certain method: Stone has all the actors who portray Macedonians speak with an Irish (and sometimes a Highland) brogue, the better to suggest the cultural relationship of the back-country Macedonians to their lofty Greek counterparts. (To poor Olympias, played with scenery-devouring glee by Angelina Jolie, he has given a peculiar Slavic drawl.)

And yet the matter of accents, however admirably motivated, also helps to illuminate a weakness that is characteristic of the film in general. For the director's clever notion ends up being an empty gesture, since there are virtually no Greeks in his film for the Macedonians to be contrasted with. Apart, that is, from a two-minute appearance by Christopher Plummer as Aristotle, who is shown lecturing to his pubescent charges among a pile of (inexplicably) fallen marble columns, describing the differences between the beneficial and the deleterious brands of same-sex love – a scene patently included in order to prepare audiences for the fact that little Alexander and Hephaistion will grow up to be more than just wrestling partners. (Provided with this Aristotelian introduction, we are supposed to breathe easy in the assumption that they're the kind who, as the great philosopher puts it, 'lie together in knowledge and virtue'.) The absence of Greeks in the movie is more than structurally incoherent: it is a serious historical omission, given that Alexander's troubles with the Greeks back home were a critical problem throughout his career.

The narrative of much of *Alexander* has, indeed, a haphazard feel: it's not at all clear, throughout the three hours of the film, on what basis Stone chose to include, or omit, various events. Vast stretches of the story are glossed, with patent awkwardness, by a voice-over narration by the aged Ptolemy (who is shown in a prologue sequence, set in his palace in Alexandria, busily writing his history forty years after Alexander's death). But in lurching from Alexander's youth to his victory at Gaugamela, the film misses many crucial opportunities to dramatize its subject: there is nothing about Egypt, no oracle at Siwah, an event of the highest importance and certainly worthy of visual representation, and no double sacrifice at Ilium, which would have nicely suggested the intensity of Alexander's attachment both to the Achilles myth and to Hephaistion – certainly more so than the silly dialogue about 'wild deer listening in the wind' that Stone puts in the lovers' mouths. (As with many an ancient epic, this one veers between a faux-biblical portentousness and excruciating attempts at casualness: 'Aristotle was perhaps prescient.') Even after Gaugamela, there are inexcusable omissions. Where, you wonder, is Darius's mother; where, crucially, is the mass interracial wedding pageant at Susa? And what about the story of the Gordian knot, a favourite that illustrated with brilliant concision and in an eminently filmable way, Alexander's approach to problem-solving?

What does get packed into the film, on the other hand, is often treated so perfunctorily as to be meaningless to those who don't already know the life; a better title for this film would have been *Lots of Things That Happened to Alexander*. Famous titbits of the biography – a reference to his tendency to cock his head to one side; another to an embarrassing episode in which his father mocked his fondness for singing – are awkwardly referred to *en passant* to no purpose other than to show that the screenwriters have studied hard and know about these details. Much that is of far greater importance is similarly poorly handled: the conspiracies against his life, the mutiny in India, and above all his ongoing and ultimately failed efforts to impose the 'prostration', the Persian ritual obeisance to the king, on Macedonians and Persians alike. These are either so briefly alluded to or so hurriedly depicted as to leave you wondering what they were about. Historical characters are similarly paraded across the screen, often without being introduced, again merely to show that the filmmakers have done their homework. The beautiful Persian eunuch Bagoas, who our sources tell us was presented to Alexander as a peace offering by a surrendering satrap, and who seems to have remained faithful to his new master for the rest of his life, suddenly appears, in this version, as little more than an extra in the harem at Babylon, and the next thing you know he's giving Alexander baths. Something, you suspect, got left on the cutting-room floor.

There is little mystery, on the other hand, about why other episodes are prominently featured. The courtship and marriage to Roxana, for instance, get a disproportionate amount of screen time – not least, you can't help feeling, because Stone, whatever the loud claims that here, at last, was a film that would fearlessly depict Alexander's bisexuality, was eager to please his target audience of 18- to 26-year-old males. Hephaistion and Alexander occasionally give each other brief, manly hugs, whereas a lengthy, stark-naked wedding-night wrestling match between Alexander and Roxana makes it clear that they, at least, were not going to be lying together in knowledge and virtue. The sexual aspect of Alexander's relationship with his longtime lover is entirely relegated to Ptolemy's voice-over: you don't envy Anthony Hopkins having to declare that Alexander 'was only conquered by Hephaistion's thighs', one of the many clunkers that evoked snickers from the audience.

The perceived obligation to cram in so much material affects Stone's visual style, which – apart from some striking sequences, such as a thrilling and imaginatively filmed battle between the Macedonians on their horses and the Indians on their elephants – is often jumbled and incoherent. There's a famous story about how, when the captive Persian royals were presented to the victorious Alexander, the queen mother, mistaking the taller and handsomer Hephaistion for the King, made obeisance to him. 'Don't worry, Mother,' Alexander is reported to have said, 'he, too, is Alexander.' This crucial encounter, so rich in psychologically telling detail, is filmed so confusingly in *Alexander* that it's impossible to tell, among other things, that the Persian lady (here, for no reason at all, it's Darius's wife rather than his mother) has made a mistake to begin with, and so the entire episode disintegrates into nonsense.

What all this betrays is a problem inherent in all biography, which is that a life, however crammed with dazzling incident, does not necessarily have the shape of a good drama. The reason it's exhausting, and ultimately boring, to sit through *Alexander* – and why the movie started disappearing from theatres so soon after its release – is that while it dutifully represents certain events from Alexander's childhood to his death, there's no *drama* – no narrative arc, no shaping of those events into a good story. They're just being ticked off a list. To my mind, this failing is best represented by the way in which the action of Stone's movie suddenly and inexplicably grinds to a halt three quarters of the way through in order to make way for an extended flashback to Philip's assassination a decade earlier. It seemed to come out of nowhere, was lavishly treated, and then disappeared, as the filmmaker scrambled to get to the next historically accurate moment. A lot of *Alexander* is like that.

*

None of this would matter much if the film had managed to convey Alexander's unique appeal. From the very beginning of his film it's clear that Oliver Stone has succumbed to the romance of Alexander, and wants us to, too. 'It was an empire not of land or of gold but of the mind,' the aged, Ptolemy muses aloud as he shuffles around his palace, which itself is a fairly typical mix of the scrupulously accurate and the inexplicably wrong. (The scrolls piled in the cubbyholes of his library rightly bear the little identifying tags that were the book jackets of the classical world; on the other hand, the tacky statuary on Ptolemy's terrace looks suspiciously like the work of J. Seward Johnson Jr.) 'I've known many great men in my life, but only one colossus,' he drones on, as a put-upon secretary scurries after him with a roll of papyrus. He would, for what it's worth, have been writing on an erasable wax tablet; costly papyrus was only for fair copying.

You can't help thinking that one reason you have to be told so explicitly and so often about the greatness of Alexander the Great is that the actor Stone has chosen to portray Alexander is incapable of conveying it himself. Colin Farrell is an Irishman with a sly, trickster's face that betrays nothing of what may be going on behind it; in films like *Phone Booth*, in which he plays a sleazy PR executive, he has a skittish authenticity. It's true that he shares certain physical characteristics with Alexander – like the Macedonian, the Irishman is small, a bantamweight who looks fast on his feet. (Alexander himself was such a good runner that for a while he was considered a candidate for the Olympic games, until he protested that he would only compete against kings.) But he simply doesn't have the qualities necessary to suggest Alexander's remarkable charisma. As he trudges through the film earnestly spouting lines that describe what we know Alexander was thinking ('I've seen the future ... these people want – need – change'), he looks more and more like what he in fact is: a

Hibernian character actor with a shaggy-browed poker face trapped in a glamorous leading man's part.

The void at the centre of this biopic must be especially embarrassing to the filmmakers, given how much fuss they made about another aspect of the film's attempts at capturing 'historical accuracy': the gruelling boot-camp training that Farrell and the actors playing his troops had to go through in order (presumably) to lend his on-screen generalship authenticity. The night before the press screening I attended, the Discovery Channel aired a documentary entitled *Becoming Alexander*, which showed Farrell jogging under the hot Moroccan sun with the loyal extras and talking about the bond that had grown up between him and the men whom he would be leading into cinematic battle. A military expert hired to advise the filmmaker opined that, as a result of this earnest process, Farrell had been transformed from 'an Irish street kid' into a 'leader of men'.

Whatever else it illuminates, the patent fatuity of this hype – if the actor hadn't attended the boot camp, would the extras have disobeyed his orders at Gaugamela? – suggests that *Alexander* gets at least one thing across successfully: the vanity of the filmmakers. With its dramatically meaningless detail and almost total failure to convey the central allure of its subject, the film at least betrays its creators' satisfaction with their own effort and expense – with, that is to say, their ability to outdo other classical epics that have sprung up since *Gladiator* was a hit a few years ago. Or betrays, perhaps, their own biographical agendas: it occurs to you that Stone, who in an early autobiographical novel reveals was the product of a rocky union between a wealthy, powerful father and a rather unstable, alluring mother, may really have been making a movie about himself.

But the reason *Gladiator* was successful was not that its characters sported togas and lolled about in Roman orgies, but that it had an irresistible story: a noble, innocent hero betrayed by an ostensible friend; a long, tormented imprisonment where the hero nonetheless acquires the arcane skills and resources that will make his vengeance possible; and then the elaborately staged, long-awaited comeback, the climactic revenge. (It's essentially a remake of *The Count of Monte Cristo*.) For all the talk of authenticity and identification with the ancients on the part of the director and actors responsible for *Alexander*, no one seems to have paused to wonder, while they spent months and millions on recreating the Battle of Gaugamela with ear-splitting, eye-popping verisimilitude, whether the 'accuracy' of such a reconstruction of the classical past actually adds anything to our understanding of that past – whether it helps tell the story or enhances our appreciation of why Alexander may be more worth making a movie about than other ancient conquerors. To my knowledge, there are no medieval romances in Armenian about Julius Caesar.

If the above sounds disappointed, it is. I became a classicist because of Alexander the Great. At thirteen I read Mary Renault's intelligent and artful novels about Alexander, *Fire from Heaven* and *The Persian Boy* (the latter told from the point of view of Bagoas the eunuch), and I was hooked. Adolescence, after all, is about nothing if not *pothos*; the combination of great deeds and strange cultures, the romantic blend of the youthful hero, that Odyssean yearning, strange rites, and panoramic moments – all spiced with a dash of polymorphous perversity which all the characters seemed to take in their stride – were too alluring to resist. From that moment on all I wanted was to know more about these Greeks. Naturally I've learned a great deal since then, and know about, and largely believe, the revisionist views of Alexander, the darker interpretation of the events I read about thirty years ago in fictional form; but I will admit that a little of that allure, that *pothos*, still clings to the story – and to the Greeks – for me.

At the age of sixteen, soon after I read Renault's novels (from which, I couldn't help noticing, a good deal in Stone's film is borrowed without credit, not least a Freudian scene illuminating the sources of Alexander's hatred of his father, and perhaps of his indifference to women), I wrote the author a fan letter which I concluded by shyly hoping that she wouldn't reply with a form letter. Her response, which was the beginning of a correspondence that lasted until her death ten years later, and which inspired me to go on and study Classics, came to my mind when I was hearing Colin Farrell described as a leader of men in *Becoming Alexander*. 'I wonder,' Miss Renault wrote to me in April 1976,

> whoever told you I'd send you a 'form letter' if you
> wrote to me. Are there really writers who do that? I
> knew film stars do. You can't blame them, really ...
> about half the people who write to them must be
> morons who think they really are Cleopatra or whoever
> ... Writers, though, write to communicate; and when
> someone to whom one has got through takes the
> trouble to write and tell one so, it would be pretty
> ungrateful to respond with something off a duplicator.

Because narcissistically deluded filmmakers are now as addled as starry-eyed fans, this new fictionalized *Alexander* isn't getting through to many people. I certainly doubt that it will inspire a young bookish boy somewhere to be a classicist, or a writer, or both.

The Strange Music of Horace

Daylight was fading on 3 June 17 BC, when there suddenly ascended into the soft air above the Palatine Hill in Rome the pure and reedy sound of fifty-four young voices singing a most unusual hymn. Anyone in the audience that evening who knew Greek literature – and you can suppose that many did – would have recognized the syncopated, slightly nervous metre of the song being sung as the one invented and made famous six centuries earlier by the Lesbian poet Sappho, who used it to convey some of her most famous lyrics of erotic yearning. ('That man seems to me to be like a god / who, sitting just across from you, / when you've spoken sweetly / hears you.')

On this particular summer night, however, burning desire was not on the poetic menu. That much became clear as soon as the two choirs of twenty-seven singers – one of boys, one of girls, each corresponding to one of the deities invoked in the hymn – called upon Apollo and Diana, 'world's brightness and darkness, worshipped forever', to

> … make our young men tractable
> and virtuous; to our old, grant peaceful health,
> give to the whole race of Romulus glory,
> descendants and wealth.

The singing of this hymn was, in fact, the high point of a magnificent and solemn civic occasion: the *ludi saeculares*, Centennial Games, which the First Citizen, Augustus Caesar (né Octavian), had ordered to be held that year – a celebration of Rome as the capital of the world, meant to commemorate the beginning of a new era, a new *saeculum*, in the affairs of human-kind. And why not? Fourteen years earlier, Augustus had defeated Cleopatra and Antony at Actium, thereby establishing, for once and for all, Rome as the single great Mediterranean power and putting a hundred years of civil conflict to an end. Since then, he had been consolidating his power abroad and at home, travelling in the East, legislating ethical and moral reforms. Only now, in the year 17 BC, could Rome and the world – and his own position as de facto emperor – be consid-ered secure enough to announce the beginning of what was clearly a New World Order.

We happen to know an unusual amount about the commis-sioning and performance of the hymn that was meant to celebrate Augustus' achievement because of the survival of two objects from antiquity: a book and a stone. The book, by Suetonius, the historian and biographer of the emperors, was written about a century and a quarter after the evening in question, and in it the author describes how Augustus 'approved so highly' of the works of a certain poet 'and was convinced that they would remain immortal that he bade him to compose … the *Carmen saeculare*'. The stone, discovered in 1890 and visible today in the Musée des Thermes, is a chunk of the official catalogue of the *ludi saeculares*, and with respect to the hymn it notes that on the third day, after a sacrifice offered on the Palatine Hill,

> twenty-seven young boys and twenty-seven young girls,
> still having their mothers and fathers, sang a hymn.
> And in the same way at the Capitol. The song was
> composed by Q. Horatius Flaccus.

We know him simply as Horace.

The poem that was sung on that long-ago evening – a Greek lyric expression of Roman civic virtues and imperial ambitions; a patriotic anthem set to the lilting poetic rhythms of erotic yearning; a grand celebration of official and communal values given definitive shape by a private individual, a solitary bard – suggests the strange tensions and seeming contradictions that characterize not only Horace's life and work, but also our awkward attitude toward him. He is, on the one hand, the august Augustan: during his lifetime, the emperor's friend as well as Virgil's, moving in the highest social, political, and literary circles, acknowledged as the 'performer on Rome's lyre', as he himself boasts; after his death, a figure absolutely central to the Western poetic tradition, having had a particular influence in the Renaissance, after languishing in comparative neglect during the Middle Ages. (He has always been more popular when reason is in vogue.) The sixteenth century in France – Ronsard, who in more than one poem rhymes 'grâce' with 'Horace', Du Bellay, Montaigne, 'the French Horace' – and the seventeenth and particularly the early eighteenth in England – Addison, Steele, Prior, Pope – would be unthinkable without him.

On the other hand, he is – well, the august Augustan: all that avuncular philosophizing about the fleeting nature of pleasure and the inevitable passage of time, from someone comfortably ensconced in the nests of privilege, comes off, today, as complacent and not terribly original, as even his admirers admit. 'Heaven knows,' the American critic Brooks Otis wrote a generation ago, in an essay called, significantly enough, 'The Relevance of Horace',

> there is nothing new about 'seizing the day' or relaxing from business or moderating one's desires or being philosophic about the future, but we all do fall into the moods that these clichés suggest and, when we do, find Horace just the man for our purposes. He was in short felicitous in his phrasing and charming in his life-style.

Indeed, Horace's lyric ouput has been reduced in the mind of the general public to a pair of clichés. One, which everyone knows even without knowing its author, concerns the poetry's content: *carpe diem*. The other concerns its form – the rigorous structures of which their creator was so proud, those formidably dense verse patterns with the funny names that sound like constellations ('Greater Asclepiad'), which have notoriously been the bane of schoolboys both real and imaginary from Shakespeare's Chiron in *Titus Andronicus* ('O, 'tis a verse in Horace, I know it well, / I read it in a grammar long ago') to the pathetic student in Kipling's short story 'Regulus', victimized by a sadistic teacher when called upon to translate Horace's paean to the Punic War hero Regulus in one of the six great 'Roman Odes' with which Book III of the *Odes* begins.

Neither the charm nor the felicity, the armchair Epicureanism nor the impregnable formality, suits the current taste. When we think of lyricists, it is Sappho who comes to mind, not Horace, who merely used her seamless metres while leaving the messy erotic stuff alone; we like our exaltation in the content, not the form, of our poetry. And yet Horace's steadfast refusal to provide such exaltation, his stubborn artisanal focus on refinements in technique rather than rawness of emotion, is the key to both the beauties and the difficulties in his greatest work, the *Odes* – to the subtle and fragile emotional textures that are so famously hard to convey, and to the elusive tonal artistry that makes it so famously difficult to translate.

Horace was born to a freedman, a former slave, on 8 December 65 BC, in Venusia, a small military colony at the heel of Italy. (In the witty and caustic *Satires* with which, at thirty, he first announced his talent to the world – the Latin title, *Sermones*, means something more like 'conversations', or perhaps better '*causeries*' – the poet amusingly recounts his schooldays with the 'burly sons of burly centurions'.) When he died, on 27 November 8 BC, in Rome, he was buried in a tomb on the Esquiline Hill next to his beloved patron, the fabulously wealthy littérateur and bon vivant Maecenas, the emperor's longtime friend. The emperor himself was his heir.

What happened between Venusia and Rome, between centurions' sons and Augustus himself, explains a great deal. The poet's childhood and early manhood witnessed some of the most traumatic years Europe has ever seen: the death throes of the Roman Republic, with its political and social instabilities, and the proscriptions, executions, and confiscations that attended them. (His shrewd, self-made father was an auctioneer's agent, responsible among other things for the disposition of confiscated properties: it's entirely possible that Horace saw firsthand the emotional trauma inflicted by the era's political violence.) As a university student in Athens, where he wrote quantities of verse in Greek – the education that made his later achievement possible – Horace became involved in the upheavals of his era, joining the cause of the 'liberators' Brutus and Cassius after their assassination of Julius Caesar in 44 BC. From the disaster at Philippi, he tells us, he barely escaped with his life. He slunk back to Italy to find his father's property confiscated for veterans of the winning side: an ironic twist of fate for the auctioneer's son. Still, he must have had some wherewithal, for he soon after bought himself a clerical post at the treasury – becoming, into the bargain, the model for many distinguished poets (Housman, his great admirer and translator, and also Cavafy) whose stultifying day jobs seem not to have extinguished the lyric impulse.

Insulated from the decade's volatile politics, he began to move in literary circles. By his late twenties he'd joined the circle of Virgil, which suggests he was already circulating poems by that point; and soon after met Maecenas, who remained an intimate for life. Two books of satires, along with a volume of epodes, scathing iambic verses modelled on the invective poetry of Archaic Greek, were published between 35 and 29 BC. It was around this time that Maecenas presented him with the gift of the Sabine farm about which he would write so lovingly – in fact a quite substantial property that allowed the poet to live henceforth as a kind of country gentleman.

It was in the comfort and security afforded by this munificent gift that Horace undertook an enormous project of a character radically different from that of the spicy, scintillating, gossipy *Sermones* and the often outrageous *Epodes*: the three books of odes, comprising eighty-eight poems in Greek metres on a wide range of subjects. Their publication in 23 BC made his name. (It was the *Odes*, certainly, and not the *Satires*, that earned him the *Carmen saeculare* commission.) There followed some verse epistles; an additional, fourth book of odes, which Augustus himself 'compelled' Horace to write, according to Suetonius; and another epistle on the writing of poetry, which has been enshrined separately as the *Ars poetica*, the 'Art of Poetry'. His last decade was darkened by the losses of friends and other poets: Virgil, Tibullus,

Propertius. In the year 8 BC, Maecenas died, admonishing Augustus on his deathbed to treat Horace as 'a second me'. He needn't have bothered: a few months later, Horace himself was dead.

Even this brief biography should help to account for much about Horace that irritates today: his ostensible embrace of the Augustan regime, his status as a poet of the establishment, his studied avoidance of ecstasy in favour of a measured appreciation of modest beauties and pleasures. For he had seen, firsthand, the worst that his century had to offer; whatever his reservations about Augustus may have been – and given his youthful politics, he must have had some – the new imperial stability was clearly to be preferred to the kind of violent upheavals he had witnessed. Who could blame him for wanting to spend the rest of the life that he had nearly lost celebrating the virtues of solid pleasures sensibly enjoyed – pleasures that are, in the *Odes* more than anywhere else in his work, both shadowed and heightened by an awareness of the violent energies always threatening to destroy them?

Yet it was not the temperate content, but rather the artful form of the *Odes* that was their great distinction – or so at least Horace declared. In the final entry to his third book of odes (the last lyric he ever planned to write, before Augustus asked him to whip up some more), he asserts that his claim to poetic fame would rest on the fact that he was the 'first to adapt Aeolian [that is., Greek, the verse forms used by Sappho and Alcaeus] verse to the Italian measure' – the very grafting of Roman onto Greek that would be replicated in the great public hymn that Augustus commissioned to celebrate the new Rome.

Why would an achievement that was, at least superficially, a technical one, matter so much – and make Horace's influence on later literature so profound? Roman authors during the last two centuries of the Republic – years marked, among other things, by the annexation of much of the Hellenistic Greek world – were acutely aware of the dominance and authority of the Greek cultural inheritance, which proved at once to be a superb model and an irritating burden. Poetry in particular was a vexed subject. The Greeks had an ancient poetic tradition, rich in its own special diction and forms; by comparison, the Roman tradition was both young and relatively impoverished. Roman poets found it was proving difficult to make Latin sound 'poetic' (which is to say, Greek). Latin as a language feels heavier than Greek: unlike Greek it has no articles, a phenomenon that lends Latin a certain chunkiness; unlike Greek, it does not have a number of monosyllabic 'particles' that can be sprinkled through lines or sentences to give subtle extra flavour – or to help meet the requirements of metre.

As a result, it was difficult to adapt Latin (so ideal for grave prose utterances) to the fluttery and complex stanzaic metres of Greek lyric verse. Horace dealt with this by altering certain conventions of the Greek models used by Sappho and her peers in ways that made them more suitable vehicles for the gravity of Latin words and rhythms (substituting spondees, for instance, where the Greek called for trochees or iambs, and placing regular caesuras, or breaks, within lines to allow for the greater stateliness of Latin speech). By eliminating the hiccuping effect of Greek metres, he achieved verse forms that for the first time sounded natural in Latin – and indeed exploited the monumental quality of the Latin tongue. It was Nietzsche who most famously put his finger on the special quality of Horatian verse, which took the stone blocks that were Latin words, ungainly and difficult to manoeuvre, and for the first time made them genuinely beautiful and artful: reading Horace, he said, was like encountering a 'mosaic of words, in which every word by sound, by position and by meaning, diffuses its influence to right and left and over the whole'.

This lapidary quality is the supreme Horatian achievement, the hallmark of his poetry. He ends his famous Mount Soracte ode ('See how deep stands the gleaming snow on / Soracte') with a description of how a flirtatious girl's lovely laughter betrays her hiding place in the corner of a Roman piazza:

> *nunc et latentis proditor intimo*
> *gratus puellae risus ab angulo …*

Each line consists of five words; literally, the words mean this:

> Now / too / of a hidden / betraying / from an intimate
> lovely / of a girl / laughter / from a corner

Any translation into syntactically correct English will shatter the cunning effect of the (syntactically correct) Latin, which is capable of a far more elastic word order. To the Roman eye and ear, the first line creates a terrific anticipation, consisting as it does of a series of adjectives describing nouns we don't encounter until the second line. When we do get there, we realize that the correct relationship between each adjective and its noun is meticulously vertical: hidden/girl, betraying/laughter, intimate/corner. So the lines in fact produce the very phenomenon they describe: a sound, a mysterious sound that you cannot at first identify because its source is deeply hidden (as is the word *angulo*) in a corner. Every line of every ode by Horace is this dense, this complex.

The problem remained of how to give poems composed in those newly useful metres the kind of intellectual heft that suited Roman sensibilities, moulded as they were by immersion in the study of rhetoric, focused as they were on the concrete, on the useful; and expressed in the rolling periods, the long, balanced, complex sentences, that so brilliantly distinguish Latin oratory. Horace's second great technical achievement was to learn to thread complicated and extended ideas through one after the other of the four-line stanzas perfected by Sappho and her peers; in so doing he hit upon an unmistakably poetic way to think like a Roman – and he provided, into the bargain, a tautness, variety, and sinew to lyric utterances that had never been achieved before. The energizing tension between the static 'mosaic' quality of his diction, which invites you to pause and admire every word, every stanza individually, and the forward-moving pull of his long arcs of thought is what gives Horatian verse its great distinction.

As it turned out, these stylistic and technical innovations perfectly served a characteristic thematic preoccupation: the relationship between pleasure and pain, between how we would like to live and what life does to us. When you carefully follow the strangely winding thread of Horace's thought from stanza to stanza, you often find yourself arriving at a destination quite different from the one the opening line might have promised. Below I have translated I.22, *Integer vitae*, 'Wholesome in life', a classic example of this characteristic Horatian sleight of hand, in which the poet's attention wavers between high Romanness and his charming girlfriend, Lalagê:

> Wholesome in life, of sin completely free:
> that man needs no Moorish spears nor bow
> nor quiver pregnant with its poisoned
>   arrows, Fuscus,

even if he's about to journey through
scorching Sidra, or the inhospitable
Caucasus, or regions that the fabled
    Jhelum laps.

For instance: a wolf – while in the Sabine woods
I once hymned my Lalagê and wandered, beyond
my usual bounds, free of all cares, unarmed –
    fled from me;

a monstrosity such as neither warlike
Apulia rears among her wide oak forests,
nor Juba's land, the arid wet-nurse of
    lions, breeds.

Place me in benumbed plains where not
a single tree is refreshed by summer's breeze,
that region of the world which mists and harsh
    Heaven oppress;

place me beneath the path of a too-close
sun, in a land denied to human habitation:
still I'll love my sweetly laughing Lalagê,
    sweetly talking.

The poem begins as if it's going to celebrate a certain kind of
Roman virtue and gravitas. (It was, indeed, often set to music and
performed at funerals in Germany and Scandinavia during the
nineteenth century.) And yet a shift occurs at the beginning of the
third stanza, which purports to give an example of the principle,
articulated in the first two, that the honest man needs no armour
but his goodness. With a flourish so grand that it suggests we are

not to take this business about virtue all that seriously, Horace posits himself as the exemplar of the heroism he lauds in the opening, all because (another letdown) a wolf once avoided him in a forest.

And just what (another shift) was he doing in the forest, anyway? Singing ditties about his darling if perhaps air-headed girlfriend (her Greek name, Lalagê, is derived from the verb 'to chatter'). The final pair of stanzas make us realize that the poem is not, after all, about purity and innocence, but rather about desire and poetry. For it is Horace's singing and his loving that will endure, however adverse the conditions; and it occurs to you to wonder whether those conditions might not, after all, include a dour cultural emphasis on wholesomeness and purity.

The sudden swerve in Horace's train of thought, so elegantly limned by his particular technique, can be found in a vast range of the odes on many subjects, both patently political and quietly personal. The penultimate poem of Book I, on Octavian's triumph over Cleopatra, famously begins with a call for celebratory drinking and foot-stomping to mark the demise of the 'demented queen' (*Nunc est bibendum*, 'Now let us drink'), but segues to an unsettling simile that compares the fleeing queen at Actium to a 'gentle dove' pursued by a hawk – which is to say, Augustus – and then ends, somewhat disorientingly, with a moving hommage to the 'fierce' dignity of her desire to 'die more nobly', 'not to be dragged, some lowly woman, in another's proud triumph'.

Such shifts are paralleled by another technique: sudden narrowings in focus from the general to the concrete, which can also subvert the poem's ostensible meaning. In the Mount Soracte ode, Horace's blithe admonishment to a young friend to enjoy love while he can takes a sudden, ferocious force from that closing evocation of the laughter of a young girl flirting in some piazza with a boy who's just snatched a love token from her finger. That flirtation was a plausible enough prospect for Horace's friend, but is, you realize, only a memory, now, for Horace himself. (And the loaded if taut manner in which the poet describes the girl's finger – *male pertinaci*, 'badly resisting' – gives some sense of the economy of expression that further characterizes his 'lapidary' diction.)

So too the Regulus ode, which so tortured Kipling's schoolboy, and which ends with a description of the dutiful soldier going off to suffer in war – an action the poet decides, almost as an afterthought, to compare to a man going off to a weekend in the country. In the context of what has preceded it, the sudden invocation of peacetime pleasures is shattering. The progressions and shifts of the poet's thought, as it moves through his meticulously fitted verses, is as unpredictable as the progress of any human experience, or human life, and it is this uncertainty that gives the poems, like the lives, their evanescent tone and fragile beauty.

All this is done with such great authority, and with such wit and panache – each of the first nine odes of Book I, the so-called 'Parade odes', is in a different Greek metre; it's the poetic equivalent of the compulsories in a sporting event, designed to show you that he's up to all the technical challenges – that it's easy to forget that nobody had ever done it before. But it made a great posterity possible. That we find it perfectly natural that a poet's project might be to express, in a wide variety of personas, something at once weighty and delicate in simple-looking four-line stanzas – to be formally structured but intellectually and emotionally varied, to be discursive and deeply poetic at the same time about a wide variety of subjects, many of them ostensibly everyday rather than ecstatic – is Horace's legacy to Western poetry.

*

The fiercely disciplined reasonableness of Horace's vision, his insistence on a poetic technique as rigorously thought out and meticulously achieved as the happiness the poems themselves endorse, have long endeared him to other poets, more, perhaps, than to the reading public at large. Auden had already put his finger on Horace's appeal in his own, very Horatian ode about the modern 'Horatians', sensible but deeply feeling people who know that they

> ... are, for all our polish, of little
> stature, and, as human lives,
> compared with authentic martyrs

> like Regulus, of no account. We can only
> do what it seems to us we were made for, look at
> this world with a happy eye
> but from a sober perspective.

The word 'polish' in the contemporary poem suggests the germ of Horace's appeal particularly to poets who, as J. D. McClatchy points out in the introduction to *Horace, The Odes*, his 2002 collection of verse renderings of the *Odes* by thirty-five well-known poets, have 'put aside their singing robes, once they think of themselves as craftsmen rather than as bards, once they attend the world as a surgery and not a party'. It is, indeed, Horace's supreme craftsmanship that has always made him at once 'wholly untranslatable', as Brooks Otis declared ('like making ropes out of sand,' Harold Mattingly once harrumphed in a book about Roman civilization), and irresistible to centuries of poets, particularly poets in English, from Dryden and Pope to Housman and (to cite the most recent of a spate of new translations of the *Odes*) David Ferry, whose much-praised translation appeared in 1997.

It is perhaps inevitable that every new translation of a great classic, like every new production of a canonical opera, needs some kind of self-justificatory new 'take' on the work: in Sidney Alexander's meticulous 1999 translation of the *Odes*, for instance, it was that he was giving us Horace as 'the quintessential Italian'. In the introduction to the new translation, McClatchy announces the distinguishing feature of his collection: 'Never before,' he writes, 'have the leading poets of the day assembled specifically to translate all the odes.' He goes on to declare that

> the variety of tone to be heard in these translations
> matches the mercurial shifts in mood and response
> the Latin poems themselves exhibit. The pairings of
> poem and translator were deliberate, and made in the
> hope of creating interesting juxtapositions. To have an
> American poet laureate write about political patronage,
> to have a woman poet write about seduction, an old
> poet write about the vagaries of age, a Southern poet
> about the blandishments of the countryside, a gay poet
> about the strategies of 'degeneracy' ... these are part of
> the editorial plot for this new book.

These *Odes* thus stand alongside recent collections of translations of a given classic, parts of which are distributed among different contemporary poets: for instance, Daniel Halpern's *Dante's Inferno: Translations by Twenty Contemporary Poets* or Michael Hoffman and James Lasdun's *After Ovid: New Metamorphoses*.

And yet while you admire McClatchy's impulse to create interesting textures between poet and translator, some of that 'editorial plot' sounds a little gimmicky to me. Surely it's enough to want to see how a group of excellent contemporary poets handle Horace, without having to suggest, *inter alia*, that Southerners know more about countrysides than (say) Midwesterners or New Englanders do, that women know more about seduction than men, or that gay men are more intimate with 'degeneracy' (scare quotes or no) than are others. For my part, I'd be happy with a gay translator who knew Latin as well as he presumably knew degeneracy: Mark Doty, a poet I much admire, seems to think that Horace was (as he says in III.14) a young man during the consulship of someone called 'Planco', probably because the words *consule Planco* appear in Horace's text; but that's just because *Planco* is the ablative form of *Plancus*, the consul's actual name. Such glitches would have been easy enough to correct, had the editorial focus been on Romans rather than Americans.

There are, to be sure, many deep pleasures to be had from individual translations you find here. Not least is that of an older poet, who has given to the incomparable Ligurinus ode, which begins with a weary rejection of love but ends in an image of heartbreaking erotic turmoil, just the right shift from bantering faux-Sappho ('So it's war again, Venus, / after all this time?') to the plaintive and poignant yearning of the poem's ending. In these last lines, the translator nicely replicates, with the long and short *i*'s, and with the *m*'s of his 'Then why, Ligurinus, why / do my eyes sometimes fill, even spill over?' both the assonant repetitions and yearning alliterative *m*'s and *n*'s of the Latin *sed cur heu, Ligurine, cur / manat rare meas lacrima per genas?* I doubt that such felicities are due simply to the fact that Richard Howard, the translator of this 'old age' poem, was born in 1929.

Similarly effective is the contribution of John Hollander, who in all of his translations, including an excellent rendering of the Soracte ode, displays a fine sensitivity in matters of enjambment, both between lines and between stanzas – always of vital importance in this poet, in whom sequences of thought are everything. Dick Davis's *Carmen saeculare*, which I quoted at the beginning of this essay, is appropriately dignified and yet manages, by means of rhymes on alternate lines, to sound like a song, which is precisely what it is. And I liked the elegant way in which Rosanna Warren handles the unenviable assignment of IV.7, *Diffugere nives*, 'The snows are fled away', the poem that A. E. Housman famously considered to be the most beautiful in ancient literature and which he himself memorably translated in a way that managed to sound both like Horace and like himself ('The snows are fled away, leaves on the shaws / And grasses in the mead renew their birth …'). Warren has managed to find new growth herself in these lines, unpacking the Latin to create fresh but not strained effects in English that make the poem sound, indeed, like poetry: 'All gone, the snow: grass throngs back to the fields, / the trees grow out new hair …'

So McClatchy's Horace has grown out some lovely new hair in which we can all luxuriate. Yet as a representation of the *Odes* as a whole (which, with its facing Latin pages, it is impossible not to take it as, whatever the editor's demurs), the new collection has deep problems, for precisely the reasons the editor proffers in order to authorize the new effort: that Horace's 'mercurial shifts in mood and response' justify the wildly different tones and degrees of formality, from free verse to rhymed couplets, on offer here.

It seems to me that this represents a fundamental misunderstanding of Horace's work. Horace's poetic identity lies precisely in the meticulous and masterly way he uses form, form above all, to solve both stylistic and intellectual problems: if he writes a poem in a stanzaic metre, it's because he wants you to feel the delicate rhythm of pausing and moving, pausing and moving, en route to the heart-stopping climax; if he casts it as a series of dense lines (as he does in the envoi to the first three books, III.30, *Exegi monumentum*, 'I have raised a monument more lasting than bronze'), it's because he wants you to feel the weight, the monumentality. Whatever his mercurial mood shifts, his absolute control and forceful personality give the poems a profound and unmistakable unity.

Indeed, each ode within the larger groupings (the individual books, and all the books taken together) is arranged with as much 'mosaic' precision as are individual words within individual odes. To cite just one example: odes II.2–11 are arranged in pairs of poems treating (roughly) the same subject, one poem in skipping Sapphics, the other in more weighty Alcaics. Part of the pleasure this sequence affords is the undulating shifts in tonality and rhythm between, first, the poems within each pair, and (then) among the pairs themselves.

Of this Horace, McClatchy's collection can give you no impression whatever. The multiple-translator approach works better for epic, whose narrative momentum helps to thread discrete cantos or books, themselves often fairly weighty and substantial, together; the continuities among lyric poems, carefully organized by their creator into a collection, are more fragile. (A device that better suits both the original work and its contemporary admirers is the one employed in R. Storr's 1959 Oxford University Press collection of 144 translations of a single ode, I.5: *Ad Pyrrham: A Polyglot Collection of Translations of Horace's Ode to Pyrrha*, a work that actually illuminates the ancient original while showing the variety of choices available to translators.)

And of course some of the approaches on display here work less well than others. Rachel Hadas's use of sing-song rhyming couplets in the Regulus ode give it a fatally Gunga-Dinish ring; Carl Phillips's decision to cast I.32, a crucial poem that quite self-consciously concerns Horace's formal achievement ('give me a Roman song, / my lyre, though Greek yourself') in loose-limbed free verse that trickles down the page makes it, in a way, far too easy – it deprives you of an essential component of the experience of reading Horatian verse, that of an aesthetic and emotional effect achieved by means of a serious intellectual effort. Horace is hard in Latin, and he should be hard in English. Without the formal rigour, the odes are reduced to little more than their apparent content, which is of course much less than what they're really 'about'.

So the individual talents of translators are on show here at the expense of Horace himself. You wonder, indeed, just who it is this collection is meant to serve. Certainly it will be of little use to those interested in ancient, as opposed to modern, poets: a major and distressing omission is the utter lack of notes of any kind. As nice as it is to think that the average intelligent reader will be able to make sense of (I have opened the collection to a random page) references to Gyges, Peleus, Magnesian Hyppolyte, Oricum, and Chloë, you suspect this is a touch optimistic. The importance of the poems' specific references isn't, as the current collection might suggest (one translation leaves out the proper names altogether, substituting blanks), pedantic: when Horace chides Venus for starting up old battles again in the Ligurinus poem, for instance, it's useful to know that Augustus claimed descent from that untrustworthy deity, and hence that the poem thus slyly questions both the erotic and political compulsions responsible for its own creation. To miss such nuances, easy enough to explain in a sentence or two, is to miss much of Horace's wit, and a lot of his seriousness, too.

The startling failure to offer even simple clarifications that would enhance ordinary readers' appreciation of Horace's deeply constructed meanings suggests again that the real focus here is on the translators; there is, indeed, a whiff of clubbiness about the present collection. (I kept wondering why none of the so-called New Formalists – Timothy Steele, Gjertrud Schnackenberg, Dana Gioia – appears in these pages: their emphasis on formal rigour, and particularly Steele's temperament, with its wry celebrations of emotional restraint, would make them ideal candidates for translating Horace.) That hermetic quality will surely have the unfortunate effect of making Horace more rather than less forbidding to the poetry-reading public. Whatever the pleasures it affords, *Horace: The Odes* isn't, finally, Horace's *Odes*. For the present *saeculum*, at least, their strange music – exotic and plainspoken, Greek and Roman, fluid and lapidary, yearning and complacent, earthy and effete – continues to hover in the air, just out of reach.

– *The New York Review of Books*, 13 May 2004

Epic Fail?

Since the end of the first century AD, people have been playing a game with a certain book. In this game, you open the book to a random spot and place your finger on the text; the passage you select will, it is thought, predict your future. If this sounds silly, the results suggest otherwise. The first person known to have played the game was a highborn Roman who was fretting about whether he'd be chosen to follow his cousin, the emperor Trajan, on the throne; after opening the book to this passage –

> I recognize that he is that king of Rome,
> Grey headed, grey bearded, who will formulate
> The laws for the early city ...

– he was confident that he'd succeed. His name was Hadrian.

Through the centuries, others sought to discover their fates in this book, from Rabelais in the early sixteenth century (some of whose characters play the game, too), to Charles I, who, during the Civil War, visited an Oxford library and was alarmed to find that he'd placed his finger on a passage that concluded, 'But let him die before his time, and lie / Somewhere unburied on a lonely beach.' Two and a half centuries after Charles lost his head, as the Germans marched toward Paris at the beginning of the First World War, a classicist named David Ansell Slater, who had once viewed the very volume that Charles had consulted, found himself scouring the same text, hoping for a portent of good news.

What was the book, and why was it taken so seriously? The answer lies in the name of the game: *sortes vergilianae*. The Latin noun *sortes* means lots – as in 'drawing lots', a reference to the game's element of chance. The adjective *vergilianae*, which means 'having to do with Vergilius', identifies the book: the works of the Roman poet Publius Vergilius Maro, whom we know as Virgil.

For a long stretch of Western history, few people would have found it odd to ascribe prophetic power to this collection of Latin verse. Its author, after all, was the greatest and the most influential of all Roman poets. A friend and confidant of Augustus, Rome's first emperor, Virgil was already considered a classic in his own lifetime: revered, quoted, imitated, and occasionally parodied by other writers, taught in schools, and devoured by the general public. Later generations of Romans considered his works a font of human knowledge, from rhetoric to ethics to agriculture; by the Middle Ages, the poet had come to be regarded as a wizard whose powers included the ability to control Vesuvius' eruptions and to cure blindness in sheep. However fantastical the proportions to which this reverence grew, it was grounded in a very real achievement represented by one poem in particular: the *Aeneid*, a heroic epic in twelve chapters (or 'books') about the mythic founding of Rome, which some ancient sources say Augustus commissioned and which was, arguably, the single most influential literary work of European civilization for the better part of two millennia.

Virgil had published other, shorter works before the *Aeneid*, but it's no accident that the epic was a magnet for the fingers of the great and powerful who played the *sortes vergilianae*. Its central themes are leadership, empire, history, and war. In it, an upstanding Trojan prince named Aeneas, son of Venus, the goddess of love, flees Troy after its destruction by the Greeks, and, along with his father, his son, and a band of fellow-survivors, sets out to establish a new realm across the sea, in Italy, the homeland that's been promised to him by divine prophecy. Into that traditional story Virgil cannily inserted a number of showstopping glimpses into Rome's future military and political triumphs, complete with cameo appearances by Augustus himself – the implication being that the real-life empire arose from a god-kissed mythic past. The Emperor and his people alike were hooked: within a century of its author's death, in 19 BC, citizens of Pompeii were scrawling lines from the epic on the walls of shops and houses.

People haven't stopped quoting it since. From the moment it appeared, the *Aeneid* was the paradigmatic classic in Western art and education; as one scholar has put it, Virgil 'occupied the central place in the literary canon for the whole of Europe for longer than any other writer'. (After the Western Roman Empire fell, in the late fifth century AD, knowledge of Greek – and, hence, intimacy with Homer's epics – virtually disappeared from Western Europe for a thousand years.) Virgil's poetry has been indispensable to everyone from his irreverent younger contemporary Ovid, whose parodies of the older poet's gravitas can't disguise a genuine admiration, to St Augustine, who, in his *Confessions*, recalls weeping over the *Aeneid*, his favourite book before he discovered the Bible; from Dante, who chooses Virgil, *l'altissimo poeta*, 'the highest poet', as his guide through Hell and Purgatory in the *Divine Comedy*, to T. S. Eliot, who returned repeatedly to Virgil in his critical essays and pronounced the *Aeneid* 'the classic of all Europe'.

And not only Europe. In America, Alexander Hamilton, Thomas Jefferson, and Benjamin Franklin liked to quote Virgil in their speeches and letters. The poet's idealized vision of honest farmers and shepherds working in rural simplicity was influential, some scholars believe, in shaping the Founders' vision of the new republic as one in which an agricultural majority should hold power. Throughout the nineteenth century, Virgil was a central fixture of American grammar-school education; the ability to translate passages on sight was a standard entrance requirement at many colleges and universities. John Adams boasted that his son John Quincy had translated the entire *Aeneid*. Ellen Emerson wrote her father, Ralph Waldo, to say that she was covering a hundred and twenty lines a day; Helen Keller read it in Braille. Today, traces of the epic's cultural authority linger on: a quotation from it greets visitors to the Memorial Hall of the 9/11 Museum, in New York City. Since the turn of the current century, there have been at least five major translations into English alone, most recently by the American poet David Ferry (Chicago), in the final instalment of his translation of Virgil's complete works.

Still, the *Aeneid* – notoriously – can be hard to love. In part, this has to do with its aesthetics. In place of the raw archaic potency of Homer's epics, which seems to dissolve the millennia between his heroes and us, Virgil's densely allusive poem offers an elaborately self-conscious 'literary' suavity. (The critic and Columbia professor Mark Van Doren remarked that 'Homer is a world; Virgil, a style.') Then, there's Aeneas himself – 'in some ways,' as even the Great Courses website feels compelled to acknowledge, 'the dullest character in epic literature.' In the *Aeneid*'s opening lines, Virgil announces that the hero is famed above all for his *pietas*, his 'sense of duty': hardly the sexiest attribute for a protagonist. If Aeneas was meant to be a model proto-Roman, he has long struck many readers as a cold fish; he and his comrades, the philosopher György Lukács once observed, live 'the cool and limited existence of shadows'. Particularly in comparison with his Homeric predecessors, Aeneas comes up short, lacking the cruel glamour of Achilles, or Odysseus's beguiling smarts.

But the biggest problem by far for modern audiences is the poem's subject matter. Today, the themes that made the epic required reading for generations of emperors and generals, and for the clerics and teachers who groomed them – the inevitability of imperial dominance, the responsibilities of authoritarian rule, the importance of duty and self-abnegation in the service of the state – are proving to be an embarrassment. If readers of an earlier era saw the *Aeneid* as an inspiring advertisement for the onward march of Rome's many descendants, from the Holy Roman Empire to the British one, scholars now see in it a tale of nationalistic arrogance whose plot is an all too familiar handbook for repressive violence. Once Aeneas and his fellow-Trojans arrive on the coast of Italy, they find that they must fight a series of wars with an indigenous population that, eventually, they brutally subjugate.

The result is that readers today can have a very strange relationship to this classic: it's a work we feel we should embrace but often keep at arm's length. Take that quote in the 9/11 Museum: 'No day shall erase you from the memory of time.' Whoever came up with the idea of using it was clearly ignorant of the context, since these high-minded words are addressed to a pair of nighttime marauders whose bloody ambush of a group of unsuspecting targets suggests that they have far more in common with the 9/11 terrorists than with their victims. A century ago, many a college undergrad could have caught the gaffe; today, it was enough to have an impressive-sounding quote from an acknowledged classic.

Another way of saying all this is that, while our forebears looked confidently to the text of the *Aeneid* for answers, today it raises troubling questions. Who exactly is Aeneas, and why should we admire him? What is the epic's political stance? Can we ignore the parts we dislike and cherish the rest? Should great poetry serve an authoritarian regime – and just whose side was Virgil on? Two thousand years after its appearance, we still can't decide if his masterpiece is a regressive celebration of power as a means of political domination or a craftily coded critique of imperial ideology – a work that still has something useful to tell us.

Little in Virgil's background destined him to be the great poet of empire. He was born on 15 October 70 BC, in a village outside Mantua; his father, perhaps a well-off farmer, had the means to provide him with a good education, first in Cremona and Milan and then in Rome. The inhabitants of his native northern region had only recently been granted Roman citizenship through a decree by Julius Caesar, issued when the poet was a young man. Hence, even after his first major work, a collection of pastoral poems called the *Eclogues*, gained him an entrée into Roman literary circles, Virgil must have seemed – and perhaps felt – something of an outsider: a reserved country fellow with (as his friend the poet Horace teased him) a hick's haircut, who spoke so haltingly that he could seem downright uneducated. His retiring nature, which earned him the nickname *parthenias* ('little virgin'), may have been the reason he decided not to remain in Rome to complete his education. Instead, he settled in Naples, a city with deep ties to the culture of the Greeks, which he and his literary contemporaries revered. In the final lines of the *Georgics*, a long didactic poem about farming which he finished when he was around forty, the poet looked back yearningly to the untroubled leisure he had enjoyed during that period:

> And I, the poet Virgil, nurtured by sweet
> Parthénopé [Naples], was flourishing in the pleasures
> Of idle studies, I, who bold in youth
> Played games with shepherds' songs.

I'm quoting David Ferry's translation of the poem. But the word that Ferry translates as 'idle' is somewhat stronger in the original: Virgil says that his leisure time was *ignobilis*, 'ignoble', a choice that suggests some guilt about that easygoing Neapolitan idyll. And with good reason: however 'sweet' those times were for Virgil, for Rome they were anything but. The poet's lifetime spanned the harrowing disintegration of the Roman Republic and the fraught birth of the Empire – by any measure, one of the most traumatic centuries in European history. Virgil was a schoolchild when the orator and statesman Cicero foiled a plot by the corrupt aristocrat Catiline to overthrow the Republic; by the time the poet was twenty, Julius Caesar, defying the Senate's orders, had crossed the Rubicon with his army and set in motion yet another civil war. It was another two decades before Caesar's great-nephew and heir, Octavian, defeated the last of his rivals, the renegade general Antony and his Egyptian consort, Cleopatra, at the Battle of Actium, and established the so-called Principate – the rule of the *princeps* ('first citizen'), an emperor in everything but name. Soon afterward, he took the quasi-religious honorific 'Augustus'.

The new ruler was a man of refined literary tastes; Virgil and his patron, Maecenas, the regime's unofficial minister of culture, are said to have taken turns reading the *Georgics* aloud to the Emperor after his victory at Actium. Augustus no doubt liked what he heard. In one passage, the poet expresses a fervent hope that Rome's young new leader will be able to spare Italy the wars that have wreaked havoc on the lives of the farmers whose labour is the subject of the poem; in another, he envisages the erection of a grand temple honouring the ruler.

Because we like to imagine poets as being free in their political conscience, such fawning seems distasteful. (Robert Graves, the author of *I, Claudius*, complained that 'few poets have brought such discredit as Virgil on their sacred calling'.) But Virgil cannot have been alone among intelligent Romans in welcoming Augustus's regime as, at the very least, a stable alternative to the decades of internecine horrors that had preceded it. If Augustus did in fact suggest the idea for a national epic, it must have been while Virgil was still working on the *Georgics*, which includes a trailer for his next project: 'And soon I'll gird myself to tell the tales / Of Caesar's brilliant battles, and carry his name / In story across … many future years.' He began work on the *Aeneid* around 29 BC and was in the final stages of writing when, ten years later, he died suddenly while returning home from a trip to Greece. He was buried in his beloved Naples.

The epic's state of completion continues to be a subject of debate. There's little doubt that a number of lines are metrically incomplete, a fact that dovetails with what we know about the poet's working method: he liked to joke that, in order to preserve his momentum while writing, he'd put in temporary lines to serve as 'struts' until the 'finished columns' were ready. According to one anecdote, the dying Virgil begged his literary executors to burn the manuscript of the epic, but Augustus intervened, and, after some light editing, the finished work finally appeared. In the epitaph he composed for himself, Virgil refers with disarming modesty to his achievement: 'Mantua gave me birth, Calabria took me, now Naples / holds me fast. I sang of pastures, farms, leaders.'

*

Virgil was keenly aware that, in composing an epic that begins at Troy, describes the wanderings of a great hero, and features book after book of gory battles, he was working in the long shadow of Homer. But, instead of being crushed by what Harold Bloom called 'the anxiety of influence', he found a way to acknowledge his Greek models while adapting them to Roman themes. Excerpts of the work in progress were already impressing fellow-writers by the mid-twenties BC, when the love poet Propertius wrote that 'something greater than the *Iliad* is being born'.

The very structure of the *Aeneid* is a wink at Homer. The epic is split between an 'Odyssean' first half (Books I through VI recount Aeneas's wanderings as he makes his way from Troy to Italy) and an 'Iliadic' second half (Books VII through XII focus on the wars that the hero and his allies wage in order to take possession of their new homeland). Virgil signals this appropriation of the two Greek classics in his work's famous opening line, 'Arms and a man I sing': the *Iliad* is the great epic of war ('arms'), while the *Odyssey* begins by announcing that its subject is 'a man' – Odysseus. Virtually every one of the *Aeneid*'s nine thousand eight hundred and ninety-six lines is embedded, like that first one, in an intricate web of literary references, not only to earlier Greek and Roman literature but to a wide range of religious, historical, and mythological arcana. This allusive complexity would have flattered the sophistication of the original audience, but today it can leave everyone except specialists flipping to the endnotes. In this way, Virgil's Homeric riff prefigures James Joyce's, twenty centuries later: whatever the great passages of intense humanity, there are parts that feel like a treasure hunt designed for graduate students of the future.

It is, indeed, hardly surprising that readers through the centuries have found the *Aeneid*'s first half more engaging. As in the

Odyssey, there are shipwrecks caused by angry deities (Juno, the queen of the gods, tries to foil Aeneas at every turn) and succour from helpful ones (Venus intervenes every now and then to help her son). There are councils of the gods at which the destinies of mortals are sorted out; at one point, Jupiter, the king of the pantheon, assures the anxious Venus (and, by implication, the Roman reader) that the nation her son is about to found will enjoy *imperium sine fine*, 'rule without end'. As for the mortals, there are melancholy reunions with old friends and family, and hair-raising encounters with legendary monsters. Virgil has a lot of fun retooling episodes from the *Odyssey*: his hero has close calls with Scylla and Charybdis, lands on the Cyclops' island just after Odysseus has left, and – in an amusing moment that does an end run around Homer – decides to sail right past Circe's abode.

And, like Odysseus, Aeneas is dangerously distracted from his mission by a beautiful woman: Dido, the queen of the North African city of Carthage, where the hero has been welcomed hospitably after he is shipwrecked. Venus, eager for her son to find a safe haven there, sends Cupid to make Dido fall in love with Aeneas in Book I, and throughout Books II and III the queen grows ever more besotted with her guest, who holds her court spellbound with tales of his sufferings and adventures. His eyewitness account of the sack of Troy, in Book II, remains one of the most powerful depictions of military violence in European literature, with a disorienting, almost cinematic oscillation between seething, smoke-filled crowd scenes and claustrophobic moments of individual panic. At one point, Aeneas, fleeing the smouldering ruins, somehow loses track of his wife, Creusa; in a chillingly realistic evocation of war's chaos, we never learn how she dies. As for Dido, her affair with the hero reaches a tragic climax in Book IV. Aeneas, reminded by the gods of his sacred duty, abandons her, and she commits suicide – the emotional high point of the epic's first half. (The curse she calls down on her former lover is the passage that King Charles selected when he played the *sortes vergilianae*.)

The *Aeneid*'s first part ends, as does the first half of the *Odyssey*, with an unsettling visit to the Underworld. Here, there are confrontations with the dead and the past they represent – Dido's ghost doesn't deign to acknowledge the apologetic Aeneas's protestations – and encounters, too, with the glorious future. One of the spirits that Aeneas meets is his father, Anchises, whom he'd carried on his back as they fled Troy, and who has since died; as Anchises guides his son through the murky landscape, he draws his attention to a fabulous parade of monarchs, warriors, statesmen, and heroes who will distinguish the history of the future Roman state, from the mythic king Romulus to Augustus himself. As they witness this pageant, the old man imparts a crucial piece of advice. The Greeks, he observes, excelled at the arts – sculpture, rhetoric – but Rome has a far greater mission in world history:

> Romans, never forget that this will be
> Your appointed task: to use your arts to be
> The governor of the world, to bring to it peace,
> Serenely maintained with order and with justice,
> To spare the defeated and to bring an end
> To war by vanquishing the proud.

This conception of Rome's strengths – administration, governance, jurisprudence, war – in relation to Greece's will be familiar to anyone who's taken a general course on world civilization. What's so confounding is that, after receiving this eloquent advice on the correct uses of power, Aeneas – as the second half of the poem shockingly demonstrates – doesn't take it.

Books VII through XII, with their unrelenting account of the *bella horrida bella* ('wars, horrible wars') that Aeneas must wage to secure his new homeland, are clearly meant to recall the *Iliad* – not least, in the event that sets them in motion. After the hero arrives in Italy, he favourably impresses a local king named Latinus, who promises his daughter, Lavinia, as a wife for Aeneas. The problem is that the girl has already been chosen for a local chieftain named Turnus, who, smarting from the insult, goes on to command the forces trying to repel the Trojan invaders. And so, like the war recounted in the *Iliad*, this one is fought over a woman who has been stolen away from her rightful mate – the difference being that this time it's the Trojans, not the Greeks, who invade a foreign country and ravage a kingdom in order to retrieve her. One challenge presented by the mythic Trojan origins of the Roman people was that the Trojans lost their great war; reshaping his source material, Virgil found a way to transform a story about losers into an epic about winners.

But what does it mean to be a winner? Anchises instructs his son that, to be a Roman, he must become (in Ferry's translation) 'governor of the world'. This rendering of Virgil's phrase *regere imperio populos* is rather mild. John Dryden's 1697 translation far better conveys the menace lurking in the word *imperium* ('the right to command'): ''tis thine alone, with awful sway, / To rule Mankind; and make the World obey.'

Just what making the world obey looks like is vividly illustrated in another vision of the future that the *Aeneid* provides. In Book VIII, there is a lengthy description of the sumptuous shield that Vulcan, the blacksmith god, forges for Aeneas before he meets Turnus and the Italian hordes in battle. The decorations on the shield meld moments both mythic and historical, past and future, from Romulus and Remus being suckled by the she-wolf to a central panel depicting the Battle of Actium, with Augustus and his brilliant general Agrippa, on one side, facing off against Antony and Cleopatra, on the other. (She's backed by her foreign 'monster gods': that 'monster' is a telling bit of Roman jingoism that Ferry inexplicably omits.) The shield also includes an image of Augustus marching triumphantly through the capital as its temples resound with the joyful singing of mothers, while – that other product of *imperium* – a host of conquered peoples are marched through the streets: nomads, Africans, Germans, Scythians.

Yet one battle into which Aeneas carries his remarkable shield ends with the hero unaccountably failing to adhere to the second part of his father's exhortation: to 'spare the defeated'. As the poem nears its conclusion, the wars gradually narrow to a single combat between Aeneas and Turnus, who, by that point, has slain a beautiful youth called Pallas, Aeneas's ward and the son of his chief ally. In the closing lines of the poem, Aeneas fells Turnus with a crippling blow to the thigh. While his enemy lies prostrate before him, the hero hesitates, sword in hand; but, just as thoughts of leniency crowd his mind – he is, after all, famous for his sense of duty, for doing the right thing – he sees that Turnus is wearing a piece of armour torn from Pallas's body. Seized with rage and grief, Aeneas rips open Turnus's breast with one blow, and the dead man's soul 'indignant fled away to the shades below'.

That is the last line of the poem – an ending so disorientingly abrupt that it has been cited as evidence by those who believe that Virgil left his magnum opus incomplete when he died. One fifteenth-century Italian poet went so far as to add an extra book to the poem (in Latin verse) tying Virgil's loose ends into a neat bow: Aeneas marries Lavinia and is eventually deified. This ending was so popular that it was included in editions of the *Aeneid* for centuries afterward.

*

As recently as the early twentieth century, the *Aeneid* was embraced as a justification of the Roman – and, by extension, any – empire: 'a classic vindication of the European world-order', as one scholar put it. (This position is known among classicists as the 'optimistic' interpretation.) The marmoreal perfections of its verse seemed to reflect the grand façades of the Roman state itself: Augustus boasted that he found Rome a city of brick and left it a city of marble.

But in the second half of the last century more and more scholars came to see some of the epic's most wrenching episodes as attempts to draw attention to the toll that the exercise of *imperium* inevitably takes. This 'pessimistic' approach to the text and its relation to imperial ideology has found its greatest support in the account of Aeneas's treatment of Dido. That passionate, tender, and grandly tragic woman is by far the epic's greatest character – and, indeed, the only one to have had a lasting impact on Western culture past the Middle Ages, memorably appearing in works by artists ranging from Purcell to Berlioz to Mark Morris.

After the gods order Aeneas to abandon Dido and leave Carthage – he mustn't, after all, end up like Antony, the love slave of an African queen – he prepares to sneak away. But Dido finds him out and, in a furious tirade, lambastes the man she considers to be her husband for his craven evasion of a kind of responsibility – emotional, ethical – quite unlike the political dutifulness that has driven him from the start:

> What shall I say? What *is* there for me to say? …
> There is nowhere where faith is kept; not anywhere.
> He was stranded on the beach, a castaway,
> With nothing. I made him welcome.

In uttering these words, Dido becomes the *Aeneid*'s most eloquent voice of moral outrage at the promises that always get broken by men with a mission. In killing herself, she becomes a heartbreaking symbol of the collateral damage that 'empire' leaves in its wake.

Aeneas's reaction to her tirade is telling. Unable to bring himself to look her in the eye, he looks instead 'at the future / He was required to look at':

> Pious Aeneas, groaning and sighing, and shaken
> In his very self in his great love for her,
> And longing to find the words that might assuage
> Her grief over what is being done to her,
> Nevertheless obeyed the divine command
> And went back to his fleet.

You wish that Ferry hadn't translated the Latin word *pius* in the first line of this passage as the English word it so closely resembles, 'pious'; here more than anywhere else, *pius* means 'dutiful', embodying a steadfast obedience to the gods' plan which overrides every other consideration. Much of the *Aeneid* is fuelled by this torturous conflict between private fulfilment and public responsibility, which was to become a staple of European literature and drama, showing up in everything from Corneille to *The Crown*. (You sometimes get the impression that Virgil himself would like to be free of his poetic duty to celebrate the empire. In Book V, a long set piece about a sailing competition that Aeneas holds for his men, filled with verve and humour, feels like a vacation for the poet, too.)

When Aeneas does reply to Dido, he's as cool as a corporate lawyer, rattling off one talking point after another. (Dido has a kingdom of her own, so why shouldn't he?) But how are we to reconcile this Aeneas with the distraught figure we're left with at the end of the poem, a man who goes berserk when he's reminded of the loss of his young ward and who brutally slays a captive supplicant? The contradiction has led to persistent questions about the coherence of Virgil's depiction of his hero. When critics aren't denouncing Aeneas's lack of personality ('a stick who would have contributed to the *New Statesman*,' Ezra Pound sniffed), they're fulminating against his lack of character. 'A cad to the last' was Robert Graves's summation.

And as with the hero so, too, with the epic itself: for many readers, something doesn't add up. If the *Aeneid* is an admiring piece of propaganda for empire triumphant, whose hero emblematizes the necessity of suppressing individuality in the interest of the state, what do you do with Dido – or, for that matter, with Turnus, who could well strike readers today as a heroic native resisting colonial incursion, an admirable prototype of Boudicca? And if it's a veiled critique of empire that movingly catalogues the horrible costs of *imperium*, what do you do with all the imperial dazzle – the shield, the parade of future Romans, the apparent endorsement of the hero's dogged allegiance to duty?

Latin is a rather chunky language. Unlike Greek, which is far more supple, it has no definite or indefinite articles; a page of Latin can look like a wall of bricks. As such, it's particularly difficult to adapt to dactylic hexameter, the waltzlike, oom-pah-pah metre of epic poetry, which the Romans inherited from the Greeks. One of Virgil's achievements was to bring Latin hexameter verse to an unusually high level of flexibility and polish, stretching long thoughts and sentences over several lines, gracefully balancing pairs of nouns and adjectives, and finding ways to temper the natural heaviness of his native tongue. Alfred, Lord

Tennyson, called the result 'the stateliest measure ever moulded by the lips of man'.

David Ferry more than succeeds in capturing the stateliness, as his translation of the Proem, the epic's introductory lines, into English blank verse shows:

> I sing of arms and the man whom fate had sent
> To exile from the shores of Troy to be
> The first to come to Lavinium and the coasts
> Of Italy, and who, because of Juno's
> Savage implacable rage, was battered by storms
> At sea, and from the heavens above, and also
> By tempests of war, until at last he might
> Bring his household gods to Latium, and build his
>   town,
> From which would come the Alban Fathers and
> The lofty walls of Rome.

Alone among recent translators, as far as I am aware, Ferry has honoured the crucial fact that, in the original, this is all one long flowing sentence and one thought: from Troy to Rome, from past to present, from defeat to victory.

But there's more to Virgil than high polish. You might compare Ferry's rendering to that of the 2007 Oxford World Classics translation by Frederick Ahl, which is far more attentive to some crucial vocabulary:

> Arms and the man I sing of Troy, who first from its
>   seashores,
> Italy-bound, fate's refugee, arrived at Lavinia's
> Coastlands, how he was battered about over land, over
>   high deep

> Seas by the power above! Savage Juno's anger
>   remembered
> Him, and he suffered profoundly in war to establish a
>   city,
> Settle his gods into Latium, making this land of the
>   Latins
> Future home to the Elders of Alba and Rome's mighty
>   ramparts.

Ahl here preserves some diction that disappears in Ferry's translation. 'Juno's anger remembered', for instance, is a smart solution for the poet's pointed description of the goddess's rage as *memorem*, 'remembering': the motif of savage wrath growing out of a compulsive remembering, a pathological inability to forget past hurts, is vital to the epic from its first lines to its final moments. Ferry's bland 'implacable' does nothing to convey this all-important motif.

Ahl's translation also preserves a certain oddness in Virgil's verse which Ferry's elegance smooths away. Because the *Aeneid*'s instantaneous status as a classic made its style a standard, it's difficult to appreciate how innovative and idiosyncratic Virgil's poetry once felt. One favourite device, for instance, is called 'hypallage', in which an adjective is pointedly displaced from the noun it should, logically, modify. Take the last line of the Proem, with its climactic vision of what Ferry renders as 'The lofty walls of Rome'. What Virgil actually wrote was stranger: 'the walls of lofty Rome'. The poet knew what he was doing – 'lofty walls' is about architecture, but 'lofty Rome' is about empire. Ferry's creamily stately rendering both here and elsewhere, which has the effect of 'correcting' the original's strangeness, is likely to leave you wondering why critics both ancient and modern have scratched their heads over Virgil's poetics – his occasionally jarring or archaic diction (mocked by one Roman littérateur who made his point by writing a parody of the poet's early work); his 'tasteless striving for effect,' as Augustus's friend and general Agrippa complained; his 'use of words too forcible for his thoughts', as A. E. Housman put it two millennia later. It's these arresting qualities that made Virgil feel modern to his contemporaries – something it's almost impossible to feel about him in this translation and so many others.

In a way, Virgil may be the victim of his own literary sophistication. The archaic force of Homer's epics makes itself felt despite the moral and cultural distance that separates them from us; the elemental qualities of their protagonists impress themselves on us, however strange their mores. This is why even adaptations that take great liberties – Alice Oswald's *Memorial* or Christopher Logue's *All Day Permanent Red*, both searing riffs on the *Iliad* – manage to feel true to the originals while completely reworking them. But for all that it's the product of a civilization much closer to our own than the Greeks', Virgil's poetry has proved curiously difficult to pin down, to make feel modern. In an essay on Virgil in English translation, the Oxford scholar Colin Burrow summed up the problem: 'Virgil has not found an Ezra Pound ... or a Christopher Logue to wrench him into modernity.'

It may be that we don't need to rely on a translation to drag the *Aeneid* into the modern era. Maybe it's always been here, and we're just looking at it from the wrong angle – or looking for the wrong things. Maybe the inconsistencies in the hero and his poem that have distressed readers and critics – the certainties alternating with doubt, the sudden careening from coolness to high emotion, the poet's admiring embrace of an empire whose moral offences he can't help cataloguing, the optimistic portrait of a great nation rising haunted by a cynical appraisal of Realpolitik at work – aren't problems of interpretation that we have to solve but, rather, the qualities in which this work's modernity resides.

This, at any rate, is what was going through my mind one day fifteen years ago, when, I like to think, I finally began to understand the *Aeneid*. At the time, I was working on a book about the Holocaust, and had spent several years interviewing the few remaining survivors from a small Polish town whose Jewish population had been obliterated by what you could legitimately call an exercise of *imperium*. As I pressed these elderly people for their memories, I was struck by the similarities in the way they talked: a kind of resigned fatalism, a forlorn acknowledgment that the world they were trying to describe was, in the end, impossible to evoke; strange swings between an almost abnormal detachment when describing unspeakable atrocities and sudden eruptions of ungovernable rage and grief triggered by the most trivial memory.

Months later, when I was back home teaching Greek and Roman classics again, it occurred to me that the difficulties we have with Aeneas and his epic cease to be difficulties once you think of him not as a hero but as a type we're all too familiar with: a survivor, a person so fractured by the horrors of the past that he can hold himself together only by an unnatural effort of will, someone who has so little of his history left that the only thing that gets him through the present is a numbed sense of duty to a barely discernible future that can justify every kind of deprivation. It would be hard to think of a more modern figure.

Or, indeed, a more modern story. What is the *Aeneid* about? It is about a tiny band of outcasts, the survivors of a terrible persecution. It is about how these survivors – clinging to a divine assurance that an unknown and faraway land will become their new home – arduously cross the seas, determined to refashion themselves as a new people, a nation of victors rather than victims. It is about how, when they finally get there, they find their new homeland inhabited by locals who have no intention of making way for them. It is about how this geopolitical tragedy generates new wars, wars that will, in turn, trigger further conflicts: *bella horrida bella*. It is about how such conflicts leave those involved in them morally unrecognizable, even to themselves. This is a story that both the Old and the New Worlds know too well; and Virgil was the first to tell it. Whatever it meant in the past, and however it discomfits the present, the *Aeneid* has, alas, always anticipated the future.

— *The New Yorker*, 15 October 2018

The Women and the Thrones

About halfway through *A Clash of Kings*, the second instalment of George R. R. Martin's epic fantasy series *A Song of Ice and Fire*, a refugee princess – she is fourteen years old but already a widow, has silver hair and purple eyes, and happens to be the mother of three dragons – stands exhausted before the walls of a fabulous, vaguely Babylonian citadel called Qarth. The last surviving scion of the deposed ruling family of a faraway land called Westeros, she has led a ragtag band of followers through the desert in the hopes of finding shelter here – and, ultimately, of obtaining military and financial support for her plan to recapture the Westerosi throne. Her first glimpse of Qarth leaves her bemused:

> Three thick walls encircled Qarth, elaborately carved. The outer was red sandstone, thirty feet high and decorated with animals: snakes slithering, kites flying, fish swimming, intermingled with wolves of the red waste and striped zorses and monstrous elephants. The middle wall, forty feet high, was grey granite alive with scenes of war: the clash of sword and shield and spear, arrows in flight, heroes at battle and babes being butchered, pyres of the dead. The innermost wall was fifty feet of black marble, with carvings that made Dany blush until she told herself that she was being a

fool. She was no maid; if she could look on the grey
wall's scenes of slaughter, why should she avert her eyes
from the sight of men and women giving pleasure to
one another?

However difficult it may be for Daenerys ('Dany') Targaryen to
make sense of the exotic city and its people, anyone familiar with
Martin's slowly metastasizing epic – it began as a trilogy in 1996
and now runs to five volumes of a projected seven, each around a
thousand pages long – will find it hard not to see in the Qartheen
decor a sly reference to the series itself. What drives *A Song of Ice
and Fire* is a war story: clearly inspired by the Wars of the Roses,
the series traces the internecine power struggles among a group of
aristocratic clans, each with its castle, lord, 'sigil' or heraldic arms,
and lineages, following the not entirely accidental death, in the
first novel, of King Robert I of the Seven Kingdoms. Robert had
seized the throne from Dany's father at the end of a previous civil
war, thereby ending the Targaryens' three-century-long rule. The
civil wars that follow Robert's death will stretch from Westeros
– whose culturally diverse regions, evoked by Martin in ingenious
detail, form the Seven Kingdoms – across the Narrow Sea to the
exotic East, where Dany Targaryen, as we know, plans to make
her own power play.

These bloody struggles take place in a world whose culture is,
on the whole, familiar-looking – Martin gives the civilization of
the Seven Kingdoms a strong medieval flavour – but whose flora
and fauna remind you why the novels are classified as 'fantasy'.
Westeros may have castles and drawbridges, knights, squires, and
jousts, 'sers' and ladies, and a capital city, King's Landing, that
looks and smells a lot like late-medieval London, but it also has
giants, shape-shifters called 'wargs', blue-eyed walking dead
known as 'wights', seasons that last for decades, red-faced 'weir-

wood' trees that grow in sacred groves called 'godswoods' – and, of course, dragons. At the end of the first novel, Daenerys emerges from a fire holding three newly hatched specimens that, you suspect, will greatly improve her chances of gaining the throne.

Against this wildly inventive natural (often supernatural) back-drop, the books' characters engage in a good deal of unsentimen-tal fornication that is not without a certain imaginative élan of its own. 'In a cushioned alcove,' one not atypical scene begins, a drunken man 'with a purple beard dandled a buxom young wench on his knee. He'd unlaced her bodice and was tilting his cup to pour a thin trickle of wine over her breasts so he might lap it off.' The pubescent Dany, as she herself acknowledges, is no innocent: deprived of the attentions of her dead husband, she now and then accepts the ministrations of a teenaged hand-maiden. Why avert her eyes, indeed?

War, fantasy, sex: averting one's eyes from at least two of these became a hot issue when *Game of Thrones*, the hit HBO television adaptation of Martin's books, began airing in April 2011. From the start, the show's graphic representations of violence (you lose count pretty early on of the times blood pumps out of gaping throat wounds) and of sexuality – of female nudity in particular – have led many critics and viewers to dismiss the series as 'boy fiction'. (Thus the *New York Times* critic; the climactic section of a shrewder, more appreciative review by the *New Yorker* critic began, 'Then, of course, there are the whores.')

Either despite or because of this, the show has been a tremendous hit. This is, in part, a testament to the way in which fantasy entertainment – fiction, television, movies, games – has moved ever closer to the centre of mass culture over the past couple of decades, as witness the immense success of the *Lord of the Rings* adaptations, the *Harry Potter* phenomenon, and the *Hunger Games* books and movies. What's interesting is that the

HBO *Game of Thrones* has attracted so many viewers who wouldn't ordinarily think of themselves as people who enjoy the fantasy genre. This has a great deal to do with the complex satisfactions of Martin's novels, whose plots, characterization, and overall tone the series reproduces with remarkable fidelity – and whose mission is, if anything, to question and reformulate certain clichés of the fantasy/adventure genre about gender and power.

At first glance, *A Song of Ice and Fire* can look like a testosterone-fuelled swashbuckler. The first novel (and the first season of the TV show; until recently, the show was tracking Martin's books at a pace of roughly one book per season) introduces the ambitious patriarchs who were on the winning side of 'the War of the Usurper' – the rebellion that had rent Westeros asunder and ended with the murder of the mad, bad King Aerys Targaryen, young Dany's father – and who, along with their clans and feudal allies, will struggle for power once again.

The present king, Robert of House Baratheon, is Henry VIII-esque in temperament – he is always roaring at terrified squires and bedding buxom wenches – but Henry VII-like in his historical role. It was he who led the rebel forces against Mad King Aerys, whose other children and grandchildren Robert's men brutally slaughtered after seizing the throne. Robert's wife, Queen Cersei (pronounced 'Circe', like the sultry witch in the *Odyssey*) belongs to House Lannister, a wealthy, golden-haired, black-souled clan who are the Boleyns to Robert's Henry VIII: the patriarch, the coldblooded Tywin Lannister, endlessly schemes on behalf of his unruly children, nephews, and siblings by whatever means may be called for.

The royal marriage was, indeed, one of political convenience. The Lannisters supported Robert's rebellion with money and arms, and Tywin aims to see his descendants on the throne. As the first novel unfolds we understand that the marriage has failed – not least because Cersei prefers her twin brother, the handsome knight Jaime, who is in fact the father of her three children. The most interesting member of the Lannister family – and by far the most interesting male character in the series – is the other brother, Tyrion, a hard-drinking, wisecracking dwarf whose outsider status gives him a soulfulness his relations lack. (The role is played with great verve by Peter Dinklage, one of many strong actors on the show.)

Staunchly loyal to Robert and just as staunchly wary of the evil Lannisters is Eddard 'Ned' Stark of Winterfell, the king's 'Hand' or chief minister, a gruffly ethical northern lord who, along with his family – his wife Catelyn, their five children, and a bastard whom he has lovingly raised as his own – provides the violent goings-on with a strong emotional focus. After Robert dies during a hunting accident engineered by his wife's relatives, Ned finds himself locked in a struggle for the regency with the Lannisters, who have placed Cersei's eldest son, Joffrey, a Caligula-like teen-aged sadist, on the throne. But because the high-minded Ned is insufficiently ruthless, his plan backfires, with fatal results for himself and the Stark family. One of the pleasures of Martin's series is the grimly unsentimental, rather Tacitean view it takes of the nature and uses of power at court. Often, the good guys here do not win.

The shocking climax of the first book – Joffrey's surprise execution of Ned, who up to this point you'd assumed was the protagonist – is a strong sign that Martin's narrative arc is going to be far more surprising than you could have guessed. 'When my characters are in danger,' the author said in an interview, 'I want you to be afraid to turn the page … you need to show right from the beginning that you're playing for keeps.' A sense that brutal, irreversible real-life consequences will follow from the characters' actions – rare in serial novels and almost unheard of in television series, which of course often depend on the ongoing presence of popular characters (and actors) for their continued appeal – is part of the distinctive tone of Martin's epic. I suspect that one reason *Game of Thrones* has seduced so many of my writer friends, people who have either no taste for fantasy or no interest in television, is precisely that its willingness to mete out harsh consequences, rather than dreaming up ways to keep its main characters alive for another season, feels more authentic, more 'literary' than anything even the best series in this new golden age of television has provided.

After Ned's death, the multiplying plotlines adhere, for the most part, to the various Starks. The widow Catelyn (splendidly played by Michelle Fairley), a complex character who oscillates between admirable strength and dangerous weakness, and her eldest son, Robb, lead a new civil war against the triumphant Lannisters. Her son Bran, crippled after being unceremoniously defenestrated by the corrupt Jaime Lannister, finds that he is gifted with second sight and has the ability to inhabit the body of a giant wolf; the beautiful young Sansa, once betrothed to Cersei's son Joffrey, now finds herself a terrified political hostage in King's Landing; and the plain but spirited Arya, a girl of nine when the story begins, is separated from the rest and starts on an unusual spiritual and emotional journey of her own.

And then there is Jon Snow, ostensibly Ned Stark's bastard. ('Ostensibly', because there are proliferating hints that he is the love child of two other significant characters, long dead.) The most sympathetic of the younger generation of male Starks, Jon is a spirited but troubled youth who, in the first novel, goes off to join something called the Night's Watch. Informally known as 'Crows', this black-clad cohort, part monk and part warrior, vowed to celibacy and trained to arms, culled from the realm's rich stores of bastards, criminals, and political exiles, man 'the Wall', a fabulous seven-hundred-foot-high edifice that runs across the entire northern border of Westeros. Clearly modelled on Hadrian's Wall (much of Westeros's topography reminds you of Great Britain's), the Wall, one of Martin's most striking creations, is meant to protect the realm against the giants, monsters, undead, and the unruly clan of 'Wildlings' who inhabit the frozen region to the north – and who, when the action of *A Song of Ice and Fire* begins, have begun, terrifyingly, to move southward for the first time in thousands of years. The novels are strewn with ominous portents – not least, a red comet that illuminates the sky for much of the second novel – of an imminent, cataclysmic confrontation between the supernatural and natural worlds.

The Wall is one of the three geographical centres of the sprawling action, the other two being King's Landing in the Italianate south, where the Lannisters endlessly machinate, and the exotic Eastern lands beyond the Narrow Sea, where Daenerys plots her comeback. (In the HBO series, shot mostly in Ireland and on Malta, each locale has its own colour palette: cool blues and hard whites for the Wall, tawny soft-focus gold for King's Landing, and saturated tropical hues for the East.)

Martin renders the Eastern cultures in particular with Herodotean gusto: the nomadic, Scythian-like, horse-worshipping Dothraki, to one of whose great warlords Daenerys is bartered when the saga begins (their unborn child is referred to as 'the Stallion Who Mounts the World'); the quasi-Assyrian city-states of Qarth, Astapur, and Meereen, with their chattering merchants and unctuous slavers (and warlocks); the decadent port of Braavos, a cross between Switzerland and Venice, whose moneylenders finance the Westerosi wars, and where young Arya finds herself, at the end of Book 5, an acolyte in a temple of death.

But what keeps you riveted, in the end, are the characters and their all-too-familiar human dilemmas. Jon Snow on the frozen Wall, torn between family loyalty and duty to his vows; Dany, both his counterpart and his opposite, far away in the burning Eastern deserts, learning the art of statecraft even as she dreams of love; the vindictive Lannisters and fugitive Starks, conniving and being betrayed by their various 'bannermen'. These people and many more suggest why Martin likes to paraphrase William Faulkner's remark, in his Nobel speech, that the only great subject is 'the human heart in conflict with itself'. A question worth raising about Martin's novels is how different they'd feel if you subtracted the dragons and witches and undead; my feeling is, not much.

One of the few serious missteps that Martin has made in his grand project was, indeed, to abandon most of these characters and locales in the fourth novel, *A Feast for Crows*, introducing instead a group of new characters, cultures, and dynastic schemers. I read each of the first three novels in a few days, happily addicted; it took me a month to get through the fourth, because I simply didn't care about these strangers. It will be interesting to see how the writers of HBO's *Game of Thrones*, which cannot afford to try the patience of its audience, handle this lapse.

This is a point worth wondering about precisely because the TV series has followed the outlines of Martin's action, and his various tangled subplots, with such fidelity. The very few deviations I noticed have no significant repercussions. Sometimes, the writers on the show have invented material that brings home Martin's important themes in a pungently dramatic way. There's an amusing scene in Season 2 when, in response to an unctuous minister's unctuous suggestion that 'knowledge is power', Cersei, now riding high as queen regent, suddenly orders her bodyguards to seize the courtier and cut his throat – and then, at the last moment, to release him unharmed. As the terrified man sags with relief, the queen looks at him and says, '*Power* is power.' (The one-note, smirky performance of Lena Headey in this crucial role is a major weakness of the TV show; far worse is the tinny portrayal of Daenerys by Emilia Clarke, an untalented lightweight who accidentally succeeds in conveying the early Dany – the cowering virgin – but can't come close to bringing across the character's touching complexity, the girlishness and the ferocity combined.)

Inevitably, the TV series can't reproduce, or must violently compress, much of the novels' most interesting techniques and most entertaining material. A striking feature of the novels is that each chapter is narrated by a different character. This device – which the directors of the HBO adaptation do not attempt to reproduce cinematically – gives the sprawling goings-on a lively texture, and can have a Rashomon-like effect, since it often turns out that the perspective we have on a character or event is partial, or biased, or simply wrong. (One pleasure of reading the novels is that you constantly have to revise your opinions and theories about the characters as the multi-layered tale evolves.) This fragmentation in the storytelling nicely mirrors Martin's larger theme: the way in which the appetite for, and the use and abuse of power, fragments societies and individuals. In a world ruled by might, who is 'right'? People often talk about Tolkien as Martin's model, but the deep, Christianizing sentimentality of the world-view expressed in *Lord of the Rings* is foreign to Martin, whose tart appreciation for the way in which political corruption can breed narrative and linguistic corruption is pure Thucydides.

So the suggestive textures of the way the novels tell their story is sandpapered away by the wholly conventional storytelling you get in the television adaptation. Also elided, of necessity, are the elaborate back-stories that give helpful context to certain plot-lines, the biographies of complicated and interesting secondary characters who, in the screen adaptation, are reduced to little more than walk-ons. (The most regrettable instance of this is the treatment of the admirable 'Onion Knight', Davos Seaworth, the loyal Hand to one of the pretenders to the throne – a man whose rise to power came at the cost of four fingers, the bones of which he good-naturedly wears around his neck as a reminder of how dangerous it is to deal with the great and powerful.) Nor is there really a way to render, in a dramatization, Martin's imaginative linguistic evocations of his invented cultures: the compound coinages that replace standard English ('sellsword' for 'merce-nary'. 'holdfast' for 'fort'), the ingeniously quasi-medieval diction and spellings of names, the perfumed language – the horses called destriers and palfreys, the gowns of vair and samite – that give you a strong sense of the concrete reality of this imagined world.

An omission on the part of the *Game of Thrones* writers that is less venial is the elision of a major theme: religion. From his earli-est published work, Martin has shown an unusually strong inter-est in serious religious questions. His first Hugo Award-winning science fiction story, 'A Song for Lya' (1974), is about two tele-paths sent to a planet whose seemingly primitive inhabitants have achieved a kind of religious transcendence unavailable to humans; in what may be his most famous single short story, the creepy 'Sandkings' (1980, also a Hugo winner), a man plays god to a colony of insectoid worshippers who are more sapient than he credits, with gruesome results. (Both stories have now been collected in the two-volume set *Dreamsongs*.)

No wonder, then, that the action of *A Song of Ice and Fire* seems to be leading not only to a resolution of the dynastic ques-tion, but to a grand showdown among three major religions whose histories, theologies, and ritual practices Martin evokes in impressive detail. There is the easy-going polytheist pantheon of 'the Seven', the religion of the indolent South (complete with priests and priestesses called *septons* and *septas*, who worship at temples called *septs*); the Druidic, tree-based animistic worship of the Northern clans, which we learn was the older religion superseded by the 'southron' gods ('The trees will teach you. The trees remember'); and the unforgiving, vaguely Semitic Eastern cult, now infiltrating Westeros, of 'the one true god' – a fiery 'lord of light' with the nicely Semitic name 'R'hllor', who insists on a furious moral absolutism, and who enjoys the occasional auto-da-fé. 'If half of an onion is black with rot,' R'hllor's terrifying priestess, Melisandre, tells Davos Seaworth, who has good-naturedly observed that most men are a mixture of good and evil, 'it is a rotten onion. A man is good, or he is evil.'

In the novels, these religious motifs are more than window dressing: there is a strong suggestion that the 'fire' of Martin's title for the entire series refers not only to Dany, with her fire-breathing pets, but to the fire-god R'hllor, and that the 'ice' refers not only to Jon Snow but to the old northern gods who animate dead men; and hence that the climax to which the entire epic is moving is not only political but metaphysical.

It's too bad then that, of all this, the writers on the series have focused only on Melisandre and her fiery deity – likely because she triggers so many plot points. I don't think that the theological preoccupations of Martin's novels – grittily realistic, for all the fantasy – raise them, in the end, to the level of, say, *Lord of the Rings*, whose grandly schematic clash of good and evil, nature and culture, homely tradition and industrialized progress gives it the high Aeschylean sheen of political parable, the enduring literary resonance of cultural myth. But the not inconsiderable appeal of *A Song of Ice and Fire* lies as much in its thematic ambitions as in its richly satisfying details, and the former ought to be a salient feature of any serious adaptation.

Martin's medieval narrative, the distinctly Anglo-Saxon milieus alternating with exotic 'oriental' locales, everywhere bears traces of the author's deep affection for the rather old-fashioned boys' adventure stories that, he has said, formed him as a writer – not least Walter Scott's crusader romance *Ivanhoe*, but also Arthur Conan Doyle's *The White Company* and Thomas B. Costain's *The Black Rose*, stories in which European men have grand adventures when they wander into exotic, often Eastern cultures and climates. On his blog, Martin recommends these texts, along with a number of classic sci-fi and fantasy titles, to readers who ask what they should be reading while waiting for the next George R. R. Martin book.

Given those literary antecedents, it's striking that a strong leitmotif of the novels is pointed criticism by various characters of 'chivalry', of romantic stories about knights and fair maidens – of, you might say, 'fantasy' itself. In the third and, perhaps, most violent novel, *A Storm of Swords*, Dany, whose ongoing political education leaves her with fewer and fewer illusions, ruefully acknowledges a childish yearning for stories 'too simple and fanciful to be true history', in which 'all the heroes were tall and handsome, and you could tell the traitors by their shifty eyes'. It's as if Martin is drawing a line between his work and an earlier, more naive phase of fantasy literature.

The purest expression of this disdain for naive 'romance' is put in the mouth of the dwarf, Tyrion, who understands better than any other male character what it means to be on the outside – on the other side of the myth. After a battle, he declares that he is

> done with fields of battle, thank you … All that about
> the thunder of the drums, sunlight flashing on armour,
> magnificent destriers snorting and prancing? Well, the
> drums gave me headaches, the sunlight flashing on my
> armour cooked me up like a harvest day goose, and
> those magnificent destriers shit *everywhere*.

The juxtaposition of 'magnificent' and 'shit' is pointed: this is a mock-medieval epic that constantly asks us not to be fooled by romance, to see beyond the glitter to the gore, to the harsh reality that power leaves in its wake, whatever the bards may sing. There's a marvellous moment in the second novel when a knight notices the sigil, or arms, of some legendary warriors above the door of a tavern. 'They were the glory of their House,' the knight mournfully observes. 'And now they are a sign above an inn.' Martin's willingness to question the traditional allure of his own genre gives his epic an unusually complex and satisfying texture.

As it happens, the knight at the inn is a woman – a most unusual character. In fact, nowhere is the unexpected subversive energy of *A Song of Ice and Fire* more in evidence than in its treatment of its female characters – the element that has provoked the strongest controversy in discussions of the HBO adaptation. (Online comment has taken the form of articles and blogs with titles such as 'Why Girls Hate Games of Thrones'; 'Misogyny and Game of Thrones'; '7 Reasons Why Game of Thrones Is Not for Women'; 'Stop Saying Women Don't Like Game of Thrones Already'; 'Why More Feminists Should Watch Game of Thrones'; etc.)

Almost from the start, Martin weaves a bright feminist thread into his grand tapestry. It begins early on in the first book, when he introduces the two Stark daughters. The eldest, Sansa, is an auburn-haired beauty who loves reading courtly romances, does perfect needlework, and always dresses beautifully; in striking contrast to this conventional young woman is the 'horsefaced' younger daughter, Arya, who hates petit point and would rather learn how to wield a sword. (Later on, she gets a sword that she sardonically names 'Needle': she too, as we will see, plays for keeps.) At one point early in the first novel Arya asks her father whether she can grow up to 'be a king's councillor and build castles'; he replies that she will 'marry a king and rule his castle'. The canny girl viciously retorts, 'No, that's *Sansa*.'

The two girls represent two paths – one traditional, one revolutionary – that are available to Martin's female characters, all of whom, at one point or another, are starkly confronted by proof of their inferior status in this culture. (In a moment from the second novel that the HBO adaptation is careful to replicate, Ned Stark's widow, Catelyn, realizes that Robb doesn't think his hostage sisters are worth negotiating for, although his murdered father would have been: they're simply not worth what a man is.) Those who complained about the TV series' graphic and 'exploitive' use of women's bodies are missing the godswood for the weirwood trees: whatever the prurient thrills they provide the audience, these demeaning scenes, like their counterparts in the novels, also function as a constant reminder of what the main female characters are escaping *from*. 'I don't want to have a dozen sons,' one assertive young princess tells a suitor, 'I want to have *adventures*.'

All the female figures in Martin's world can be plotted at various points on the spectrum between Sansa and Arya Stark. It's significant that the older generation tend to be less successful (and more destructive) in their attempts at self-realization, while the younger women, like Arya and Daenerys, are able to embrace more fully the independence and power they grasp at. Cersei

Lannister is a figure whose propensity to evil, we are meant to understand, results from her perpetually thwarted desire for independence, as is made clear in a remarkable speech she is given at the end of *A Clash of Kings* (reproduced faithfully in the TV series):

> When we were little, Jaime and I were so much alike
> that even our lord father could not tell us apart.
> Sometimes as a lark we would dress in each other's
> clothes and spend a whole day each as the other. Yet
> even so, when Jaime was given his first sword, there
> was none for me. 'What do *I* get?' I remember asking.
> We were so much alike, I could never understand why
> they treated us so *differently*. Jaime learned to fight with
> sword and lance and mace, while I was taught to smile
> and sing and please. He was heir to Casterly Rock,
> while I was to be sold to some stranger like a horse,
> to be ridden whenever my new owner liked, beaten
> whenever he liked, and cast aside in time for a younger
> filly. Jaime's lot was to be glory and power, while mine
> was birth and moonblood.

Among other things, this is an arresting echo of the Greek notion that childbirth is for women what warfare is for men.

Cersei is a portrait of a tragic pre-feminist queen – someone out of Greek drama, a Clytemnestra-like figure who perpetrates evil because her idea of empowerment rises no higher than mimicking the worst in the men around her. (She ruefully remarks at one point that she 'lacked the cock'.) By contrast, Dany Targaryen can be seen as a model of a new feminist heroine. Apart from the Starks, it is she who commands our attention from book to book, learning, growing, evolving into a real leader.

We first see her as a timid bride, sold by her whiny brother Viserys, the Targaryen pretender, to a savage nomadic warlord whose men and horses the brother wants to secure for his own claim. But eventually Dany edges her brother aside, wins the respect of both the warlord and his macho captains, and grows into an impressive political canniness herself.

This evolution is pointed: whereas Viserys feels entitled to the throne, what wins Dany her power is her empathy, her fellow feeling for the oppressed: she, too, has been a refugee, an exile. As she makes her way across the Eastern lands at the head of an increasingly powerful army, she goes out of her way to free slaves and succour the sick, who acclaim her as their 'mother'. She doesn't seize power, she earns it. What's interesting is that we're told she can't bear children: like Elizabeth I, she has substituted political for biological motherhood. Unlike the frustrated Cersei, Daenerys sees her femininity as a means, rather than an impediment, to power.

And so Martin's saga goes to considerable lengths to create alternatives to the narratives of male growth, the boys' *Bildungsromane*, that have, until relatively recently, been the mainstay of so many myths and so much fantasy literature. 'Boy's fiction'? I don't think so. Characters such as the feisty Arya are, if anything, antecedents of the protagonists of such popular contemporary Young Adult series as *The Hunger Games*, in which the 'heroes' are girls. Whatever climax it may be leading to, however successfully it realizes its literary ambitions, George R. R. Martin's magnum opus is a remarkable feminist epic.

– *The New York Review of Books*, 7 November 2013

Unsinkable

In the early 1970s, my Uncle Walter, who wasn't a 'real' uncle but had a better intuition about my hobbies and interests than some of my blood relatives did, gave me a thrilling gift: membership in the Titanic Enthusiasts of America. I was only twelve, but already hooked. The magnificence, the pathos, the enthralling chivalry – Benjamin Guggenheim putting on white tie and tails so he could drown 'like a gentleman' – and the shaming cowardice, the awful mistakes, the tantalizing 'what if's: for me, there was no better story. I had read whatever books the local public library offered, and had spent some of my allowance on a copy of Walter Lord's indispensable *A Night to Remember*. To this incipient collection Uncle Walter added the precious gift of a biography of Thomas Andrews, the man who designed the ship. (It has always been among the first books I pack when I move.) A little later, when I was in my mid-teens, I toiled for a while on a novel about two fourteen-year-old boys, one a Long Islander like myself, the other a British aristocrat, who meet during the doomed maiden voyage. Needless to say, their budding friendship was sundered by the disaster.

I wasn't the only one who was obsessed – or writing. It may not be true that 'the three most written-about subjects of all time are Jesus, the Civil War, and the *Titanic*', as one historian has put it, but it's not much of an exaggeration. Since the early morning of

15 April 1912, when the great liner went to the bottom of the Atlantic Ocean, taking with it five grand pianos, eight thousand dinner forks, an automobile, a fifty-line telephone switchboard, twenty-nine boilers, a jewelled copy of *The Rubáiyát* of Omar Khayyam, and more than fifteen hundred lives, the writing hasn't stopped. First, there were the headlines, which even today can produce an awful thrill. ALL SAVED FROM TITANIC AFTER COLLISION, the New York *Evening Sun* crowed less than twenty-four hours after the sinking. A day later, brute fact had replaced wishful conjecture: TITANIC SINKS, 1500 DIE. Then there were the early survivor narratives – a genre that has by now grown to include a book by the descendants of a Lebanese passenger whose trek to America had begun on a camel caravan. There were the poems. For a while, there was such a glut that *The New York Times* was moved to print a warning: 'To write about the *Titanic* a poem worth printing requires that the author should have something more than paper, pencil, and a strong feeling that the disaster was a terrible one.' Since then, there have been histories, academic studies, polemics by enthusiasts, and novels, numbering in the hundreds. There's even a *Titanic for Dummies*. This centennial month alone will see the publication of nearly three dozen titles.

The books are, so to speak, just the tip of the iceberg. Between 1912 and 1913 more than a hundred songs about the *Titanic* were published. A scant month after the sinking, a one-reel movie called *Saved from the Titanic* was released, featuring Dorothy Gibson, an actress who had been a passenger in first class. It established a formula – a love story wrapped around the real-life catastrophe – that has resurfaced again and again, notably in a 1953 tearjerker starring Barbara Stanwyck, and in James Cameron's 1997 blockbuster, which, when it was released, was both the most expensive and the highest-grossing film of all time. (The film was rereleased during the week of the centenary, after an $18 million conversion to 3D.) There have been a host of television treatments: the most recent is a four-part miniseries by Julian Fellowes, the creator of *Downton Abbey*. And that's just the English-language output. German dramatizations include a Nazi propaganda film set aboard the ship – *not* the same movie as the Leni Riefenstahl *Titanic* movie. A French entry, *The Chambermaid on the Titanic* (1997), based on a novel, fleshes out the story with erotic reveries.

The inexhaustible interest suggests that the *Titanic*'s story taps a vein much deeper than the morbid fascination that has attached to other disasters. The explosion of the *Hindenberg*, for instance, and even the torpedoing, just three years after the *Titanic* sank, of the *Lusitania*, another great liner whose passenger list boasted the rich and the famous, were calamities that shocked the world but have failed to generate an obsessive preoccupation. The aura of significance that surrounds the *Titanic*'s fate was the subject of another, belated headline, which appeared in a special publication of the satirical newspaper *The Onion* in 1999, stomping across the page in dire block letters:

WORLD'S LARGEST METAPHOR HITS ICE-BERG

The 'news' was accompanied by an archival image of the ship's famous four-funnelled profile. The subhead pressed the joke: TITANIC, REPRESENTATION OF MAN'S HUBRIS, SINKS IN NORTH ATLANTIC. 1,500 DEAD IN SYMBOLIC TRAGEDY.

The Onion's spoof gets to the heart of the matter: unlike other disasters, the *Titanic* seems to be *about* something. But what? For some, it's a parable about the scope, and limits, of technology: a 1997 Broadway musical admonished us that 'in every age mankind attempts / to fabricate great works at once / magnificent and impossible.' For others, it's a morality tale about class, or a foreshadowing of the First World War – the marker of the end of a more innocent era. Academic historians dismiss this notion as mere nostalgia; for them, the disaster is less a historical dividing line than a screen on which early-twentieth-century society projected its anxieties about race, gender, class, and immigration.

All these interpretations are legitimate, even provocative; and yet none, somehow, seems wholly satisfying. If the *Titanic* has gripped our imagination so forcefully for the past century, it must be because of something bigger than any fact of social or political or cultural history. To get to the bottom of why we can't forget it, you have to turn away from the facts and consider the realm to which the *Titanic* and its story properly belong: myth.

If the facts are so well known by now that they seem more like memory than history, it's thanks to Walter Lord. More than fifty years after its publication, *A Night to Remember* (1955) remains the definitive account; it has never gone out of print. In just under 150 pages, the author crisply lays out a story that, he rightly intuited, needs no added drama. He begins virtually at the moment of impact. 'High in the crow's nest' of the sumptuous new ship – the largest ever built, widely admired for its triple-propeller design, and declared by the press to be 'unsinkable' – two lookouts peering out at the unusually calm North Atlantic suddenly sight an iceberg 'right ahead'. Within a couple of pages, the ship's fate is sealed: Lord gives us the agonizing thirty-seven seconds that elapsed between the sighting and the collision, and then the eerily understated moment of impact, the 'faint grinding jar' felt by so many passengers and crew. ('If I had had a brimful glass of water in my hand not a drop would have been spilled,' one survivor recalled.) Only then does he fill in what led up to that moment – not least the decision to speed through waters known to be strewn with icebergs – and what followed.

Until Lord's book, what most people had read about the *Titanic* came from the initial news stories, and then, as the years passed, from articles and interviews published on anniversaries of the sinking. Lord was the first writer to put it all together from a more distanced perspective. The unhurried detachment of his account nicely mirrors the odd calm that, according to so many survivors' accounts, long prevailed aboard the stricken liner. 'And so it went,' Lord wrote. 'No bells or sirens, no general alarm.' His account has no bells or sirens, either; the catastrophe unfolds almost dreamily. There are the nonchalant reactions of passengers and crew, many of whom felt the sinking ship was a better bet than the tiny lifeboats. ('We are safer here than in that little boat,' J. J. Astor declared. He drowned.) There are the oddly revealing decisions: one socialite left his cabin, then went back and, ignoring the $300,000 in stocks and bonds that he had stashed in a tin box, grabbed a good-luck charm and three oranges. There is the growing realization that there weren't enough lifeboats; of those, many were lowered half full. There are the rockets fired off in distress, which one passenger recalled as paling against the dazzling starlight. And then the shattering end, marked by the din of the ship's giant boilers, torn loose from their housings, hurtling downward toward the submerged bows.

There are iconic moments of panache and devotion, and of cowardice. Benjamin Guggenheim really did trade in his life jacket for white tie and tails. Mrs Isidor Straus really did refuse to leave her husband, a co-owner of Macy's: 'Where you go, I go,' she was heard to say. Among the songs written after the sinking was one in Yiddish, celebrating the couple's devotion. And – an anecdote that has been repeated in everything from a poison-pen letter sent soon after the sinking to an episode of *Rod Serling's*

Night Gallery – a woman in a lifeboat turned out not to be a woman at all. It was just a terrified Irish youth wrapped in a shawl.

Lord had access to many survivors, and the details that had lodged in their memories have the persuasive oddness of truth. One provides an unsettling soundtrack to the dreadful hour and a half between the sinking, at 2:20 in the morning, and the appearance of a rescue ship. Jack Thayer, a teenage passenger from Philadelphia's Main Line, who was one of only a handful of people picked out of the water by lifeboats, later recalled that the sound made by the many hundreds of people flailing in the twenty-eight-degree water, drowning or freezing to death, was like the noise of locusts buzzing in the Pennsylvania countryside on a summer night.

The closest that *A Night to Remember* comes to engineering drama is an account, shrewdly spliced into the larger narrative, of the doings of two ships that would become intimately associated with the disaster. One was the little Cunard liner *Carpathia*, eastbound that night en route from New York to the Mediterranean. Fifty-eight miles away from the *Titanic* when it picked up her first distress calls, it was the only ship to hasten to the big liner's rescue, reversing its course and shutting off heat and hot water in an attempt to maximize fuel efficiency. The other was the *Californian*, a small steamer that had stopped about ten miles from the *Titanic* – unlike the doomed ship, it had heeded the ice warnings – and sat there all through that terrible night, disregarding the *Titanic*'s frantic signalling, by wireless, Morse lamp, and, finally, rockets. Not all of this was as inexplicable as it seems: the *Californian* didn't have a night-time wireless operator. (All passenger ships were subsequently required by law to have around-the-clock wireless.) But no one has ever sufficiently explained why the *Californian*'s captain, officers, and crew failed to respond to what seemed like obvious signs of distress. The second officer merely thought it strange that a ship would be firing rockets at night. If Lord had been given to large interpretations, he might have seen in the one ship a symbol of the urgent force of human striving and, in the other, the immovable resistance of sheer stupidity.

About halfway through *A Night to Remember* – this is just after the ship has gone under, and an English socialite in a lifeboat turns to her secretary and sighs, 'There is your beautiful night-dress gone' – Lord interrupts his narrative for a few pages of musings about what it all means. The themes he finds are charac-terized by an appealing combination of nostalgia and scepticism. One notion is that the sinking marked 'the end of the old days' of nineteenth-century technological confidence, as well as of 'noblesse oblige'; another is a sense that people behaved better back then, whether noblesse, steerage, or crew. When one officer was finally picked up from his lifeboat, he carefully stowed the sails and the mast before climbing aboard the rescue ship. But overshadowing everything is the problem of money and class.

The *Titanic*'s story irresistibly reads as a parable about a gilded age in which death was anything but democratic, as was made clear by a notorious statistic: of the men in first class – who paid as much as $4,350 for a one-way fare at a time when the average annual household income in the US was $1,800 – the percentage of survivors was roughly the same as that of children in third class. For all his sentimentality about gentlemanly chivalry, Lord doesn't shy away from what the sinking and its aftermath revealed about the era's privileges and prejudices. 'Even the passengers' dogs were glamorous,' begins a tongue-in-cheek catalogue in *A Night to Remember* that includes a Pekingese called Sun Yatsen – part of the entourage of Henry Harper, of the publishing family, who, Lord laconically reports, had also picked up an Egyptian dragoman during his pre-embarkation travels, 'as a sort of joke'.

The book traces a damning arc from the special treatment enjoyed by the pets to the way in which third-class passengers were, at the end, 'ignored, neglected, forgotten'.

Even so, Lord kept his sermonizing to a minimum. His book ends on a grace note: the seventeen-year-old Jack Thayer climbing into a bunk on the *Carpathia*, which saved 706 of the *Titanic*'s 2,223 souls, and falling asleep after swallowing his first ever glass of brandy. *A Night to Remember* left the love stories, stolen diamonds, handcuffs, axes, and underwater lock-picking to others.

One sign of how efficiently Lord did his job is the air of embarrassment that hangs over the latest studies. John Maxtone-Graham, whose fond and thoroughgoing *The Only Way to Cross*, published in 1972, is considered a classic history of the ocean-liner era, interrupts his *Titanic Tragedy: A New Look at the Lost Liner* halfway through in order to admit that he'd spent a long time trying to avoid the subject altogether. John Welshman's *Titanic: The Last Night of a Small Town* aims to 'both build upon and challenge *A Night to Remember*'. His subtitle is a phrase borrowed from Lord's book.

Yet, perhaps surprisingly, there seems to be no shortage of new angles. Because the allegedly unsinkable ship sank, its design and construction, as well as the number and disposition of the life-boats, have often been the subject of debate. But Maxtone-Graham shifts the technological focus, by pointing up the crucial role of wireless communication. The *Titanic* was one of the first ships in history to issue an SOS. ('Send SOS,' the 22-year-old Harold Bride, the *Titanic*'s junior wireless operator, who survived, told the 25-year-old Jack Phillips, the senior officer, who died. 'It's the new call, and it may be your last chance to send it.') And the sinking was among the first global news stories to be reported, thanks to wireless radio, more or less simultaneously with the events. One of the early headlines, which appeared as the rescue ship carried survivors to New York – WATCHERS ANGERED BY CARPATHIA'S SILENCE – suggests how fast we became accustomed to an accelerating news cycle. The book winningly portrays the wireless boys of a hundred years ago as the computer geeks of their day, from their extreme youth to their strikingly familiar lingo. What is the matter with u? came one response to the *Titanic*'s distress call.

In *Titanic: The Last Night of a Small Town*, Welshman works hard to 're-balance' another narrative – the one about privilege. There's a scene in a not at all bad 1979 TV movie about the sinking, *SOS Titanic*, in which a pair of second-class passengers standing on deck observe the struttings of the first-class neighbours to one side and the antics of some steerage passengers on the other. 'This is a funny place to be,' one of them, an American schoolteacher played by Susan Saint James, remarks to the other, a British schoolmaster with whom she's been flirting. 'We're in the middle.' Indeed. In his new book, Welshman persuasively argues that narratives about second-class passengers have tended to be neglected, lacking as they do the glamour of first class or the extreme pathos of steerage. Drawing in particular on the published memoirs of a British science master named Lawrence Beasley (he's the character in the TV movie who gets a crush on Susan Saint James), the author shines welcome light on this overlooked corner of *Titanic* history. His technique of providing little biographies of characters in all classes probably tests the limits of the human-interest approach ('the export of butter from Finland was growing rapidly'), but it pays off in some wonderfully idiosyncratic details. Beasley felt an odd 'sense of security' once the ship came to a stop, 'like standing on a large rock in the middle of the ocean'; another survivor, a boy of nine at the time, realized long after settling with his family in the Midwest that he couldn't bring himself to go to Detroit Tigers games because the noise that greeted home runs reminded him of the cries of the dying.

The impulse to reappraise is not new. The best dissection of *Titanic* mythmaking is Steven Biel's *Down with the Old Canoe: A Cultural History of the Titanic Disaster*, first published in 1996 and now updated for the centenary. Biel, a Harvard historian, showed how the *Titanic*'s story has been made to serve the purposes of everyone from anti-suffragettes to the labour movement to Republicans. He argues that, while the sinking was 'neither catalyst nor cause', it 'did expose and come to represent anxieties about modernity'. One of these was race: an assault on one of the wireless operators during the ship's final minutes was blamed on a nonexistent 'Negro' crew member. Another was the influx of 'new', non-Anglo-Saxon immigrants. Reports by crew members and coverage in the press revealed a prejudice against southern Europeans so pervasive that the Italian ambassador to the United States was moved to make a formal complaint.

Sometimes, the fancy critical frameworks get out of hand: Welshman's eagerness to talk about 'the lifeboat as metaphor' seems a bit grotesque, in this case. One reason that the *Titanic* grips the imagination even today is, if anything, that it poses the big, enduring questions we associate with much larger historical events: as Nathaniel Philbrick writes in the introduction to a new edition of Lord's book, 'Who will survive?' and 'What would I have done?' These hover over Frances Wilson's *How to Survive the Titanic; or, The Sinking of J. Bruce Ismay*, a biography of one of the most controversial figures in this story: the man who was the managing director of the company that owned the ship. Ismay was widely reviled for having entered a lifeboat rather than going down with his ship; worse, perhaps, it seems to have been he who pressed the *Titanic*'s experienced captain, E. J. Smith, to maintain a relatively high speed even though the ship had been receiving ice warnings.

Twining Ismay's story around a series of reflections on Joseph Conrad's *Lord Jim*, a novel about a ship's mate who abandons his vessel, Wilson at once confirms and undercuts the familiar cartoon of Ismay. To be sure, there are the sense of entitlement and the convenient ethics. 'I cannot feel I have done anything wrong and cannot blame myself for the disaster,' he wrote to the widow of one drowned passenger. And yet Wilson deftly evokes the often startling emotional complexities beneath. Drawing on an unpublished correspondence, she reveals that, during the voyage, Ismay fell in love with young Jack Thayer's mother, Marian, and paid her epistolary court after the sinking left her a widow. Even here, though, a self-serving coldness prevailed. When Marian asked for help with her insurance claim, Ismay replied, 'I am deeply sorry for the loss you have sustained and of course I know any claim you put in would be absolutely right, but you must agree with me that all claims must be dealt with on the same basis now don't you?'

If you were writing a morality play about class privilege, you couldn't do better than to dream up a glamorous ship of fools and load it with everyone from the A-list to immigrants coming to America for a better life. The class issue is, indeed, one major reason the *Titanic* disaster has always been so ripe for dramatization. And yet the way we tell the story often reveals more about us than it does about what happened. If the indignant depictions of the class system in so many *Titanic* dramas coexist uneasily with their adoring depictions of upper-crust privilege, that, too, is part of the appeal: it allows us to demonstrate our liberalism even as we indulge our consumerism. In Cameron's movie, you root for the steerage passenger who improbably pauses, during a last dash for a boat, to make a sardonic comment about the band as it famously played on ('Music to drown by – now I know I'm in first class'), but you're also happy to lounge with Kate Winslet on a sunbathed private promenade deck while a uniformed maid cleans up on her hands and knees after breakfast.

Perhaps not surprisingly, the strongest treatment of this issue was the 1958 film of Lord's book, made in Britain – which is to say, by people who had a better feel for class distinctions than Lord (an American) did, and who were working at a time when the class system was under tremendous strain, and was the object of relentless examination in literature and theatre. It says something that the only star in the film (the popular actor Kenneth More) played a comparatively lowly, though heroic, character – Second Officer Herbert Lightoller, who managed to keep thirty men alive while they all stood on an overturned lifeboat. The film, like the book, depends for its effectiveness on a straightforward presentation of information and an accumulation of damning detail. A short scene in which a group of Irish steerage passengers breaks through a metal gate as they make their way to the lifeboats – they suddenly find themselves in the first-class dining room, set for the next morning's breakfast, and at first can barely bring themselves to penetrate this sacred space – tells you more about the class system than Cameron's cruder populism does.

It certainly tells you more than the ham-handed treatment of the subject in the new Julian Fellowes miniseries. In his hugely popular *Downton Abbey*, and in the script for the 2001 Robert Altman film *Gosford Park*, Fellowes showed a subtle feel for the ironies of class, but his *Titanic* sinks under the weight of its ideological baggage: the sneering condescension of the first-class passengers is so caricatured that it ends up having no traction.

('We are a political family,' a snooty countess observes. 'You, I think, have always been in *trade*.') There's even a fugitive Russian anarchist aboard to give free lessons in politics: 'Europe was wrong for me.' Worse, the production looks cheap: the first-class dining room has the ad hoc fanciness of a high school cafeteria on prom night. This is a *Titanic* drama in which the class outrage feels synthetic and there's no compensatory luxe.

If the underlying theme of all *Titanic* dramatizations has been class, the engine driving the plot has nearly always been romance. Apart from *A Night to Remember*, movies and television have tended to ignore the *Carpathia–Californian* drama, preferring to use the *Titanic* as a lavish backdrop for tragic passions and eleventh-hour lessons about the redemptive value of love. Fellowes takes this to new heights, or perhaps depths: whereas previous adapters of the story have made their star-crossed lovers fictional, he foists an invented upper-class suffragette on an actual first-class passenger, Harry Widener, to whose death Harvard students owe their university library, built as a memorial by Harry's mother. If I were a Widener, I'd sue.

The yoking of romance to the disaster narrative began with *Saved from the Titanic*, the 1912 movie with the weirdly prescient 'reality' angle – it's the one that starred an actual survivor. In it, the heroine must overcome her fear of the sea so that her naval officer fiancé can fulfil his duty. The sinking haunts a 1929 British talkie, *Atlantic*, which sets an adulterous affair on a *Titanic*-like liner, and a bizarre 1937 tragicomedy called *History Is Made at Night*, in which Jean Arthur plays a wealthy American who falls for a famous headwaiter (!) played by Charles Boyer, and travels to Europe with him on a liner that hits an iceberg on its maiden voyage.

The actual *Titanic* makes an important appearance in Noël Coward's *Cavalcade*, a big hit on both stage and screen in the early 1930s. But it took another twenty years for Hollywood to inject romantic melodrama into the real-life story. In Jean Negulesco's *Titanic* (1953), Barbara Stanwyck plays Julia Sturges, a midwestern woman unhappily married to a wealthy man (Clifton Webb) from whom she's become estranged while living an empty life of the beau monde – 'the same silly calendar year after year … jumping from party to party, from title to title, all the rest of your life,' as she says, when explaining why she has absconded with their two children, a marriageable girl and a boy on the verge of adolescence. The arc of the drama traces the husband's evolution from a superficial cad to a self-sacrificing hero; more important, it outlines the couple's trajectory from estrangement to an inevitable last-minute reconciliation that makes them both realize what's really valuable – not money but love.

If the *Titanic* is a vehicle for working out our cultural anxieties, the 1953 film makes it clear that one of those, during the first years of the Cold War, was the question of who the good guys were. 'We're Americans and we belong in America,' Julia declares. Middle-class Americans, too. You learn that Julia had started out as a 'girl who bought her hats out of a Sears, Roebuck catalogue'; on board the *Titanic*, her prissy, Europeanized daughter is being wooed by a handsome American undergraduate who pointedly remarks that the 'P' on his letter shirt stands for Purdue, not Princeton. Steven Biel's *Down with the Old Canoe* makes a further argument: that the film represents Cold War-era nostalgia for a more manageable kind of apocalypse – not the blinding thermo-nuclear flash but the slow freeze that left you time to write your own ending.

*

With its focus on feminine suffering and self-sacrifice, and, especially, in its presentation of an ill-fated romance between the unpretentious young man and the class-bound society girl, the 1953 *Titanic*, which won an Oscar for Best Story and Screenplay, anticipated Cameron's 1997 movie, which won Oscars for just about everything. A lot of the dialogue that Cameron put in the mouth of his frustrated debutante, Rose DeWitt Bukater (Winslet), reminds you of Barbara Stanwyck's lines: 'I saw my whole life as if I'd already lived it,' Rose recalls, explaining her attraction to a carefree young artist named Jack Dawson (Leonardo DiCaprio). 'An endless parade of parties, cotillions ... the same mindless chatter.' But Cameron gave his film a feminist rather than a patriotic spin. Rose, of a 'good' but impoverished Main Line family, is being married off to the loathsome Cal Hockley, who seals their engagement with the gift of a blue diamond that had belonged to Louis XVI. ('We are royalty,' he smugly tells her as he drapes the giant rock around her neck.) 'It's so unfair,' she sighs during a conversation with her odiously snobbish mother, who, in the same scene, is lacing Rose tightly into a corset. 'Of course it's unfair,' the mother retorts. 'We're women.' Small wonder that nearly half the female viewers under twenty-five who saw the movie went to see it a second time within two months of its release, and that three quarters of those said that they'd see it again.

Rose isn't the only troubled girl who's being manhandled. Like all ships, the *Titanic* was a 'she', and Cameron went to some lengths to push the identification between the ship and the young woman. Both are, to all appearances, 'maidens' who are en route to losing their virginity; both are presented as the beautiful objects of men's possessive adoration, intended for the gratification of male egos. 'She's the largest moving object ever made by the hand of man in all of history,' a smug Ismay boasts to some appreciative tablemates at lunch. Later, as Rose goes in to dinner, one of Cal's fat-cat friends commends him on his fiancée as if she, too, were a prized object: 'Congratulations, Hockley – she's splendid!'

Cameron underscored the parallels between the young woman and the liner in other ways. The scene in which Jack holds Rose by the waist as she stands at the prow, arms outstretched, heading into what will be the *Titanic*'s last sunset, has become an iconic moment in American cinema. (And indeed in life: a couple was married in a submersible parked near that very spot.) But far more haunting is the way the image of the speeding prow in this scene morphs, seconds afterward, into a by now equally famous image from real life – the same prow as it looks today, half buried in Atlantic mud under two and a half miles of seawater, drained of colour, purpose, and life. In this movie, there's only one other beautiful 'she' that is transformed in this way: we see the flushed face of Kate Winslet as the young Rose, on the night she poses nude for Jack, suddenly wither into the wrinkled visage of Gloria Stuart, the actress whom Cameron cannily chose to play Rose in the modern-day sequences of the narrative. Stuart, a star of the 1930s, was less than a generation younger than Dorothy Gibson, the lead in the 1912 film.

When you compare Cameron's movie to its 1953 predecessor, the evolution in attitudes is striking. The emotional climax of the earlier film is marked by Julia Sturges's agonized realization that she belongs with her husband after all; the disaster brings this shattered family back together again. Cameron's picture is about breaking the bonds of family, a point made by means of a clever contrast between its two leading ladies – Rose and the *Titanic*. At the start of the movie, the ship speeds confidently forward while Rose is described as being 'trapped' and unable to 'break free' (that corset, that mother); by the end, the ship is immobilized, while the girl strikes off on her own, literally and figuratively. After the sinking, she has to abandon the piece of panelling she's climbed onto – and tearfully let go of Jack (now a frozen corpse), which she'd promised never to do – in order to swim for help.

Rose, in other words, saves herself; in the end the *Titanic* is the sacrifice, the price that must be paid for Rose's rebirth as a girl who acts by and for herself. Or, rather, a woman: she memorably makes love to Jack during her journey, and gets to New York (there's a beautiful little scene in which we see her huddled form on the *Carpathia*'s deck as it glides under the Statue of Liberty), while the ship remains a maiden forever. This is another reason we can't get the story out of our heads. If the *Titanic* had sunk on her twenty-seventh voyage, it wouldn't haunt us in the same way. It's the incompleteness that never stops tantalizing us, tempting us to fill in the blanks with more narrative.

Toward the end of *A Night to Remember*, Walter Lord briefly nodded to 'the element of fate' in the story, which teases its audience with a sense at once of inevitability and of how easily things might have turned out differently. It is, he says, like 'classic Greek tragedy'.

He was right. All the energy spent pondering the class injustices and the romance, the dissertating about the ship's design, size, and luxury, the panegyrics of the heroics (or the denunciations of the cowardice) of the passengers and crew, the tortured debates over the captain's or Ismay's guilt, the hypothetical pirouetting about what the *Californian* might or might not have done, the endless computations of just how many people perished (still never resolved), have distracted from what may, in the end, be the most obvious thing about the *Titanic*'s story: it uncannily replicates the structure and the themes of our most fundamental myths and oldest tragedies. Cameron intuited this, when he made the ship itself both the double and the opposite of his teenaged heroine. Like Iphigenia, the *Titanic* is a beautiful 'maiden' sacrificed to the agendas of greedy men eager to set sail; the 46,000-ton liner is just the latest in a long line of lovely girl victims, an archetype of vulnerable femininity that stands at the core of the Western literary tradition.

But the *Titanic* embodies another strain of tragedy. This is the drama of a flawed and self-destructive hero, a protagonist of great achievements and overweening presumption. The ship starts out like Oedipus: admired, idolized, hailed as different, special, exalted. Sophocles' play derives its horrible excitement from a relentless exposition of its protagonist's fall from grace – and from the fact that his confidence and his talents are what prevented him from seeing the looming disaster. Cameron understood this, too. The enormous resources at his disposal enabled him to give us that other hero: the ship itself, recreated in overwhelming detail. The scene in which the liner puts out to sea, the stokers filling the boilers, the steam gauges rising, the *chunk-chunk* of the engines gathering speed as the pistons thrust up and down – culminating in an underwater shot of the triple propellers starting to churn the water – sets up what you could call 'the mechanical tragedy'. The director knew what the Greeks knew: that there is a profound theatrical pleasure, not totally free of Schadenfreude, in watching something beautiful fall apart.

Either mythic strand, the virgin sacrifice or the grandiose self-destruction, would be enough to rivet our attention: as a culture, we're hard-wired to respond to these narratives. To have them conflated into one story is overpowering. The reason we keep watching Cameron's movie is the same reason we can't stop thinking about the *Titanic* itself: it irresistibly conflates two of the oldest archetypes in literature.

So much about the story, when you think about it, makes it feel more like an artistic composition than a real-life event. The ship's mythic name – the Titans were a race of superbeings who fought the gods and lost – points up the greatest of all classical tragic themes: hubris punished. ('God himself could not sink this ship.') Steven Biel reproduces the lyrics of a song sung by South Carolina cotton-mill workers who clearly grasped this: 'This great ship was built by man / That is why she could not stand / She could not sink was the cry from one and all / But an iceberg ripped her side / And He cut down all her pride.' In real life, too, people seem to have understood the disaster in this ancient way. A rumour that started circulating at the time of the disaster maintained that her sister ship, the *Britannic*, was supposed to have been called the *Gigantic* but was given a less fate-tempting name.

The structure of the *Titanic*'s story has the elegant symmetry of literature, too: in it, you get a doomed heroine caught between an energetic saviour (the *Carpathia*) and an obtuse villain (the *Californian*). And there's something else that suggests a quality of having been designed as a dramatic spectacle. One big difference between the *Titanic* and other wrecks – the *Lusitania*, say – is the way her story unfolded in real time. Torpedoed by a U-boat in May 1915, the Cunard liner sank in eighteen minutes – too short an interval, in other words, to generate stories. The *Titanic* took two hours and forty minutes to founder after hitting the berg; which is to say, about the time it takes for a big blockbuster to tell a story.

Greek tragic protagonists, classical themes, perfect structure, flawless timing: if you'd made the *Titanic* up, it couldn't get any better. But then, someone did make it up. Perhaps the most unsettling item in the immense inventory of *Titanic* trivia is a novel called *Futility*, by an American writer named Morgan Robertson. It begins with a great ocean liner of innovative triple-screw design, 'the largest craft afloat and the greatest of the works of men ... Unsinkable – indestructible.' Speeding along in dangerous conditions, the ship first hits something on its starboard side ('A slight jar shook the forward end'); later on, there is a terrifying cry of 'Ice ahead', and the vessel collides with an iceberg and goes down.

As the title suggests, the themes of this work of fiction are the old ones: the vanity of human striving, divine punishment for overweening confidence in our technological achievement, the futility of human effort in a world ruled by indifferent nature. But the writing comes to life only when Robertson focuses on the mechanical details, as in the scene of the aftermath of the collision:

> Seventy-five thousand tons – dead-weight – rushing
> through the fog at the rate of fifty feet per second, had
> hurled itself at an iceberg ... She rose out of the sea,
> higher and higher – until the propellers in the stern
> were half exposed ... The holding-down bolts of twelve
> boilers and three triple-expansion engines, unintended
> to hold such weights from a perpendicular flooring,
> snapped, and down through a maze of ladders, gratings
> and fore-and-after bulkheads came these giant masses
> of steel and iron, puncturing the sides of the ship ...
> the roar of escaping steam, and the bee-like buzzing
> of nearly three thousand human voices, raised in
> agonized screams and callings ... A solid, pyramid-like
> hummock of ice, left to starboard.

Down to the most idiosyncratic detail, all this is familiar: the bee-like buzzing seems like a nod to Jack Thayer's comparison of the sounds of the dying to locusts on a summer night. And yet it couldn't be. Robertson – who gave his fictional ship the name *Titan* – published his book in 1898, fourteen years before the real liner sailed. If the *Titanic* continues to haunt our imagination, it's because we were dreaming her long before the fresh spring afternoon when she turned her bows westward and, for the first time, headed toward the open sea.

– *The New Yorker*, 16 April 2012

Not Afraid of Virginia Woolf

At the beginning of the novel in question, it is a fine June day in a great city, and a fifty-two-year-old woman named Clarissa goes shopping for flowers. She is giving a party that evening, and as she walks to the flower shop, a host of thoughts tumble through her mind. Not all of them are about her party. (Her party!) She worries, for instance, that her beautiful teenaged daughter is in thrall to a humourless middle-aged woman who is, somehow, her, Clarissa's, mortal enemy. (The woman's fierce ideological views make Clarissa feel slightly shabby in comparison; and indeed Clarissa supposes that she is, when all is said and done, quite 'ordinary'.) She is embarrassed to run into someone whom she hasn't invited; she has reveries about a long-ago summer in a house in the country when she and some friends indulged in illicit love affairs. (As she thinks these thoughts she is glimpsed by a neighbour who sternly, but not unkindly, judges her looks: she has aged.) She thinks, often, about death. As she stands in the shop buying the flowers, there is commotion outside – a loud noise – and when Clarissa and the florist go to the window to see what it might be, they get a glimpse of a famous head emerging from a vehicle, someone everyone knows from the papers, from pictures.

The famous head, glimpsed from afar by curious, even prurient crowds, has been placed there by the author of this novel for the purpose of contrast. This head reminds us of the great world out there, and the values by which it measures things: fame, importance, power, rank, distinction – and hence stands in stark contrast to Clarissa's head, filled as it is with a quotidian, haphazard jumble of thoughts that are of no particular importance to anyone except Clarissa herself. Clarissa's life is meant, indeed, to be one of those existences, neither brilliant nor tragic, that moved Virginia Woolf, in *A Room of One's Own*, to ponder what the proper subject and style of an authentic women's literature might possibly be. The values of novels, she argued, reflect the values of life, which novels must mirror; and it was, furthermore, 'obvious' that

> the values of women differ very often from the values
> which have been made by the other sex; naturally,
> this is so. Yet it is the masculine values that prevail.
> Speaking crudely, football and sport are 'important';
> the worship of fashion, the buying of clothes 'trivial'.
> And these values are inevitably transferred from life to
> fiction. This is an important book, the critic assumes,
> because it deals with war. This is an insignificant
> book because it deals with the feelings of women
> in a drawing-room. A scene in a battlefield is more
> important than a scene in a shop – everywhere and
> much more subtly the difference of value persists.

Part of the proper work of women's writing, Woolf suggested, was to recuperate for literature 'these infinitely obscure lives [that] remain to be recorded'. Let men preoccupy themselves with 'the great movements which, brought together, constitute the historian's view of the past'. As Woolf grew as an artist, she experimented with ways to record and 'bring ... to life' another kind of experience altogether, one hitherto buried in the interstices of those great movements.

One way to do so was, indeed, to focus on the concrete minutiae of women's everyday existences – everything that men's literature, by its very nature, overlooked, an omission that led to yet larger gaps and inaccuracies. 'So much has been left out unattempted,' Woolf complained. 'Almost without exception [women] are shown in their relation to men ... not only seen by the other sex, but seen only in relation to the other sex.' And so, she told the audiences of the lectures that would become *A Room of One's Own*,

> you must illumine your own soul with its profundities
> and its shallows, and its vanities and its generosities,
> and say what your beauty means to you or your
> plainness, and what is your relation to the everchanging
> and turning world of gloves and shoes and stuffs
> swaying up and down among the faint scents that
> come through chemists' bottles down arcades of dress
> material over a floor of pseudomarble.

That which men's literature dismissed as trivia must be taken up and forged into a new kind of literature that would suggest how great were the hidden worlds and movements in women's lives; such a literature was long overdue. 'There is the girl behind the counter,' she wrote toward the end of *A Room of One's Own*. 'I would as soon have her true history as the hundred and fiftieth life of Napoleon or seventieth study of Keats and his use of Miltonic inversion which old Professor Z and his like are now inditing.'

Hence Clarissa, with her random thoughts of flowers and parties and sewing and old love affairs: she is (for all the differences in social status) that girl, just as the famous head is a reminder of the other world, the world of great movements, of Napoleons and Miltons. And indeed Clarissa is the heroine of the first great example of the literary project that Woolf advocates in *A Room of One's Own*: *Mrs Dalloway*, first published in 1925, a few years before the essay in which she explicated that project.

And yet the novel I began this essay by describing is not, in fact, *Mrs Dalloway*. Or, I should say, is not only *Mrs Dalloway*. It is, rather, Michael Cunningham's *The Hours*, the 1999 Pulitzer Prize winner which is at once an homage to and an impersonation of the earlier work of fiction. (Woolf had long planned to call her novel *The Hours*, but decided on *Mrs Dalloway* in the end.) In it, three narratives about three women, each connected in some way to *Mrs Dalloway*, are intertwined; in each of the three, numerous elements from Woolf's novel – characters, names, relationships, tiny details of phrasing, individual sentences, whole scenes (not least, the world-famous head poking momentarily from the big vehicle) – are reincarnated with almost obsessional devotion. But perhaps the most remarkable achievement of *The Hours* is to preserve Woolf's project – to avoid the banal ways in which male novelists often see women, either dramatizing them or trivializing them, and thereby making them more comfortable for consumption by men.

'The design is so queer & so masterful,' Woolf wrote in her journal, in June 1923, of the book she was struggling to write; the same words, with additional overtones, could well be used of Cunningham's reinterpretation of it. Cunningham takes his Woolfian donnée and splits it into three narratives, each a kind of riff on some aspect of *Mrs Dalloway*. Each takes place, as does *Mrs Dalloway*, in the course of a single day: each focuses on the inner life of one woman. The sections called 'Mrs Dalloway', set in the 1990s, are about a lesbian book editor in New York City named Clarissa Vaughan (whom her best friend and onetime lover, a poet now dying of AIDS, enjoys calling 'Mrs Dalloway'; she's giving a party to celebrate the prestigious literary award he's won). The sections called 'Mrs Brown', set in 1949, recount one fraught day in the life of an LA housewife, Laura Brown, who's torn between reading *Mrs Dalloway* for the first time and planning a birthday party for her husband. And the 'Mrs Woolf' sections envision Virginia Woolf herself on a day in 1923 when she conceives how she might write *Mrs Dalloway*. In each section, Cunningham ingeniously uses Woolf's novel as a template: like Woolf's Clarissa, each of his three heroines plans a party, has an unexpected visitor, escapes, in some sense, from the house, and tries to create something (a party, a cake, a book).

The central story is the story of Clarissa Vaughan, the woman whose preparations for a grand party, like those of Woolf's Clarissa Dalloway, are the vehicle for a stream-of-consciousness narrative that suggests a contemporary, wryly self-aware Everywoman: 'an ordinary person (at this age, why bother trying to deny it?)'. While this Clarissa prepares for her party, the dying poet, whose name is Richard (the given name of Mr Dalloway in Woolf's story) worsens: just as the Great War and the Spanish flu gave poignancy and weight to Clarissa Dalloway's musings about the essential goodness and beauty of everyday existence ('life; London; this moment in June'), AIDS gives substance to the similar thoughts of Cunningham's Clarissa ('What a thrill, what a shock, to be alive on a morning in June ...').

Both Clarissas, for all that they are haunted by thoughts of death, are strong. In Cunningham's novel, as in Woolf's, it is the men surrounding the women who keep falling apart. In *Mrs Dalloway*, Clarissa's old flame, Peter Walsh, disintegrates in tears when he shows up for an unexpected visit. (He's having an affair with a much younger married woman; sensible Clarissa knows she was right to refuse his offer of marriage, long ago.) In a different part of town, meanwhile, the mad poet Septimus Smith disintegrates and flings himself from a window. Cunningham's novel reproduces these elements while updating them. His Clarissa lives in Greenwich Village with another woman, Sally (the name Woolf gave to the girl her Clarissa once kissed, long ago, in a country house); in his novel, it's an old flame of Richard's – his onetime lover, Louis – who shows up for an unexpected visit and, while Clarissa is preparing for the party, dissolves into tears. Like Woolf's Peter Walsh, Cunningham's Louis is foolish in love: he's having an affair with a male theatre student who 'does the most remarkable performance pieces about growing up white and gay in South Africa'.

And in Cunningham's novel, too, it's a mad poet, Richard (to whom the author gives some of Septimus's lines: both characters believe they hear animals speaking ancient Greek), who spectacularly kills himself toward the end of the book – the kind of theatrical self-immolation that Western literature has typically reserved for women, whose staged disintegrations have long served as the climaxes of so many dramas and novels. In *A Room of One's Own*, Woolf hinted that behind the empire-building noise that men made, women were strong, too; that because of the patriarchal economy, their creations were more often than not children, households, families; but they did create, and could of course create art, too, if they had the means. It was just that no one had written of this strength, this creativity. In *Mrs Dalloway*, she wrote of it – and of men's weakness; and in *The Hours*, Cunningham does too.

*

The other two strands of Cunningham's tripartite narrative recapitulate this important if subtle motif of Woolf's story in various ways. His 'Mrs Woolf' section is a fantasy of what might have gone through Woolf's mind on the day that *Mrs Dalloway* took shape. On that summer's day, she wakes up in Richmond (the suburb to which she and her husband, Leonard, had retreated for the sake of her fragile mental health), thinks about her book, entertains her sister, Vanessa Bell, and 'Nessa"s children to tea (they come unexpectedly early), and tries, unsuccessfully, to run off to London, whose noise and bustle she misses. (A frantic Leonard catches up with her outside the train station and fetches her home.) It is no easy or safe thing for a contemporary novelist to ventriloquize a great author who was a novelist herself, but Cunningham approaches his task with terrific delicacy – and no little erudition: much of the 'Mrs Woolf' section of his book is based on careful reading of Woolf's journals. The 'escape' scene, for instance, is based on an episode that Woolf records in a diary entry on 15 October 1923:

> I felt it was intolerable to sit about, & must do the
> final thing, which was to go to London … Saw men
> & women walking together; thought, you're safe &
> happy I'm an outcast; took my ticket; and 3 minutes
> to spare, & then, turning the corner of the station
> stairs, saw Leonard, coming along, bending rather,
> like a person walking very quick, in his mackintosh.
> He was rather cold & angry (as, perhaps was
> natural).

Cunningham delicately transforms it into a parable about Woolf's artistry, and her bravery – her yearning to have a full life out of which to create her art, whatever the risks.

But the real delight of the 'Mrs Woolf' portions of Cunningham's *The Hours* is its delicate, detailed, and sometimes witty suggestions about how Woolf might have come up with some of the material that appears in *Mrs Dalloway*. In *The Hours*, Vanessa Bell's children find a dying bird in the garden, and the youngest, her daughter, Angelica Bell, makes an elaborate bier for it out of grass and roses. Peering at the tiny dead thing in its improbable nest, Virginia thinks to herself that 'it could be a kind of hat. It could be the missing link between millinery and death.' Readers of *Mrs Dalloway* will remember that the wife of Septimus Smith is an Italian girl who makes hats; she is, indeed, making one just before her shell-shocked husband flings himself out the window. The hat-like bier gives Cunningham's Virginia an even more important idea: that it is not Clarissa who must die (she loves life, the world, too much), but the mad poet. 'Clarissa', Virginia thinks, 'is the bed in which the bride is laid.' Clarissa's life, that is to say – and her love of life, the quotidian thoughts and feelings that suggest how good she finds life, and how strong she is – must be the surround, the context, in which the death of the poet, the young man, will stand out as anomalous, impossible to integrate, 'other'. Another way of putting this is that Virginia will do to her male characters what so many male authors do to their female characters.

It is the third of Cunningham's three women who has no clear referent in either *Mrs Dalloway* or the life of its author. But this is not to say that Laura Brown, the housewife whose reading of Woolf's novel, one summer's day in 1949, transforms her life, has no basis in Woolf's work. In *A Room of One's Own*, Woolf wryly comments on the ironic way in which (as was the case in ancient Athens, she thinks; one recalls that she worked on her Greek every day) woman is 'imaginatively' – i.e., in the works of male writers – 'of the greatest importance', while being 'completely insignificant' in real life. Hence what one must do to create a fully real woman is

> to think poetically and prosaically at one and the same moment, thus keeping in touch with fact – that she is Mrs Martin, aged thirty-six, dressed in blue, wearing a black hat and brown shoes; but not losing sight of fiction either – that she is a vessel in which all sorts of spirits and forces are coursing and flashing perpetually.

In Cunningham's novel, Laura Brown is, in fact, just this combination of prose and poetry. Her life is an ostensibly ordinary one – her day consists of sending her husband Dan, a former war hero, off to work, and then baking a birthday cake for him with her little son Richie – but she is not, nor has she ever been, the homecoming queen type. Cunningham goes to considerable lengths to make sure we understand how starkly she stands out against her bland background, 'the foreign-looking one with the dark, close-set eyes and the Roman nose', with her Polish maiden name and her passion for books. Privately Laura thinks she could be 'brilliant' herself. Tormented by inner demons, seething with inchoate creativity, striking-looking, she is clearly meant to bring to mind Woolf herself; her tragedy, the author suggests, is that her time, culture, and circumstances provide no outlets for her lurking creativity other than domestic ones. Baking cakes, for instance: as Laura sets about her day's work, 'she hopes to be as satisfied and as filled with anticipation as a writer putting down the first sentence'.

It's really Laura who's the fulcrum of the novel, a hybrid of Clarissa, with her everyday bourgeois preoccupations, and Virginia, the dark, half-mad high priestess of art. And indeed, in the novel's deeply moving conclusion, we get to see how Laura is the bridge that connects Woolf, in 1923, to Clarissa Vaughan, in the 1990s: little Richie, it turns out, grows up to be Clarissa's friend Richard, the poet. It is Laura who, through her reading of Woolf (she flees to a hotel in order to finish the book in peace and quiet), understands that the life she's living is somehow terribly wrong for her: she feels she's going mad. And it is Laura who finds reserves of terrible strength to preserve her own sanity, her authentic self. By the end of *The Hours* she's decided to abandon her family after the birth of her second child; we learn later that she moves to Toronto, where she becomes a librarian – another position that places her midway, as it were, between literature and life. Throughout *The Hours*, as throughout *Mrs Dalloway*, it's the women who are strong, who choose life, who survive.

And so Cunningham's novel is a very interesting form of 'adaptation' indeed: much more than being merely a clever repository of allusions to its model (although these are many and dazzling, and make *The Hours* a kind of scholarly treasure hunt for Woolf lovers), it transposes into a different key, as it were, the constituent elements of Woolf's novel, for the purposes of a serious literary investigation of large (and distinctively Woolfian) themes – the nature of creativity, the role of literature in life, the authentic feel of everyday living.

Cunningham has, indeed, found just the right equivalents in today's world for many of the elements you find in *Mrs Dalloway*. Take that famous head, for example – the apparition, in Woolf's book, that serves as symbol for the world that is made by men, for men's literature and men's values – the great world, with its preoccupation with importance and fame and status. In Woolf's novel, people wonder who that briefly glimpsed head could belong to – 'the Queen's, the Prince of Wales's, the Prime Minister's?' In Cunningham's book, the scene is replicated, but this time the VIPs come from a slightly different milieu. 'Meryl Streep?' they wonder. 'Vanessa Redgrave?'

By a bizarre coincidence that the author of *The Hours* cannot have foreseen, the invocation of Streep's and Redgrave's names invites us to consider another kind of adaptation altogether. As it happens, Vanessa Redgrave was the star of the film adaptation of *Mrs Dalloway*, which appeared in 1998, the same year that Cunningham's novel was published; while Meryl Streep is the star of the film that seems poised to win this year's Best Picture Oscar: Stephen Daldry's recent adaptation of *The Hours*. Daldry's film is, like its model, a grave and beautiful work, and an affecting one, too; like its model, it goes to great lengths to suggest how litera-ture can change the way we lead our lives. For those reasons, it deserves the acclaim it has got. And yet elements of the adapta-tion suggest that it has done to *The Hours* what *The Hours* would not do to *Mrs Dalloway*.

Stephen Daldry's film adaptation of Cunningham's book shows a good deal more visual imagination than did – which is to say, is a good deal more cinematic than was – his 2000 film *Billy Elliot*, a sentimental Cinderella fable about a working-class boy who dreams of becoming a ballet dancer. The new film is still, essen-tially, mainstream moviemaking; it saves its energies for commu-nicating, as clearly as possible, the shape of its three narratives, which as in the book are interwoven, episode by episode. (You wouldn't want Daldry to make a film of *Mrs Dalloway* itself. Indeed, the adaptation of Woolf's novel that starred Vanessa Redgrave, from a script by the actress Eileen Atkins, who played Woolf onstage in her *Vita and Virginia*, failed to convey the frag-mented stream-of-consciousness that was Woolf's great achieve-ment in the novel – her new way of 'bringing to life' the experience of her ostensibly ordinary heroine.) And yet there are many effective, and affecting, visual touches that reproduce, in filmic terms, the tissues in Cunningham's novel that connect its three female figures. I am not talking here so much of the recurrent images – of eggs being broken, of flowers being placed in pots, of women kissing other women – that appear in each of the three narratives in the film, as I am of smaller but very telling touches, such as the ingenious cross-cutting between the Woolf, Vaughan, and Brown narratives. At the beginning of the film, when it is morning in all three worlds, we see Virginia bending down to wash her face; the head that rises up again to examine itself in the mirror is that of Meryl Streep, as Clarissa Vaughan.

Daldry and his screenwriter, David Hare, have, moreover, clearly thought hard about how to represent elements which, in the book, seem not to be of the highest importance, but which in the film convey the book's concerns in sometimes ravishing visual language. Early on in the novel's presentation of Laura Brown, Cunningham describes the young woman's feelings as she allows herself to be swept away by Woolf's fiction:

> She is taken by a wave of feeling, a sea-swell, that rises
> from under her breast and buoys her, floats her gently,
> as if she were a sea creature thrown back from the sand
> where it had beached itself.

Daldry and Hare transpose this minor moment to Laura's visit to the hotel, where it becomes an image that reminds us, in a complex way, just how 'carried away' a woman can get by writing. In one of the film's most original moments (one spoiled, for the audience, by its inclusion in the theatre trailers and television commercials for the film, which has resulted in a deadening of its impact in the cinema), we see the pale, beautiful Julianne Moore, who plays Laura, lying on her hotel bed when suddenly the rushing waters of a river – the Ouse, surely – flood the room, buoying and then submerging her and the bed. It's just after the striking fantasy sequence involving the river waters that Laura realizes she can't kill herself. (In Daldry's film – but not in the book – the young mother has brought a number of bottles of prescription pills with her to the hotel, and we're meant to understand that she intends to take her life there.)

More of a problem, inevitably, was the film's representation of Woolf herself. Much has been made of the prosthetic nose used to transform Nicole Kidman into Woolf for the purposes of the film, but while the fake nose has the virtue of making Kidman look less distractingly like an early-21st-century movie star, it also coarsens the Woolf that we do see; the frumpy creature we see on screen, clumping around in a housedress, breathing heavily through a broad, flat, putty-coloured nose, bears little resemblance to the fine-boned, strikingly delicate woman that you see in almost any photograph of Woolf, whose mother was a famous beauty, and who herself was memorably described by Nigel Nicolson, who knew her, as 'always beautiful but never pretty'. Without the prosthesis, Kidman is pretty without being beautiful; with it, she is neither.

The physical appearance of the film's Woolf is only worth mentioning because it may be taken as a symbol of the ways in which the film's attempts to invoke Woolf herself, or her work, have the effect of flattening or misrepresenting her – not only Cunningham's carefully researched, if idiosyncratically reimagined, character, but also the real person. In Hare's script, for instance, Virginia announces that she's not going to kill off Mrs Dalloway, as she'd originally intended; instead, she says, she's going to kill off the mad poet. (This is the bit that corresponds to Woolf's insight about the 'bride of death' in the novel.) After

Vanessa and the children have left, Leonard asks Virginia why she has to kill the poet. Because, Virginia announces, 'someone has to die in order that the rest of us should value life more. The poet will die. The visionary.' It is true that you can go back to *Mrs Dalloway* and find there a climactic passage in which Clarissa Dalloway muses, on hearing of Septimus's suicide (it turns out that the young man's doctor is a guest at her party, and so she hears, as a piece of idle gossip, what has happened to him), that 'she felt glad that he had done it; thrown it away ... He made her feel the beauty; made her feel the fun.' But this is an implied comment on Clarissa, and how she thinks about things; the scene in the film, by contrast, suggests that it's a philosophical state-ment by Virginia Woolf herself: that poets must die so that the rest of us will appreciate the beauty of life, and so forth.

It is true that the film, like the book, focuses on a small sliver of Woolf's life: the moment in Richmond immediately prior to her return to London. But it is still a serious problem that little about this frumpy cinematic Woolf suggests just why she loves London so much; you get no sense of Woolf as the confident, gossip-loving queen of Bloomsbury, the vivid social figure, the amusing diarist, the impressively productive journalist expertly manoeuvring her professional obligations – and relationships. (There's a lot more of the real Virginia Woolf in her Clarissa Dalloway than this film would ever lead you to believe.) If anything, the film's Woolf is just one half (if that much) of the real Woolf, and it's no coincidence that it's the half that satisfies a certain cultural fantasy, going back to early biographies of Sappho, about what creative women are like: distracted, isolated, doomed.

*

There are other shifts from the novel to the film that distort the female characters in Cunningham's book just as much, and to similar ends. It is strange, coming directly from the novel to Daldry's movie, to see the central element of Clarissa Vaughan's story – the unexpected visit from Richard's old lover Louis, who bursts into tears; a canny reincarnation of the scene in *Mrs Dalloway* in which Clarissa's old flame Peter Walsh comes to see her and weeps uncontrollably – turned inside out. For in the film, it's Clarissa who goes to pieces in front of Louis. 'I don't know what's happening,' Meryl Streep says as she stands in her kitchen, cooking for her party. 'I seem to be unravelling ... Explain to me why this is happening ... It's just too much.' Her voice, as she says these lines, cracks on the verge of hysteria. Cunningham's (and Woolf's) book places Clarissa at the centre of her story: she is the subject of ruminations about objects that are male – surprisingly weak or emotionally fractured males. Daldry and Hare's film may look as if it's putting Clarissa at the centre of her story – Streep's the star, after all, or one of the three gifted stars – but what the makers of the film are doing, it occurs to you, is exactly what Woolf worried that men did in their fictional representations of women: seeing women from the perspective of men.

In the film these men include, indeed, not only Louis, who in the scene I've just described sympathetically comforts the helpless Clarissa, but Richard too. In Cunningham's novel, there's a passing moment in which Clarissa Vaughan ruefully thinks to herself that she is 'trivial, endlessly trivial' (she's fretting because Sally, a producer of documentaries, hasn't invited her along to lunch with a gay movie star); but in the film, she's worried that *Richard* thinks she's trivial. 'He gives me that look to say *your life is trivial, you are trivial*,' Streep says, her voice quavering. For Hare and Daldry, a 'woman's story' must, it seems, involve the spectacle of women losing their self-possession in front of their men – men within the drama, and outside of it, too. Their subtle recasting of Cunningham's words makes the character into an object (of Richard's derision, of the audience's pity) when she had, in the original, been a subject.

This shift in emphases is even clearer in the Laura Brown portions of the film. Gone are Laura's darkness, her hidden 'brilliance', her foreign looks and last name: here, she is transformed into the exceedingly fair Julianne Moore, who has made a name for herself in a number of films about outwardly perfect young women who are losing their inner balance (as in this year's *Far from Heaven*, and the 1995 film *Safe*). But to make Laura into a prom queen inverts the delicate dynamic of the novel – the structure that makes you aware of Laura's latent poetic qualities, her latent similarities to Woolf. In the book, her madness is that of a poet who has not found a voice; in the film, she's yet another fifties housewife whose immaculate exterior conceals deep, inchoate dissatisfactions. I found it interesting that in the film, the date for the Mrs Brown sections has been moved from 1949, as in Cunningham's novel, to 1951; I suspect it's because the latter dovetails better with our own cultural clichés about the repressed fifties. Laura's maiden name has been changed, too, from Zielski, as it is in the book, to McGrath.

And in the film, we should remember, Laura goes to the hotel for the day not to read, but to commit suicide, whereas in the novel the idea of self-annihilation occurs to her only once she's in the hotel, and then only fleetingly. (That Laura may have more dire intentions is suggested by an abstruse literary allusion on Cunningham's part that has nothing to do with Woolf. Laura checks in to Room 19 at the Normandy Hotel – the same room and hotel where the heroine of Doris Lessing's story 'To Room Nineteen' commits suicide.)

And so this Laura, rather than being unusual and complex, is closer to a cliché of domestic repression than she is to Cunningham's character. No wonder that, in a key scene in the film – one that gives away its creators' prejudices, you suspect – this Laura gets *Mrs Dalloway* so wrong. When she has a visit from her neighbour Kitty (whose vibrancy and seeming good health are intended by Cunningham to suggest those of Vanessa Bell, whom the real Virginia Woolf thought 'the most complete human being of us all'), Kitty – clearly not a great reader – asks about the copy of *Mrs Dalloway* she sees lying on the kitchen counter. Laura replies by describing it as a story about a woman who's giving a party and 'maybe because she's confident everyone thinks she's fine, but she isn't'.

The problem with this sound bite about *Mrs Dalloway*, interpolated by the filmmakers, you suspect, for the sake of an audience that may not have read that novel, is that Woolf's Clarissa *is* fine; as are Cunningham's Clarissa and his Woolf, and even his Laura, three women who understand, in their different ways, that, as Clarissa Vaughan realizes on the last page of the novel, 'it is, in fact, great good fortune' to be alive. 'Everyone thinks she's fine, but she isn't' is, on the other hand, a perfect description of Laura as she appears in this film: flawless, the American dream, on the outside, but unravelling on the inside. Which is to say, a character in a film we've seen many times.

At the conclusion of *A Room of One's Own*, Woolf summed up her reasons for thinking that women should have a literature of their own: 'The truth is, I often like women,' she wrote. 'I like their unconventionality. I like their subtlety. I like their anonymity. I like – but I must not run on in this way.' I think Michael Cunningham likes women, too; his book's female characters are unconventional and subtle – the 'anonymous' housewife more so, if anything, than the others. I also think that, at one level, the makers of the new film of Cunningham's book like women, too. Rarely has a mainstream film offered three more interesting roles for three more accomplished actresses, each of whom makes the most of an admittedly rare opportunity: there are moments – not least, a climactic encounter in Clarissa Vaughan's apartment between Clarissa's young daughter, Julia, and the now aged Laura Brown – that will make you cry. (I did.)

But I think these filmmakers like women in the way Virginia Woolf feared that male writers liked, and used, women; their female figures are, in the end, more conventional, less subtle than what either Cunningham or Woolf had in mind. They are, in other words, more like the women we already know from the books and films that men make about women: the self-destructive, glowering, mad poetess; the picture-perfect fifties housewife slowly cracking up in her flawless mid-century modern decor; the contemporary lesbian frazzled by the effort of caring for her best friend with AIDS, a woman who goes to pieces on her kitchen floor while wearing rubber gloves.

Still, *The Hours* is a serious and moving film, one that achieves many of its goals; among other things, it will presumably have many, many more people reading *Mrs Dalloway* than Woolf could ever have dreamed of. That is no mean accomplishment. Perhaps it was inevitable that, of all the elements you find in her great novel, the one that the film should have reproduced most successfully is Mrs Dalloway's sense that what is truly strange, unconventional, and subtle must be sacrificed so the rest of us might feel the beauty, feel the fun.

White or Grey?

The heroine of *A Streetcar Named Desire* is famously alert to the significance of names; 'Blanche DuBois', she flirtatiously asserts early on in the play, means 'white woods'. ('Like an orchard in spring!') But the most meaningful name in the play may be the one that, unlike that of Blanche or her sister Stella – 'Stella for star!' – is never parsed or etymologized by the characters themselves.

Throughout the published text of *A Streetcar Named Desire*, the name of the plantation once inhabited by the DuBois family – the 'great big place with white columns' that pointedly represents the elevated sensibility to which the white-clad Blanche so pathetically clings – appears as 'Belle Reve' (pronounced 'bell reeve'). At first glance, the name looks as if it should mean 'beautiful dream': *belle* after all means 'beautiful' and *rêve* means 'dream', and Williams's masterwork is, as we all know, about the tragic destruction of the dreams of beauty to which Blanche, like so many other of Williams's heroines, so pathetically clings. But of course *belle rêve* means absolutely nothing in French. For the French noun *rêve* (the 'e' is short) is masculine; if the French Huguenot ancestors of whom Blanche boasts (in the scene in which she translates her name) had wanted to call their estate 'beautiful dream', they would have called it Beau Rêve. What they almost certainly did call it was Belle Rive, 'Beautiful Riverbank', which is, in fact, pronounced 'bell reeve', and which is a perfectly sensible name for a house in the Mississippi Delta.

The elision of the sensible if rather ordinary 'riverbank' in favour of the far more poetic if grammatically illogical 'dream' is – whether Williams intended it or not – a deeply symbolic one. On the one hand, it may be said to represent the heroine's approach to life. From the moment she shows up on the seedy doorstep of Stella and her crude husband, Stanley Kowalski, it becomes increasingly clear that Blanche's aim is to replace the mundane, even the sordid – poverty, disgrace, loneliness, encroaching middle age, all the unflattering realities that she associates, in a telling little outburst early in the play, with the naked light bulb that hangs over Stella's matrimonial bed – with romantic illusions, using whatever means she has to hand: liquor, deceit, costumes, coloured paper lanterns. 'I don't want realism,' she cries during her climactic encounter with her suitor, Mitch, after he's learned that Blanche's affected refinements conceal a dirty past, 'I'll tell you what I want. Magic!' The action of the play consists of the process by which Blanche's magic is eroded and ultimately pulverized by contact with hard reality, embodied by her brother-in-law, Stanley. It is no accident that Stanley is a sexual brute who smirkingly boasts of having pulled his plantation-born wife 'down off them columns' into, presumably, the mire of sexual pleasure – of having, in a way, retransformed 'Belle Reve' into the muddy 'Belle Rive'.

But the original metamorphosis, the enhancement of common delta clay into the stuff of illusory dreams, of 'Belle Rive' into the impossible 'Belle Reve', may be said to reflect another sleight of hand that takes place in the text of *Streetcar*. Here I refer to the character of Blanche herself. In a notoriously vitriolic denunciation of the play composed immediately after its March 1948 New York premiere, Mary McCarthy described the 'thin, sleazy stuff of this character', the kind of stock figure – the annoying in-law who comes for overlong visits – who, to McCarthy, belongs more properly to the genre of comedy:

> … thin, vapid, neurasthenic, romancing, genteel,
> pathetic, a collector of cheap finery and of the words
> of old popular songs, fearful and fluttery and awkward,
> fond of admiration and overeager to obtain it, a refined
> pushover and perennial and frigid spinster … the
> woman who inevitably comes to stay and who evokes
> pity because of her very emptiness, because nothing can
> ever happen to her since her life is a shoddy magazine
> story she tells herself in a daydream.

It is, to say the least, difficult to reconcile this rude vision of Blanche DuBois with the iconic status she has achieved in the half-century since the play's premiere: the vanquished but somehow ennobled female victim of male violence, gallantly exiting on the arm of her executioner, the heroically wounded prophetess of art and beauty in the face of crassly reductive visions of what life must be – an emblem, in short, of culture itself. 'When, finally, she is removed to the mental home,' Kenneth Tynan wrote, 'we should feel that a part of civilisation is going with her.'

For a production of *Streetcar* to work, McCarthy's and Tynan's wildly opposed characterizations of Blanche must both feel true. Precisely what makes the part so insinuating is the way in which it manages to hold Blanche's awfulness and her nobility in a kind of logic-defying suspension. There can be little doubt that the decision to endow her with both monstrousness and pathetic allure was a deliberate one on Williams's part. As he recalled in his memoirs, Williams began writing bits and pieces of what ended up being *Streetcar* in 1944:

> Almost directly after *Menagerie* went into rehearsals I
> started upon a play whose first title was *Blanche's Chair
> in the Moon*. But I did only a single scene for it that
> winter of 1944–45 in Chicago. In that scene Blanche
> was in some steaming hot Southern town, sitting
> alone in a chair with the moonlight coming through a
> window on her, waiting for a beau who didn't show up.
> I stopped working on it because I became mysteriously
> depressed and debilitated and you know how hard it is
> to work in that condition.

The close relationship between *Streetcar* and *Menagerie* explains a great deal about the later play, and in particular about the special quality of the role of Blanche. The two female leads in *Menagerie* (based loosely on Williams's mother and sister) represent – very roughly speaking – two extremes of theatrical femininity: the manipulative monster and the pathetic victim. It seems quite clear, from the passage in Williams's memoirs, that even at the earliest stages of her creation, the character of Blanche DuBois was meant to be an amalgam in one character of both female leads in the earlier play – the manic, yearning woman who trades in destructive illusions and the tragic, passive victim of those illusions. 'Waiting for a beau who didn't show up' calls to mind both Amanda Wingfield, who as we know was deserted by her husband, and her shy daughter Laura, whose lameness will, Amanda fears, doom her to spinsterhood. Desire, Blanche asserts toward the end of *Streetcar*, in part as an obscure justification of her own promiscuous past, is the 'opposite' of death. As a figure who represents both desire and death, who embodies that typical Williamsesque grasping at beauty and the equally typical failure to seize hold of it, Blanche fuses within herself the confused, frenetically 'desiring' Amanda Wingfield with the almost marmoreally passive and funereal figure of the futile Laura. (Blanche's trajectory from desire to death is famously symbolized by the fact that she's taken streetcars named 'Desire' and 'Cemeteries' to arrive at the neighbourhood called 'Elysian Fields'.)

This is why, for *Streetcar* to succeed – for the play to evoke the idiosyncratic quality that is so important to Williams's sensibility, the tragic allure of broken beauty, the way in which our illusions can be lovely and destructive simultaneously – Blanche must be convincing as both a monster and a victim. Another way to put this is that she has to delude the audience as successfully as she has deluded herself; must force us, as she forces the other characters (at least for a time) to see her as she wants to be seen, as well as how she really is. It's a fine and difficult line for an actress to walk. If she's played as a delicate neurasthenic, her tragedy has no traction – she's just a loon. She is, after all, not an innocent victim: she's cruel to Stella, irritatingly (and ultimately dangerously) flirtatious with Stanley, manipulative and deceitful with Mitch; and as we know, she herself is guilty of the kind of deliberate cruelty to another human being which Williams held to be particularly reprehensible. (We learn that, years ago, her young homosexual husband killed himself after she humiliated him at a dance.) If, on the other hand, you strip away all the pathos, she's just an alcoholic fabulist – the comic strip figure of McCarthy's vision, the pesky in-law who hogs the bathroom.

It is precisely between the pathological delusions and the unpleasant manipulativeness that the fascination of this character lies. Blanche is enormously appealing, both to the many actresses who yearn to play her and to the audiences who continue to yearn to see her again and again having her nervous collapse, because she has the same kind of outsized, illogical but nonetheless irresistible character that Medea and Clytemnestra do. None of the three is conventionally sympathetic, since they all do reprehensible things, and yet they are unmistakably heroines, too. Like her Greek tragic sisters, Blanche is caught in a hard world, ruled by aggressive men; however repellent the few tricks women have at their disposal – deception, seduction, 'magic' – these characters must somehow evoke our sympathies more than our revulsion.

I've dwelt at some length on the character of Blanche DuBois because she is, in a way, a kind of template for the play itself, which like Blanche suffers from a certain degree of illogic, perhaps even self-delusion. I am not referring to certain aspects of the plot or narrative that other critics have found troublesome, in particular the way in which Williams, for neither the first nor the last time, overloads his characters and action with rather an excess of psychological and historical baggage. (Would our sense of the play, or even its meaning, be radically different if Blanche, in addition to being a drunk, having lost the family estate, and having been run out of town for being a tramp, hadn't also had a gay first husband who'd shot himself at a cotillion? Probably not.)

But it's interesting how this play, like others in the Williams repertoire, never seems to work through a coherent position with respect to the key terms with which it seeks to create its meanings, terms such as 'realism' and 'beauty' and 'lies' and 'truth' and 'art'. Perhaps its greatest sleight of hand is to have convinced so many people that it's about the losing battle between beauty, poetry, and fantasy, on the one hand, and crassness, vulgarity, and brute 'realism' on the other – and convinced them to root for the former – without ever quite engaging the provocative question of why 'reality' must always be ugly, and why 'art', in these plays, is always presented as a liar, why it always has such an aversion to the truth, to reality – as of course good art does not. In a way, the play, like Blanche, succeeds only if it doesn't make you wonder about such internal inconsistencies – doesn't, as it were, make you wonder about 'Belle Reve'.

The special complexity and richness necessary for a performance of *Streetcar* to succeed on its creator's terms are wholly lacking in the big new production of the play that has just opened on Broadway, starring Natasha Richardson and John C. Reilly. As with the equally vacuous production of *Glass Menagerie* which is running concurrently, the problem lies essentially in a failure by the director and the lead actress to understand the central female part – a particularly costly error when performing Williams. And here again, a concomitant misapprehension about the lead male role makes nonsense of the play's themes.

Precisely because so much of what Blanche actually does on stage is part of the monstrous aspect of her character – her baiting of her sister, her seductive teasing of Stanley, the toying with Mitch, and of course the ceaseless lying – Williams again and again in his script insists on a certain visual and verbal delicacy and flutter, which are expressions of the other Blanche, the vulnerable and wounded creature who must somehow capture our sympathy. Her 'delicate beauty', he instructs, 'must avoid a strong light. There is something about her uncertain manner, as well as her white clothes, that suggests a moth.' Indeed, as we know, from the very earliest stages of writing the play Williams conceived of Blanche as a nocturnal creature; we remember that first image of Blanche, before there was even a play for her to inhabit, 'sitting alone in a chair with the moonlight coming through a window on her, waiting for a beau who didn't show up'. The nervous fluttering of moth wings is audible in the speeches that Williams wrote for Blanche, too – in her stammering hesitations and nervous repetitions. ('But don't you look at me, Stella, no, no, no, not till later, not till I've bathed and rested! And turn that over-light off! Turn that off!')

These qualities are admirably conveyed in Vivien Leigh's definitive performance in the 1951 film version of the play – a film that every Blanche, and perhaps even more every Stanley, must somehow contend with. It is true that a certain degree of nuance is possible in film, with its close-ups and immaculate sound, that the stage actor must forgo. But even accounting for this, you're struck by the ingenuity and effectiveness of Leigh's performance, from the slightly desperate way she clutches Stella's arm when the two sisters embrace at their first meeting, to the slightly hysterical way her voice hits the word 'tired' when she tells Stella, coming off the streetcar, that she's 'just all shaken up ... and hot ... and dirty ... and tired'. And yet she also uses her slightly worn beauty with just the right degree of aggressiveness in her first scene with Stanley – a reminder that the fragility coexists with a certain hardness.

Neither physically nor temperamentally is Natasha Richardson, the star of the new production, suited for this exquisitely complicated role. Part of the equipment that stage actors, far more than movie actors, must work with in creating a character are the bodies and faces that God (or whoever) gave them, and in this respect it must be said Ms Richardson has much to overcome when it comes to roles that require confusion and vulnerability. She has the unthreatening, scrubbed, pleasant blond looks you associate with captains of girls' hockey teams; quite tall to begin with, she has inexplicably been given what looked to me to be six-inch heels to wear in this new production, with the result that she clomps around the stage looming over the other actors, exuding the healthy if sexless glow of an Amazon – or, given her colouring, perhaps a Valkyrie. To my mind, the heartiness of Richardson's physique is reflected in her acting. Like Gwyneth Paltrow, another daughter of a famous and gifted actress, Richardson is a star whose performances feel more than anything like the result of an elaborate series of calculations; you feel the will, the determination behind every word and gesture. In this performance, she seemed to be compensating for a lack of natural sympathy with the character by means of exaggerated tics: in particular, her hands shook violently every time she was called upon to suggest anxiety or instability – a caricature rather than a true performance.

And indeed, as I watched Ms Richardson on two occasions, moving around the enormous and awkwardly designed set (Stella's two-room apartment is raised on a platform centre stage, so the actors are constantly having to step clumsily up or down), I kept trying to think what the awkward bigness, the loping strides, the vague quality of caricature, the fraught avidity reminded me of. It wasn't till I'd left the theatre that I remembered what it was: drag performers 'doing' Blanche. In this *Streetcar*, you don't get Williams's Blanche, with all her desperate contradictions, so much as a Blanche who's been mediated by the performances we've already seen – not Blanche but 'Blanche', the quippy camp queen (Richardson plays a good many lines for laughs – as for instance her remark that 'only Mr Edgar Allan Poe' could do justice to Stella's rundown neighbourhood – that, as Leigh's performance makes clear, are all the more telling if downplayed); Blanche the cultural icon of affirmation and determination, qualities we like to admire in women today. For all the obvious twitching and slurring, Ms Richardson's Blanche looked like a powerful young woman at the top of her game. Watching her I found it hard not to draw comparisons between this Blanche and Jessica Lange's Amanda Wingfield. In both performances, the appalling, neurotic aspects of the characters (as opposed to mere tics) were being edged out, as it were, by the 'strong' side – the side that has greater appeal, in other words, for today's audiences, the side that allows these women to be heroic in a way we want women to be today.

The big, sexless Blanche of Edward Hall's new production finds her match in a sexless, big Stanley Kowalski. An obvious problem of casting this part is the gigantic shadow cast by the remarkable, career-making performance by Marlon Brando, which electrified Broadway audiences and was, no doubt to the chagrin of every actor who's undertaken the role ever since, admirably preserved in the 1951 film. Hall clearly believed that the best way to avoid invidious comparisons was to avoid altogether the idea of casting someone straightforwardly sexy as Stanley (someone even like Alec Baldwin, who played Stanley opposite Jessica Lange's Blanche in the 1992 revival on Broadway).

But the perverse casting of the excellent but grotesquely inappropriate John C. Reilly in the role of Stanley Kowalski, while it makes us aware that we are in the presence of a director who is eager to 'rethink' a classic, suggests that the director does not understand the play. Here is what Williams asks for in his Stanley:

> He is of medium height, about five feet eight or nine,
> and strongly, compactly built. Animal joy in his being
> is implicit in all his movements and attitudes. Since
> earliest manhood the centre of his life has been pleasure
> with women, the giving and taking of it, not with
> weak indulgence, dependently, but with the power and
> pride of a richly feathered male bird among hens ... his
> emblem of the gaudy seed-bearer.

Reilly, who has the physique of a character actor – he's a big, soft-bellied man who slides easily into roles of long-suffering blue-collar husbands, such as the one in the Los Angeles sequences in *The Hours* – fails to suggest any of the qualities Williams seeks. The problem is not that he's rather pleasantly homely, or that he appears to spend less time in the gym than Ms Richardson does. The problem is that he isn't someone who strikes you as a cocky 'seed-bearer', or gives you the slightest impression that 'pleasure with women' has been the centre of his life from earliest manhood. There are large actors – John Goodman, for instance – who have no trouble convincing you that they're good in bed. Reilly is not one of them.

An intelligent actor, Reilly compensates by giving a performance that emphasizes another much-discussed aspect of Stanley's character, which is the fact that he's a working-class American of Polish descent. His Stanley is loud, bearish, crude – someone who corresponds more or less exactly to what Blanche clearly has in mind when she refers to him, contemptuously, as a 'Polack'. But the horrible irony of casting Reilly, or of Reilly's understandable default decision to play him as a crass vulgarian, is that the Stanley you end up getting in this *Streetcar* is itself a kind of delusion. As the entire action of the play makes clear, Blanche's harping on the class issue – her insinuations that the 'Polack' is an inappropriate match for a DuBois – is a cover for what's really bothering her, which is his raw sexual allure, to which she responds flirtatiously from the very start and which of course comes back to destroy her in the latter part of the play, when Stanley finally rapes her. ('We've had this date from the beginning,' he gloats, and he's right.) To play Stanley as more vulgar than sexy is precisely to shy away from what's at the heart of the play – sex – as determinedly as Blanche, in her delusional mode, does.

It's unfortunate that neither of the leads in the current production is able to convey sexual heat, since there is evidence that Williams himself recognized that it was precisely that energy, flowing across the stage, that could dissolve some of the objections to the play's ostensible inconsistencies. In his memoirs, he tells an amusing anecdote about the 1948 New Haven tryout of *Streetcar*:

> After the New Haven opening night we were invited
> to the quarters of Mr Thornton Wilder, who was in
> residence there. It was like having papal audience. We
> all sat about this academic gentleman while he put the
> play down as if delivering a papal bull. He said that it
> was based upon a fatally mistaken premise. No female
> who had ever been a lady (he was referring to Stella)
> could possibly marry a vulgarian such as Stanley. We sat
> there and listened to him politely. I thought, privately,
> This character has never had a good lay.

Wilder's objection arises out of the same critical impulse that fuelled McCarthy's. ('She must', she complained of Blanche, 'also be a notorious libertine who has been run out of a small town like a prostitute, a thing absolutely inconceivable for a woman to whom conventionality is the end of existence …') But the power of 'a good lay' – and, indeed, of desire – explains a lot of what happens in the play, from Stella's connection to Stanley to Blanche's pathetic behaviour – her confusion of sex with desire, of desire with love, an emotion to which, in her life, only generic 'kindness' has ever come close.

You could, indeed, say that sex is the very core of *Streetcar*'s commentary on illusion, reality, truth, and lies, since it's the object of Blanche's hypocrisy, the vehicle of her undoing. Sex and desire serve the same purpose in this play that poverty and vanity do in *The Glass Menagerie*: they are the solvents that corrode the characters' pretensions, the hard surfaces against which their delusions shatter, leaving the vulnerable and pathetic interior visible to our shocked, and ultimately sympathetic, gaze. (The final scene of *Streetcar* should leave you with the same almost shamed horror that the final scene of *Menagerie* does.) For the revelation to which this drama leads is that despite her veneer of plantation-bred gentility, Blanche is not as white as her name so famously suggests; she was, we learn, run out of Laurel, Mississippi, for her promiscuity, which culminates in her seduction of an underage boy.

This is why it's important for the actress portraying Blanche to be able to convey the confused sexual avidity that lurks beneath her blurred and desperate gentility. She may denounce Stanley as an 'animal', but she herself is all too familiar with the animal pleasures he represents. (Similarly, she chastises her relatives for having bankrupted the family through 'their epic fornications' – 'the four letter word deprived us of our plantation' – although she too, as we know, is an epic fornicator.) Our desire to see Blanche simplistically, as a heroine of the poetic, has made it easy to forget about her carnality, about the fact that she is, in many ways, not the opposite but the double of Stanley. What is moving about Blanche is what is moving about so many of Williams's pathetic, tortured females: not that she isn't what she claims to be – some kind of virginal 'beauty' violated by Stanley's reductive, goat-like 'reality' (Stanley, after all, has intense romantic feelings, and waxes poetic about lovemaking) – but that she can still cling to her notions of beauty after wallowing in so much ugly reality herself.

The tortured complexity typical of the play's characters extends to its presentation of sex: the action leads to a climactic sexual encounter between the two that is at once a rape and the inevitable culmination of Blanche's hidden desire. In the film, the sexual energy between Leigh and Brando crackles from the minute she drinks in the sight of him; the fact that Brando – it can be hard to remember this – looked almost shockingly, prettily boyish in the film, despite his muscles, gives texture to the relationship, since we know that Blanche has a special interest in teenagers. At one point, she makes a play for a newspaper boy.

But on the stage of Studio 54, there's no sexual energy, and hence no climax, no provocative complexity – there's just a lot of noise. Reilly in particular compensates for his lack of allure by turning up the volume, and so you feel the potential of violence in Stanley (a character who, as even his wife admits, loves to smash things) but not the potential seductiveness – the thing that got Stella to come down off of them columns. At a certain moment during one of the performances of this *Streetcar*, I realized that Reilly reminded me of Jackie Gleason's Ralph Kramden in *The Honeymooners* – another big galoot who's rough with the women around him. Without the transformative power of sex – the power that for Williams, in so many plays, can effect the metamorphosis of the ordinary into the sublime, a power that is, like so much else in this author's work, like Blanche herself, at once base and exalted – the play had indeed become precisely the play that Mary McCarthy said it was: a simplistic farce about annoying in-laws who outstay their visit.

Stripped of its key element, stranded between the 'daring' pretensions of its director and subtle text of the play itself, between the tragedy it is meant to be and the comedy into which it can so awkwardly descend, this *Streetcar* doesn't take you anywhere – not to desire, not to cemeteries, certainly not to the blissful Elysian Fields. You leave Studio 54, in fact, with no strong emotions at all – certainly none of the deep feelings that Williams at his best can evoke: the odd and illogical admixture of horror and pity and shamed pathos, those tenderer and more awkward emotions whose unflinching exploration is his great talent as a dramatist, his great accomplishment as a humanist.

And a *Streetcar* thus denatured, one that leaves you politely tepid, that's about people with no particularly interesting passions, is not only a play Williams wouldn't have written – it's a play he went out of his way not to write. What else, after all, can you conclude from another, final oddity in the text of this play that has to do with the meaning of names – with the way in which verbal conventions can get elided by wishful thinking? I have always wondered why, if Blanche DuBois was indeed married at an early age to a tragic young homosexual – and if she is as invested in social propriety as she claims – she is not known, in the play, by her married name. But then, who would want to sit through a drama about a character named Blanche Grey?

– *The New York Review of Books*, 9 June 2005

The Two Oscar Wildes

At the climax of Oscar Wilde's comic masterpiece, *The Importance of Being Earnest*, we learn that a baby has been mistaken for a book. Until that improbable revelation, the play – Wilde's wicked exposé of the artificiality of conventional morality, and his one unequivocally great work – is concerned less with procreation than with recreation. *Earnest* follows two fashionable young heroes, Algernon Moncrieff and Jack Worthing, as each leads an elaborate double life, complete with false identities and imaginary friends, that allows him to seek unrespectable pleasures while presenting a respectable face to his local society at home: London for Algy, whose fictional invalid friend, Bunbury, provides frequent excuses to escape to the countryside; Hertfordshire for Jack, whose assumption of a false identity of his own (that of an invented ne'er-do-well brother named Ernest) allows him to misbehave in town.

Those artificial façades start crumbling when both men fall victim to natural impulses. Jack has fallen in love with Algy's cousin, Gwendolen Fairfax, and Algy becomes besotted with Jack's young ward, Cecily Cardew, during a mischief-making visit to Jack's house in the country. (He arrives pretending to be the made-up black-sheep brother, Ernest – which is just as well, since Cecily, like Gwendolen, has always yearned to marry a man named Ernest – and Jack, although irritated, can't expose Algy without exposing himself.) Jack's matrimonial aims, however, are seriously impaired by the fact that he has no pedigree. As he sheepishly reveals during an interview with Gwendolen's mother and Algy's aunt, the formidable Lady Bracknell, he was discovered, as an infant, in a large handbag in the cloakroom in Victoria Station, and subsequently adopted by the kindly gentleman who found him, Mr Worthing.

Just how the baby got into the handbag is revealed in the play's final moments, when it evolves that Miss Prism, the tutor currently employed by Jack to educate Cecily, was once a nursemaid in the employ of Lady Bracknell's sister (Algy's mother) – the same nursemaid who'd gone for a promenade with Algy's elder brother twenty-eight years ago and subsequently disappeared, along with her charge. As the shocked company looks on, Prism describes how, 'in a moment of mental abstraction', she had switched the baby she was taking care of and the manuscript of the novel she was writing, placing the former in her handbag, which she deposited in the railway station cloakroom, and the latter in the pram, which she took for a stroll. On realizing that she'd lost the baby, Miss Prism fled London and never returned.

Miss Prism's inability to distinguish between a human being and a work of fiction may have been the result of mental abstraction, but for Oscar Wilde, the conflation of life and art was always deliberate. The result, for us, is that it has never been easy to separate how Wilde led his life – particularly his personal craving for notoriety – from his aesthetic and creative impulse to subvert. As early as the 1870s, before he'd left Oxford for London, the Dublin-born student of both Pater and Ruskin was playing the young artiste with a flair for self-promotion that caught the attention of the wide world. The character of Bunthorne in the Gilbert and Sullivan operetta *Patience* was based on him; his post-collegiate debut as a public figure was at the splashy opening of the new Grosvenor Gallery, which the twenty-two-year-old Wilde attended in a coat cut to look like a cello.

Not everyone was seduced by the precocious youth and his attention-getting shenanigans. 'What has he done,' the actress Helena Modjeska complained, 'this young man, that one meets him everywhere? … He has written nothing, he does not sing or paint or act – he does nothing but talk.' Nonetheless, Wilde had become sufficiently famous as a proponent of Aestheticism by his mid-twenties that he went on a two-year lecture tour of the United States, during which he gave tips to the colonials on how to make life more aesthetic. 'The supreme object of life is to live,' went Wilde's refrain. 'Few people live.'

By 'living', Wilde in his Aesthete mode meant living beautifully, down to the last detail. Despite its apparent superficiality – or indeed, because of its apparent superficiality – the insistence that every aspect of lived life be exquisite and unconventional was part of a philosophical and artistic project of subversion; the emphases on surfaces, appearances, and style flew in the face of conventional middle-class Victorian sensibility, with its leaden earnestness and saccharine sentimentality. This creed was intended to be a red flag waved in the face of bourgeois society, and was understood as such by those sophisticated enough to see what he was up to. 'So much taste will lead to prison,' Degas murmured while Wilde visited Paris just before *Earnest* opened early in 1895.

Wilde's life was intended to be a demonstration of his artistic philosophy – was intended, that is to say, to seem like a work of art. The self-consciously dandyish clothes, the flowing locks that he wore provocatively long, the promenades down Piccadilly holding a lily, the unconventional all-white decor in the house at

16 Tite Street, where he eventually lived with his wife, Constance, and their two children, and which, like the famous blue china that adorned his Oxford rooms, was the subject of much comment; the polished epigrams he kept in a notebook at the ready ('you have a phrase for everything,' a disapproving Walter Pater scolded him): all these suggested that there was not a little truth in that famous remark to Gide, one that – typically of Wilde, for whom 'a truth in art is that whose contradictory is also true' – assumed a distinction between art and life even as it sought to blur that distinction. 'I have put my genius into my life,' he declared. 'I have only put my talent into my works.'

The statement was probably true of everything except *Earnest*. Even at Oxford, where he showed extraordinary promise as a Classics student, it was clear that Wilde saw his intellectual gifts as a passport to celebrity; that he happened to be brilliant enough to earn fame in any number of honourable ways was merely a means to an end. 'God knows,' the young Magdalen graduate replied, when asked what he wanted to do after university. 'I won't be a dried-up Oxford don, anyhow. I'll be a poet, a writer, a dramatist. Somehow or other I'll be famous, and if not famous, notorious.'

He got everything he hoped for. Like many Victorian youths who had a literary bent and a restless nature, Wilde set out to be a poet. His early efforts were not without some success: he won the prestigious Newdigate Prize at Oxford with a poem called 'Ravenna'. Yet for all their surface dazzle and facility, and despite a patent eagerness to shock with 'decadent' material – in 'Charmides' a youth makes love to a statue of Athena, who takes predictably humourless revenge – Wilde's verse was always studied, and now seems dated, lacking the epigrammatic crispness and fluency of his prose, which by contrast seems surprisingly modern. (*Punch* dismissed his first volume of poems as 'Swinburne and water'.) Pater had sensed early on that Wilde's real voice was the sound of speech, not song: 'Why do you always write poetry?' he chided Wilde. 'Why do you not write prose? Prose is so much more difficult.' One reason was that it was as a poet that the young Wilde thought he could garner the most attention; his early career strongly suggests that he loved posing as a littérateur as much as he loved writing itself. '*Pour écrire il me faut du satin jaune,*' he announced. He insisted on writing the draft of his early play *The Duchess of Padua* on fabulously expensive stationery.

It was in prose that Wilde found his real voice, which was clearly that of a critic. The provocative titles of some of the essays – 'The Truth of Masks', 'The Decay of Lying', 'The Critic as Artist' – suggest, *in ovo*, the scope and character of his future artistic and philosophical project, which Wilde's biographer Richard Ellmann succinctly characterized as 'conducting, in the most civilized way, an anatomy of his society, and a radical reconsideration of its ethics'. The most ambitious prose vehicle for that project was *The Picture of Dorian Gray*, which, for all its haphazard construction, still suggests – with its almost prurient and (whatever his post-facto demurs) never quite unadmiring portrait of beauty wholly divorced from morals – why Gide could have thought of Wilde as 'the most dangerous product of modern civilization'. That judgment may seem excessive to our modern ears, but in the wake of *Dorian* – and of Wilde's French-language drama *Salomé*, written at the same time and characterized by the same self-conscious desire to shock by means of decadent sexuality – it would have seemed quite justifiable. 'Since Oscar wrote *Dorian Gray*,' Constance Wilde sighed in 1890, when her husband's novel was being denounced as decadent and immoral, 'no one will speak to us.'

Five years later, people weren't only speaking to Wilde, they were begging for him. By then, it was evident that even *Dorian*

Gray, with its famous inversions of substance and reflection – of life and art – hadn't been the ideal vehicle for his gifts; Wilde himself knew perfectly well he wasn't really a novelist. 'I am afraid it is rather like my own life – all conversation and no action,' he said of *Dorian Gray*. But what is a weakness in a novel can be a strength in a play. Helena Modjeska had been prescient: Wilde was, at bottom, a great Irish talker, and his true métier, as the course of his career would soon demonstrate, was dialogue – real dialogue, rather than the rococo verses he'd put in the mouths of his early characters. It's the voice of Wilde the brilliant talker – amusing, incisive, economical, wicked, feeling, fresh, contemporary, *right* – that you hear in the plays. (And in the letters, too, which have the same quality of intellectual vivaciousness and delightfulness of expression that his best dialogue has.) It wasn't until he allowed that real-life voice to be heard in his work that Wilde achieved true distinction in art as well as life, however briefly. 'Talk itself is a sort of spiritualized action,' he declared in May 1887, at a time when he'd begun writing down narratives and dialogues as a kind of training for his mature dramatic work, of which *Earnest* – with its razor-like epigrams and perfect inversions of the natural and the artificial, of life and art, of babies and books – was the most exquisite, and devastating, expression.

Typically, the creative breakthrough marked by Wilde's great comedy was deeply entwined with another, personal watershed: his authentic artistic self emerged into view at the same time that his authentic emotional self was being revealed. After being initiated into homosexual sex by the precocious Robbie Ross in 1886 – Ross was seventeen, Wilde thirty-one – Wilde became increasingly involved in enacting the Greek love to which he'd always enjoyed alluding, even when he didn't actually practise it. (He'd scandalized his fellow Oxford undergraduates by observing, of a school athlete, that 'his left leg is a Greek poem'; but back then he really was all talk.) Wilde's marriage had begun to unravel after his wife's second pregnancy, which left him physically repelled: 'I ... forced myself to touch and kiss her ... I used to wash my mouth and open the window to cleanse my lips in the open air.' By the late Eighties and early Nineties, he was spending his free time first with Ross, and then, after their fateful 1891 meeting, with the pale-skinned, fair-haired Lord Alfred Douglas – 'Bosie'. And, soon after, with the telegraph boys and rent boys and other lower-class youths of the homosexual demimonde, whose company gave Wilde – the gay among straights, the Irishman among Englishmen – the delicious, gratifying thrill of danger: 'like feasting with panthers'.

Wilde's consummation of his Hellenic urges, after such a long courtship, put an end to all kinds of unresolved tensions. The art/life dialectic that Wilde made the basis of so many of his on- and off-stage pronouncements was just one of many that structured his life and work; temperamentally, he preferred to hesitate between such poles rather than commit to either one. Just as he had hovered endlessly on the verge of conversion to Catholicism as an undergraduate, just as he could never quite choose between Ruskin's moralistic aesthetics or Pater's pagan 'gem-like flame', he had vacillated, from his earliest youth, between the classical and the medieval, the Greek and the Gothic. Between, that is to say, the form, the style, the profane 'sanity' of his beloved Greeks on the one hand, and religious feeling combined with Romantic exaltation on the other. One of the things that 'Ravenna' is about is, indeed, the keenly felt tension between the Hellenic and the Gothic. Its narrator wobbles between ecstatic apostrophes of Greece ('O Salamis! O lone Plataean plain!') and invocations of Gaston de Foix and 'hugelimbed Theodoric, the Gothic king'. 'To be Greek one should have no clothes: to be medieval one should have no body: to be modern one should have no soul,' he wrote. But it was to the Greeks that he eventually returned.

It is tempting to read Wilde's 'anatomy of his society' – his 'radical reconsideration of its ethics' by means of a playful reordering, even deconstruction, of key terms – as the product of his Greek rather than his Gothic side; Hellenism was the rubric under which his intellectual and emotional passions could, for once, coexist in peace. In an essay he wrote at twenty-five for the Oxford Chancellor's Prize, he entwines style, illicit sexuality, and the classical exaltation of form above all things:

> The new age is the age of style. The same spirit of exclusive attention to form which made Euripides often, like Swinburne, prefer music to meaning and melody to reality, which gave to the later Greek statues that refined effeminacy, that overstrained gracefulness of attitude, was felt in the sphere of history.

Wilde identified the Greek aesthetic as 'essentially modern', and inasmuch as he, in his Greek mode, became the first popular modern writer to attempt to divorce aesthetics from morality, he was accurate. The Wilde we love, the Wilde of the epigrammatic wit, the Wilde who so devastatingly skewers puffed-up convention by turning his fictive worlds inside out, is the pagan, the Greek Wilde. The forms with which we identify him today – epigram, satire, the conventionalized situational comedy – are Greek forms. The Romantic Wilde, the deeply nineteenth-century Wilde, the Wilde of the cloying sonnets and the highly perfumed blank verse of early plays like *Véra; or, The Nihilists* and *The Duchess of Padua*, we tend to ignore. It was – significantly –

only after his disgrace, in the bitter, belated paroxysm that was eventually published as *De Profundis*, that Wilde (who'd once remarked that the chief argument against Christianity was the style of Saint Paul) championed spirituality in its traditional 'medieval' forms, emphatically rejecting his erstwhile allegiance to classical style, to

> the dreary classical Renaissance that gave us Petrarch,
> and Raphael's frescoes, and Palladian architecture,
> and formal French tragedy, and St Paul's Cathedral,
> and Pope's poetry, and everything that is made from
> without and by dead rules, and does not spring from
> within through some spirit informing it.

Indeed, even in the Wilde that we do treasure, particularly the three English-language plays that precede *Earnest* – *Lady Windermere's Fan* (1892), *A Woman of No Importance* (1893), and *An Ideal Husband* (1895) – it's clear that the author belonged as much to the dying century as he did to the one that lay ahead. The spirit of these works, which seek to subvert stuffy conventions, may look forward to the twentieth century, but the plays themselves are, essentially, clanking nineteenth-century melodramas, with their illegitimate births suddenly revealed, their plots that hinge on stolen jewels and letters, their eleventh-hour revelations. Even Wilde's contemporaries were able to see this. After attending a 1907 revival of *A Woman of No Importance*, Lytton Strachey described the play to Duncan Grant as 'a complete mass of epigrams, with occasional whiffs of grotesque melodrama and drivelling sentiment … Epigrams engulf it like the sea.' In almost every dramatic work but *Earnest*, we feel the two Wildes – the sentimental, 'Gothic' Wilde, and the crisp, classical Wilde – at war. It was only in *Earnest*, with its architectural symmetries, its self-consciously toy-like, artificial characters, its bejewelled style, that he achieved the ideal 'Greek' harmony in which form and content were entirely at one.

Still, if *Earnest* is a perfect vehicle for the expression of Wilde's intellectual and aesthetic concerns, it can also be read as an allegory for the writer's life – one that was torn between a hunger for acceptance and a flair for subversion. ('*Le bourgeois malgré lui*' was Whistler's canny description of his one-time friend.) Like the drama of his life, much of the drama that Wilde wrote was concerned with the tension between the public masks we wear and the messy private impulses that they often hide; with sudden reversals of fortune and last-minute recognitions; with true natures – and true identities – ruefully revealed at the last minute. This is particularly true of the two works whose debuts early in 1895 marked the apogee of his professional life and the onset of his personal disintegration: *An Ideal Husband* and *The Importance of Being Earnest*. The former premiered to delirious reviews in January 1895; the latter, on Valentine's Day of the same year. Four days later, the marquess of Queensberry, Bosie's father, left his famously misspelled calling card, which referred to Wilde as a 'somdomite'; two months later, Wilde had been condemned for 'gross indecencies'.

Unsurprisingly, both plays use the same structural devices (switched identities, long-buried secrets) and both treat identical themes (the catastrophic tensions between public and private selves), and yet they are radically different in tone, temperament, and style. *An Ideal Husband* seems, indeed, to belong to the nineteenth century, and looks backward to what we may call the 'Gothic' Wilde. Its interest lies, if anywhere, in its imperfections: the famous epigrams ('To love oneself is the beginning of a lifelong romance') sparkle brightly, but are at odds with the melodramatic structure and patent sentimentality – and with overwrought passages in which the playwright seems to be using his characters as mouthpieces for personal concerns. When the play's tortured main character, a man revealed to have a terrible secret in his past, addresses a series of lengthy, impassioned, and nakedly illogical pleas for sympathy to his wife – a woman whom he goes on to chastise for having insufficient sympathy for his flaws – it is impossible not to think of Wilde himself.

Earnest, on the other hand, has the high aesthetic elegance and irrefutable, mechanical efficiency of a theorem: in this case, a theorem about art and society. Here, significantly, all emotion, all feeling – all real 'life' – have been purposefully pared away. With its nihilistic inversions of surface and content, attitude and meaning, triviality and seriousness, the play flashes and gleams dangerously like the scalpel it was meant to be, the instrument with which Wilde dissected Victorian ethics, thereby making twentieth-century aesthetics – an aesthetics divorced from false sentiment – possible.

The story of the paradoxical process by which Wilde evolved from a poseur who put life before art into a real artist, from the composer of florid poems on ostentatiously lofty themes into the author of comedies whose flippancy concealed a serious intellectual and critical purpose, is a fascinating one. So it is a great irony that Wilde's life story has come to overshadow his work in a way that has blunted our understanding of just what it is that made him an interesting artist. Today we think of Wilde as an icon of martyrdom in the cause of sexual freedom; and yet our seeming familiarity with him – our sometimes too-hasty sense that we know what he's about, which happens to be something we're interested in today – has dulled our appreciation of his creations. This is nowhere more apparent than in the recent film version of

The Importance of Being Earnest. It was directed by the Englishman Oliver Parker, who also directed the 1999 film version of *An Ideal Husband*; in both films, a knowing familiarity with Wilde the icon has all too frequently transformed his artistic creations into the opposites of what they were intended to be.

To get *The Importance of Being Earnest* right – to convey the danger, as well as the delight, inherent in those artfully constructed double lives, danger and delight that Wilde himself knew so well, and which ultimately destroyed him – you need to maintain its artificiality, the self-conscious conventionality of form that the playwright uses to highlight his ideas about the artificiality of social and moral conventions. In Anthony Asquith's flawless 1952 film version of the play, the director emphasizes the theatrical nature of his material: the movie opens with an image of people being seated at the theatre, followed by the appearance of a title card reading, 'Act 1. Scene 1. Ernest Worthing's Room in the Albany.' The performances themselves – particularly those of the incomparable Joan Greenwood as Gwendolen and Dorothy Tutin as Cecily – are shaped to be as robotic as possible. The young women tinkle their slyly nonsensical lines ('Mamma, whose views on education are remarkably strict, has brought me up to be extremely short-sighted') like the wind-up toys they are.

In his new film version of *Earnest*, by contrast, Oliver Parker does what many filmmakers do when translating plays onto celluloid, which is to attempt to 'open out' the work. This allows him to present many splendid images: of the grotesquely ornate residence in which Lord and Lady Bracknell live; of Jack's impressive country seat, where Algy arrives by means of a hot-air balloon; and of Lady Bracknell's awesome hats, which appear to have decimated more than one aviary. But film's inherent tendency to naturalize what it shows us works, if anything, against the grain of the play – as does the inevitable tendency of film to translate into images motifs and ideas that are conveyed on stage by means of words. The latter is particularly unfortunate when treating the work of a great talker; the visual temptations of film make nonsense of some of Wilde's sharpest and best-known lines. 'I never travel without my diary,' Gwendolen famously says with glacial sweetness on meeting Cecily at Jack's country house. 'One should always have something sensational to read in the train.' Parker's film makes you wonder just when she gets to read that famous document, since in this version she prefers to motor down from London in a clanking automobile which she can barely keep on the road. This makes for visual interest, but destroys the comic point.

It may be that the purpose of showing Gwendolen's perilous drive is to demonstrate her independence of mind. (Parker writes in a scene in which we see her having the name 'Ernest' tattooed on her derrière – a vulgar and otiose intrusion.) But, of course, Wilde's Gwendolen *has* no 'mind', or at least not in the sense Parker thinks she does. The most salient aspect of Gwendolen's character is, if anything, her artificiality of mind: it is her and Cecily's inane, lifelong yearning to marry men named 'Ernest' that drives the perverse action of the play, forcing both Jack and Algy to maintain their elaborate double lives as Ernests. Indeed, Parker's eagerness to give his characters inner lives often means that his direction is at odds with the directions Wilde provides. Like all of *Earnest*'s females, young Cecily is as tough as nails beneath an elaborate, doll-like politesse; this is part of Wilde's satire of contemporary expectations that high-born girls be hothouse flowers. Jack understands his creator's important point, and goes so far as to articulate it – one of the rare moments in the play when a character says, and means, something that happens to be true: 'Cecily is not a silly, romantic girl, I am glad to say. She has got a capital appetite, goes on long walks, and pays no attention at all to her lessons.' Parker, however, has ideas of his own. His Cecily is the opposite of Wilde's – a dreamy young thing who, during long, beautifully photographed fantasy sequences, imagines herself as a misty Burne-Jones heroine, decked out in medieval gowns while tied to a tree awaiting rescue by hunky knights. Wilde's point is that contemporary artistic fantasies of young maidenhood run counter to some tough natural truths; Parker's joke is that – well, there is no joke.

Of course, the two young women are merely embryonic versions of the most artfully constructed of all of Wilde's females, Lady Bracknell, that epigram-breathing dragon of self-assurance. Like all great humour characters, she is utterly without a past or future, without motivation or reason of any kind: like the mandarin systems of class and taste and privilege that she represents, she merely, monstrously, is. Parker, however, gives her a sordid past as a lower-class showgirl who (as we see in a flashback) entrapped Lord Bracknell into marriage by getting pregnant – a scenario as unlikely as it is, ultimately, unilluminating. However clever, such details undermine the entire project of Wilde's dramaturgy, which always proposes as being quite 'natural' that which is the most artificial of motivations, and vice versa.

Parker's failure to understand the structures and meanings of Wilde's play is clearest in his direction of the final scene – the denouement in which Miss Prism tells all, and all ends happily. At the end of the play, after it is established that Jack is the long-lost child of Lady Bracknell's sister – and hence is Algy's brother – there is a frantic scrambling to find out what his real given name had been. (Remember, Gwendolen will only marry an 'Ernest'.) All that Lady Bracknell can recall was that the child was named for its father, the late General Moncrieff, whose first name she can no longer remember. Jack eagerly consults the Army Lists, where he triumphantly discovers that his dead father's name had, in fact, been Ernest John, and hence that both his real and his assumed names are, indeed, 'true' – so that Jack has been both Ernest and 'earnest' all his life. 'It is a terrible thing,' he declares at this revelation, 'for a man to find out suddenly that all his life he has been speaking nothing but the truth.' It is this discovery that prompts his newfound aunt's withering final observation: 'My nephew, you seem to be displaying signs of triviality.' The disdain she evinces for the discovery of this authentic 'Ernest' mirrors Wilde's disdain for all that is 'earnest'.

Bizarrely, Parker contorts this concluding moment, with its typically Wildean condemnation of earnestness, into its exact opposite. In his cinematic *Earnest*, we see Jack's finger going down the list of entries in the Army Lists and landing on the name 'Moncrieff', but the first name here, as we can all too clearly see, is simply 'John'. Nonetheless – in order to win the hand of Gwendolen – Jack announces to everyone that his late father's name was Ernest. Lady Bracknell sees and comprehends the deceit, but still goes on to make her disdainful closing remark about her nephew's 'signs of triviality': the result is that in this version, her barb is directed not at Jack's 'earnestness', but at his deceitfulness, which she alone has glimpsed. For her to condemn deception rather than sincerity doesn't merely miss the point, it inverts it: Parker's film ends up implicitly endorsing the conventional morality that the play – a drama, let us not forget, by the author of 'The Truth of Masks' and 'The Decay of Lying' – so hilariously lampooned.

The reasons for Parker's failure – the reasons his *Earnest* is cute rather than lethal – are not hard to locate, and may best be understood by comparing two other films having to do with Wilde. Like the two film versions of *Earnest*, one dates from the Fifties and the other is very recent; both are biographies of Wilde himself.

The 1959 Ealing Studios picture *Oscar Wilde*, starring Robert Morley as the corpulent Wilde and Ralph Richardson as his forensic nemesis, Sir Edward Carson, dwells on Wilde's tragedy. Nearly a third of this movie – which came out when *Regina v. Wilde* was still a living memory for some people – is devoted to the trials, the almost Greek-tragic climax of which was one small comment made by Wilde during the course of his cross-examination. Asked whether he'd kissed a certain boy, Wilde disdainfully replied that he had not, as the boy in question was 'singularly plain'. This, we now know, was the turning point of the trial: by suggesting that Wilde would have kissed the boy had he been pretty, it gave Wilde's foes the ground they needed to condemn him. (The organizers of the British Library exhibition 'Oscar Wilde, 1854– 1900: A Life in Six Acts', which opened late in 2000 and subsequently travelled to the Morgan Library in New York City, also realized this point: the exhibition featured a copy of the official court transcript of Wilde's trial, opened to the page on which this crucial remark appears. Queensberry's calling card was also on display.) And so, in a final, terrible failure to distinguish between reality and art, Wilde's need to perform, to amuse the spectators, came at the cost of his freedom – and, eventually, his life.

The film ends, as Wilde's life did, ignominiously, with a drunken Wilde drinking absinthe in a French bar, cackling dementedly to himself. If the film focuses on the tragic repercussions of Wilde's actions ('Why did I say that to Carson?' he cries: it's a good question), it does so no more than Wilde did himself. 'I thought life was going to be a brilliant comedy,' Wilde wrote from prison to Bosie in the immensely long, tortured letter of recrimination (and self-recrimination) that became *De Profundis*. 'I found it to be a revolting and repellent tragedy.'

Brian Gilbert's 1997 film *Wilde*, by contrast, ends not in defeat but in erotic victory. By the time Gilbert made his film, anyone who remembered the sordid reality of Wilde's humiliation and defeat had died; living memories had been replaced by a political and cultural need to see Wilde purely as a martyr – not as a self-destructive hero-martyr, in the Greek-tragic mould that Wilde would have well understood, but as a wholly passive victim, a role that erases everything about what happened to him that is interesting from a moral and psychological point of view. You wonder how many people recall that it was Wilde, in a moment of monumental delusion, who sued Queensberry for libel; it was during this prosecution that it was revealed, in a way that the earlier film showed but the more recent one does not, that the marquess's 'libel' – 'somdomite' – was, in fact, all too true.

Gilbert's biopic is intended above all as a celebration of 'the love that dare not speak its name'; only a few moments are devoted to the trials – presumably because we all take for granted that Wilde was the hapless victim of Victorian sexual hypocrisy. This film ends not with the end of Wilde's life, but with his reunion with Bosie in Italy after his release from prison. As Wilde stands in a sunlit piazza, the beautiful face of Jude Law, who plays Bosie, comes into view, smiling ecstatically. Freeze-frame, then credits. This puerile moment isn't so much misleading as dishonest. In real life, as we know, the grossly mismatched love between what Auden called 'the underloved and the overloved' failed miserably to conquer all, and the awful squabbles between Wilde and the dreadful Bosie continued, as did the terrible arguments about money.

You can't understand why Wilde was important, and you certainly can't understand why *Earnest* is great, without recognizing the aspect of danger and tragedy that lurked beneath the glittering surface of his best comic creation – and of his life. Wilde the classicist understood that the flip side of *Earnest*, with its misplaced baby and last-minute recognitions between near relations, was *Oedipus Rex*. The stylistic master of dualities, of truths that were also their own opposites: in order to do justice to Wilde, to both the life and the art, we must always strive to see not only the exaltation but the humiliation, not only the pathos and suffering but the hubris and arrogance, not only the dazzling clarity of vision about the flaws in his society but a penchant for self-deception that suggested a profound self-destructiveness; not only the beauty but the peril. Wilde himself saw it all too clearly, if too late. An intricate appreciation of the complex and often deceptive relationship between things as they really are and things as we wish them to be is, after all, the whole point of his final work for the stage.

The recent film biography's failure to understand what Wilde's life was about is mirrored, in Parker's film of *Earnest*, by a failure to understand what his art was about. Both movies are characterized by a certain familiarity, a certain presumptiveness, about who Wilde was and what he meant. It's significant that Parker's direction constantly underscores the most famous witticisms and inversions of the normal ('her hair has gone quite gold with grief') with intense close-ups – the cinematic equivalent of winking. Parker isn't doing Wilde; he's doing 'Wilde'. Our own need to see Oscar Wilde as one thing only – as a cartoon martyr, as the poster boy of a modern-day movement – has dulled our vision, and reduced Wilde, both as a man and as an artist. In an irony that Wilde himself would have appreciated, we have all become too earnest to do *Earnest*.

The Tale of Two Housmans

Tom Stoppard's play about A. E. Housman opens with a perceptive bit of shtick. As the curtain rises, the eminent Cambridge Latinist and author of *A Shropshire Lad* has just died at the age of seventy-seven – the year is 1936 – and is waiting to be ferried across the Styx. Charon, the infernal ferryman, is waiting, too: he keeps peering over 'Professor Housman's' shoulder, looking for the other passenger he thinks he's supposed to be picking up:

> CHARON: He's late. I hope nothing's happened to
> him …
> AEH: Are you sure?
> CHARON: A poet and a scholar is what I was told.
> AEH: I think that must be me.
> CHARON: Both of them?
> AEH: I'm afraid so.
> CHARON: It sounded like two different people.
> AEH: I know.

Stoppard wastes no time, then, getting to the heart of the Housman conundrum – the 'psychological puzzle' as C. O. Brink, in his 1986 history of English classical scholarship, puts it, that even today makes the poet-scholar someone who can arouse 'attention, admiration, fear, irritation, criticism, evasion, or downright detestation' in those who study him. For to all appearances, Housman *was* two different people. To study his life and work – and Stoppard clearly has studied them; his play is filled with knowing citations of Housman's letters and published writings – is to confront again and again the stark divisions, rigid distinctions, and odd, almost schizoid doublings that characterize nearly everything about him.

Housman himself set the tone. Sundering, separation, and halving are motifs in several of his best-known and most striking verses. 'I shook his hand and tore my heart in sunder / and went with half my life about my ways', goes one posthumously published poem, presumably about his farewell to Moses Jackson, the hearty, heterosexual Oxford companion for whom he had a disastrously unrequited passion that was the pivotal emotional experience in his life. Demarcation and bifurcation are themes in his scholarly writing as well: hence his lifelong insistence, impossible to take seriously any longer, on divisions between intellect and scholarship, on the one hand, and emotion and literature, on the other. 'Meaning is of the intellect, poetry is not,' goes one typical aphorism. Occasionally, the poetic and the scholarly came together:

> The stars have not dealt me the worst they could do:
> My pleasures are plenty, my troubles are two.
> But oh, my two troubles they reave me of rest,
> The brains in my head and the heart in my breast.

'He very much lived in water-tight compartments that were not to communicate with each other,' his sister Kate Symons observed after his death. She was referring to Housman's homosexuality, which forced him, as it did many homosexuals of his era, to live a 'double life'. But duality is the leitmotif of his entire existence, professional as well as personal.

Who were the 'two' Housmans? The 'two different people' – a poet, a scholar – for whom Stoppard's clueless Charon waits are particularly apt symbols for the two discordant halves into which Housman's personality seemed, even to his contemporaries, to fall. (The title of W. H. Auden's review of *A.E.H.*, a 1937 memoir of Housman written by his brother Laurence, who was a popular and prolific poet and playwright in his own right – his *Victoria Regina*, starring Helen Hayes, was a huge Broadway hit – was 'Jehovah Housman and Satan Housman'.) There was the heavenly poet of *A Shropshire Lad*, first published in 1896 – the elegy on dead or soon-to-be-dead youth which was so loved in its time that its author was, in George Orwell's words, 'the writer who had the deepest hold upon the thinking young' in the years immediately before and after World War I; and yet there was also the devilishly forbidding classics scholar who, in the damning words of a contemptuous 1939 sonnet by Auden, 'Deliberately … chose the dry-as-dust':

> In savage footnotes on unjust editions
> He timidly attacked the life he led
> And put the money of his feeling on
> The uncritical relations of the dead.

Auden knew his classics, and the 'dry-as-dust' criticism wasn't a casual bit of Philistinism: Housman devoted thirty years of his professional life to producing a five-volume critical edition of an obscure verse treatise on astronomy and astrology called the *Astronomica*, by the minor first-century AD poet Marcus Manilius.

And there were also the tender Housman, whose sympathy for the doomed young men he wrote verse about – the soldiers marching off to die in wars not of their making, the forlorn, possibly homosexual suicides, the prematurely dead village athletes, the petty criminals about to be hanged – was apparently limitless; and the vindictive Housman, whom the ineptitude of other scholars could rouse to bursts of famously annihilating – and, it must be said, quite funny – contempt. One eighteenth-century edition of Manilius, Housman dryly wrote, 'saw the light in 1767 at Strasburg, a city still famous for its geese'. (Luckily, the editor responsible for the offending Strasburg edition was long dead: Housman went on to write that his 'mind, though that is no name to call it by, was one which turned as unswervingly to the false, the meaningless, the unmetrical, and the ungrammatical, as the needle to the pole'.)

Finally, there was the man whom friends recalled as 'an admirable raconteur', the *bon vivant* who loved good food and wine and (as Housman once slyly hinted to some High Table companions) was perfectly willing to fly to Paris for lunch, the tablemate whose 'silvery', 'boyish, infectious' laughter made an impression on all who heard it, the kind and surprisingly sensitive colleague who, as his friend the classicist A. S. F. Gow noted, took pains, in the everyday business of academic life, to 'defer to suggestions made by junior colleagues'. How little that Housman had in common with the aloof misanthrope recalled by the British-born classicist Bernard Knox. As a Cambridge undergraduate in the Thirties, Knox would occasionally glimpse Housman marching stiffly across the courts of St John's College in his elastic-sided black boots, his 'thousand-yard stare' intended, as was the out-of-the-way location of his rooms, to discourage casual contact.

In his 1985 history of English classical scholarship, one fourth of which is devoted to Housman (a discussion divided, significantly enough, into two chapters: 'Life and Poetry' and 'Critic and Scholar'), C. O. Brink warns against indulging the seemingly irresistible urge to create one coherent figure out of all these Housmans, which seem to fall so naturally into two groups roughly aligned with 'two such apparent incompatibles as pure poetry and pure scholarship'. (Those 'two different people' again.) 'The bearing of the one on the other,' he writes, 'cannot be direct.' But the risks that the cautious academic historian, bound by the available evidence, fears to take are the bread and butter of the artist. It is to writers like Stoppard that we turn to find the answers to 'puzzles' like the one seemingly posed by Housman's life.

There are many pleasures to be had from Stoppard's play, which was presented this spring in Philadelphia, in a visually striking staging. Like all of his plays, this one is a clever and artic-ulate work written for a large, popular audience. Like his 1993 hit *Arcadia*, the new play seeks, often successfully, to create drama out of technical intellectual material. (The quite emotional climax of one scene in *The Invention of Love* turns on the correct reposi-tioning of a comma in Catullus' poem about the marriage of Achilles' parents.) And yet the playwright hasn't solved the puzzle. Or, to be more precise, he isn't interested in the puzzle. The reason for this is that the real hero of *The Invention of Love* isn't Housman at all, but a contemporary of his who cut a far more dashing figure, someone who was, if anything, the Anti-Housman – in nearly every way his temperamental, creative, and intellectual opposite; someone who, after being gossiped about, invoked, admired from a distance, and quoted throughout Stoppard's play, finally appears at its close for a climactic showdown: Oscar Wilde.

Wilde's life certainly *looks* more dramatic. 'With Housman,' his most recent and most judicious biographer, Norman Page, has written, 'the extent of our knowledge of the various aspects of his existence is usually in inverse proportion to their interest or significance.' We know, in other words, a tremendous amount about the meals Housman ate, the trips he took, his opinions about publishing matters ('I want the book to be read abroad, and continental scholars are poorer than English,' he wrote when urging Grant Richards, his longtime friend and publisher, to keep the sale price of the first Manilius volume low), his opinions about bibliophiles who wrote to him asking for autographs ('an idiotic class ... the only merits of any edition are correctness and legibility'), and little if anything about the kind of emotional dramas that typically make for engrossing theatre. In Housman's case, there were two such dramas which, perhaps predictably, represent, between them, the heart and the mind: his unrequited love for Moses Jackson, which seems to have affected him profoundly for the rest of his life; and his mysterious, apparently deliberate failure at Oxford, the humiliation of which took him ten dreary years to recover from.

Alfred Edward Housman was born in March 1859 into a respectable if troubled middle-class Worcestershire family. (Shropshire, as he never tired of pointing out, was a place he wasn't very familiar with; the topographical details described in his poem were, he wrote two years before his death, almost always 'wrong and imaginary'. The place's resonance for him was, if anything, symbolic: 'Shropshire was our western horizon, which made me feel romantic about it.') Both of his grandfathers had been clergymen. His father, who had no luck with money, drank, and seemed to have been somewhat unbalanced: Edward Housman would sometimes assemble his children at bedtime and shout his favourite Tory slogans at them. Young Alfred's adored mother, Sarah, died just before his twelfth birthday, an event that apparently precipitated his abandonment of his grandfathers' High Church religion. 'I became a deist at thirteen and an atheist at twenty-one,' he wrote to an interviewer in 1933. One of seven children, Housman was particularly close to his sister Kate, to whom he wrote frequently, warmly, and wittily throughout his life; for his brother Laurence, also homosexual, he seemed to have less esteem. Most Housman scholars agree that Alfred's decision to appoint Laurence as his literary executor was based on the cynical belief, eventually borne out, that Laurence would, contrary to his instructions, make public some revealing poems of a personal nature that Housman had never published: a passive-aggressive coming-out if ever there was one.

Housman found refuge from family troubles in reading. Despite an early passion for astronomy, his 'affections', he recalled in old age, were already 'attached to paganism' by the time he was eight, when, as he put it, a copy of Lemprière's classical dictionary fell into his hands. After distinguishing himself in the local village school he went up to St John's College, Oxford, on a scholarship in the fall of 1877, at the age of eighteen. Oscar Wilde had arrived three years earlier and made a big splash with his blue china decor and his assiduous courting of Pater and Ruskin; by contrast, Housman 'lived a quiet student's life', according to a fellow student, 'reading hard, and not taking any interest in the general life of the College'.

Housman did well enough, but his great passion, already at this early age, was in the unglamorous field known as textual criticism. The printed texts of the Greek and Latin classics which we read today are based on ancient and often erroneous medieval manuscripts that were themselves copied from even older and, likely, error-riddled manuscripts. Only close reading of, and comparison among, various manuscripts of an ancient author allow a scholar to surmise what that ancient author most likely wrote, assuming such a scholar has total mastery of language, grammar, manuscript tradition, lexicography, and the author's style, taste, and diction. This mastery Housman had, at an astonishingly early age. As an undergraduate, he blithely ignored the assigned readings in philosophy and instead was hard at work on a new edition of the Roman love elegist Propertius. This intellectual inclination went against the grain of the rather romantic mid-Victorian cult, led by Benjamin Jowett, the Master of Balliol, that celebrated classical education as a means of improving moral tone among the ruling classes, and which was dismissive of what Jowett condescendingly referred to as 'exact scholarship'.

Housman's Oxford experience was marked, characteristically it would seem, by not one but two distinct disasters. The first was emotional. In his first year he met, and struck up a friendship with, Moses Jackson, an athlete and engineering student who was utterly different from him: a contemporary remembered Jackson as being 'a perfect Philistine … quite unliterary and outspoken in his want of any such interest'. However reticent the documentary record may be about the content of the relationship between the two, it seems clear that Housman fell swiftly and deeply in love with Jackson, whom in later life he referred to as 'the man who had more influence on my life than anyone else'. Even though his feelings were not returned, Housman persisted in his obsessive crush, and he and Jackson (and Jackson's brother Adalbert, who according to Laurence Housman became Housman's lover) lived together in Bayswater for three years after Housman was sent down in 1881 and subsequently went to work in the Patent Office, doggedly following Jackson, who'd got a position there after successfully completing his degree.

The extreme emotional tensions bound to make themselves felt in a ménage like the one in which Housman and his two love objects found themselves aren't hard to imagine, and it broke up in 1885, apparently after some kind of blow-up between Housman and Moses Jackson. (Stoppard has the nice conceit of making the proximate cause of the break the news of the passage, in that year, of the infamous Labouchère Amendment to the Criminal Law Amendment Act, which made acts of 'gross indecency' even between consenting adult men punishable by up to two years' hard labour, and under which Wilde would be convicted.) Moses soon left England for India, returning briefly in 1889 to marry, but by that time the relationship was over; Housman heard about the wedding second-hand. Jackson retired in 1911 and moved to Canada, where he died of cancer in 1923. Adalbert Jackson died at twenty-seven, in 1892. Till the end of his life, Housman kept portraits of the two brothers over the mantel in his rooms at Trinity, Cambridge. It is worth noting that Housman's two bursts of poetic activity – the composition of *A Shropshire Lad* in the mid-1890s, and that of *Last Poems* (1922) in the early 1920s – coincided with crises related to Jackson: in the first case, the awful, awkward separation, in the second, the news that Jackson was seriously ill.

The second disaster was an academic one. For reasons that have never been satisfactorily explained, and about which Housman himself remained silent, he failed his final exams in May 1881. Housman was a scholarship boy from a financially beleaguered family; his failure meant that avenues of possibility that Oxford could have opened for him were (or at any event seemed at the time) forever closed. What is striking is the almost wilful manner of his downfall: one of the examiners later reported that he had barely written anything at all in response to the examination questions. Various explanations for the catastrophe have been put forth over the years. A week before he sat the exams, Housman had received news that his father had suffered a life-threatening breakdown; Housman had contemptuously ignored the set curriculum, heavy as it was with philosophy, in order to work on his edition of Propertius; there was some kind of confrontation with Jackson about the true nature of Housman's feelings for him.

A posthumously published lyric that appears as *More Poems* XXXIV – 'For me, one flowery Maytime, / It went so ill that I / Designed to die' – suggests that the real explanation was, in fact, a combination of all three. Indeed, this allegedly great mystery of Housman's life won't seem very mysterious to anyone who has gone to college. It is easy to imagine that Housman, upset by the terrible news from home, was at long last jarred out of the rebellious undergraduate fantasy that he didn't have to prepare the set curriculum; with only days before the exams, he panicked. In his overwrought state, we can further imagine, he sought comfort from Jackson, and in so doing inadvertently betrayed the intensity of his feelings – or, indeed, was made aware of their intensity for the first time. (It may even be that he unconsciously welcomed the crises as a way of finally forcing a confrontation with Jackson.) Hence the disaster, the willed collapse, the 'design to die': if not literally then, certainly, symbolically.

The Oxford and Bayswater fiascos marked the nadir of Housman's life; from that point, it was, more or less, all uphill. Even during the decade between 1881, when he left Oxford, and 1892, when he got his first professorial position at University College, London – a period to which Norman Page refers as 'the years of penance' – a typical bifurcation is in evidence. By day, Housman worked at the Patent Office and lived as an ordinary working man, an existence the details of which he described in vivacious letters to his stepmother, Lucy Housman, which display the often outrageous humour that characterized so much of his prose writing (a quality that the 'dry-as-dust' school of Housman critics conveniently ignores). 'One butcher's man,' he wrote to her in 1885 after having served with great glee on a coroner's jury, 'cut his throat with a rusty knife and died a week after of erysipelas (moral: use a clean knife on these occasions).'

Nights he spent in the reading room of the British Museum, where he began producing a series of papers on the texts of Horace, Propertius, Ovid, and other classical authors that almost immediately won the admiration of the international scholarly community – the more so because the author had no official academic affiliation. His first published paper, 'Horatiana', appeared when he was twenty-three, and reads like the work of a man three times as old. Housman's reputation was sufficiently established ten years after flunking out of Oxford that he won the appointment to the Chair of Latin at University College, London. In 1903 he published the first volume of his magnum opus on Manilius, and by 1911, when he was elected Kennedy Professor of Latin at Cambridge University, his reputation as a scholar who deserved to be ranked with his intellectual idols, Scaliger and Bentley, was secure. He remained at Cambridge until his death. The last of the millions of words he wrote appeared on a postcard to Kate, mailed five days before his death. 'Back to Evelyn nursing home today (Saturday). Ugh.'

In an onstage conversation that took place in December 1999 at the Wilma Theatre in Philadelphia, where *The Invention of Love* had its American premiere, Tom Stoppard rightly asserted that 'the appeal [of Housman as a dramatic subject] was to write the play about two people who inhabited the same person'. There are indeed two Housmans in Tom Stoppard's play – but they're the wrong ones. With the exception of a few disparaging references to *A Shropshire Lad* in the second act, which Stoppard puts in the mouth of the journalist and Wilde memoirist Frank Harris ('I think he stayed with the wrong people in Shropshire. I never read such a book for telling you you're better off dead'), Housman the well-loved sentimental poet is virtually nonexistent. Instead, *The Invention of Love* focuses on the formation of Housman the classical scholar, who is here split in two: the young, emotional, idealistic 'Housman' and the dead, cynical 'AEH' whose postmortem reveries of his youth, from his Oxford days through his appointment to his first academic position and the age of thirty-three, constitute the play's dreamlike action. What contrast there is between them is less a matter of the suggestive differences between Poetry and Criticism, or angels and devils, than one of age. 'Housman', who spends the play getting into as much of a lather about misspellings and misplaced punctuation as he does about Jackson, and into whose mouth Stoppard puts many of the more acidulous aphorisms for which Housman became famous ('the passion for truth is the faintest of all human passions'), isn't different in kind from 'AEH', who says pretty much the same things; he's just more wide-eyed and enthusiastic.

To be sure, much of Stoppard's presentation of Housman the developing scholar is engrossing; certainly the Philadelphia audience thought so. (The run there was extended several times; at the time of writing, there are no plans to bring the play to New York. The rumours are that cautious producers fear that the subject matter is too esoteric.) Few playwrights delight in the surface dazzle of intellectual activity – the theorems, the Latin phrases, the arcane allusions – as much as Stoppard does, and – superficially, at least – he seems to honour his subject's intellectual energy and love of learning for its own sake. There's a wonderful scene toward the end of the first act in which the young Housman exults, apropos of that correction in the Catullus passage, that

> by taking out a comma and putting it back in a
> different place, sense is made out of nonsense in a
> poem that has been read continuously since it was first
> misprinted four hundred years ago. A small victory over
> ignorance and error.

When I saw the play in March with a classicist friend of mine, we were amazed to see that the audience was rapt as Housman explained, in technical language that refused to condescend to the nonclassicist, how his emendation worked. ('So *opis* isn't *power* with a small "o", it's the genitive of Ops who was the mother of Jupiter. Everything comes clear when you put the comma back one place.')

But as the play proceeds, it becomes evident that Stoppard himself isn't all that preoccupied with the kind of small victories over ignorance and error to which Housman devoted his life as a scholar. In the Inaugural Lecture he gave on assuming his position at University College, London, Housman the scrupulous scholar warned against what he called 'dithyrambic' tendencies: self-indulgence on the part of the critic, reckless emotionality and idealization in interpreting texts, as opposed to cautious evaluation and strict consciousness of the author's, rather than the interpreter's, tastes and cultures. For all his interest in intellectual esoterica, Stoppard has always been the dithyrambic sort – a romantic at heart. However much it fussed over Fermat's last theorem, and some of its characters' worries about 'the decline from thinking to feeling', *Arcadia* ultimately celebrates the imperfectability of knowledge, and exalts the messiness of love and sex ('the attraction which Newton left out'). Henry, the playwright protagonist of *The Real Thing*, which is currently enjoying an excellent revival on Broadway, may be impatient with intellectual softness, and may have no patience for vulgar politicized writing, but everyone else realizes – with relief – that he's really 'the last romantic', despite his reputation as someone who doesn't get 'bothered' by things (as Housman was thought not to). The point of this popular play of love and infidelity among very clever people is to make Henry realize this, too. 'I don't believe in behaving well,' he exclaims toward the end of the play, when he realizes how fiercely he loves his second wife. 'I believe in mess, tears, pain, self-abasement, loss of self-respect, nakedness. Not caring doesn't seem much different from not loving.'

As it happens, similar words mark the climax of *The Invention of Love*, where a character rapturously catalogues the effects of love: 'the self-advertisement of farce and folly, love as abject slavery and all-out war – madness, disease, the whole catastrophe owned up to …' The character is Housman, but he's describing not love itself but love poetry – as near to the real thing, we are meant to feel, as this erotically thwarted man ever got. The structure of his play suggests that – as Auden might have done – Stoppard believes that Housman's devotion to the life of the mind was essentially a repressive (and depressive) reaction to, and a sublimation of, his failed love for Jackson.

This is where Wilde comes in: emotionally foolhardy, aesthetically flamboyant, Stoppard's Wilde is clearly intended as a foil to his Housman. (Stoppard's Wilde is valued here for his emotional messiness rather than his intellectual brilliance.) References to Wilde run like a basso continuo through the play from the very beginning, first in breathless undergraduate rumours of his notorious 'Aesthete' excesses while at Oxford, and then in more grown-up gossip about his trial and conviction. In the climactic scene, set after Wilde's release from prison, he and Housman finally meet. (They never actually did, but Housman sent Wilde a copy of *A Shropshire Lad*, and we know that Wilde's intimate friend Robbie Ross recited some of the poems to Wilde when he was in prison.) There's little question of where your sympathies are meant to lie. It's no accident that in this play, the news of Wilde's trial and conviction comes at precisely the moment when Housman gets his first academic appointment, as if Housman's success were somehow predicated on Wilde's failure. And as Wilde himself is rowed across the Styx in the last scene, he recites some of his wittiest and most famous aphorisms, while Housman, standing upstage, recites some of his most vicious and mean-spirited.

'I'm very sorry,' AEH says to Wilde in this final exchange:

> Your life is a terrible thing. A chronological error.
> The choice was not always between renunciation and
> folly. You should have lived in Megara when Theognis
> was writing and made his lover a song sung unto
> all posterity ... and not *now*! – when disavowal and
> endurance are in honour, and a nameless luckless love
> has made notoriety your monument.

If Housman stands for renunciation in Stoppard's eyes, Wilde stands for glorious folly:

> Better a fallen rocket than never a burst of light ...
> Your 'honour' is all shame and timidity and compliance
> ... You are right to be a scholar. A scholar is all scruple,
> an artist is none ... I made my life into my art and it
> was an unqualified success ... I awoke the imagination
> of the century. I banged Ruskin's and Pater's heads
> together, and from the moral severity of one and the
> aesthetic soul of the other I made art a philosophy that
> can look the twentieth century in the eye ... I lived at
> the turning point of the world where everything was

> waking up new – the New Drama, the New Novel,
> New Journalism, New Hedonism, New Paganism, even
> the New Woman. Where were you when all this was
> happening?
>
> AEH: At home.

This exchange got a big laugh when I saw the play, but I have to think that it came at the price of intellectual fairness: Housman, after all, was an artist too, and a very good one. But then, it often seems like the point of *The Invention of Love* is to make Housman into the representative of timid, thwarted, dry-as-dust 'scholarship' and 'science', so that Wilde can become the heroic and tragic representative of 'poetry' and 'emotion' – a dithyrambic type for whom the playwright evidently has more feeling. And in fact, in his Philadelphia comments, Stoppard acknowledged as much: he talked there about Housman as an outwardly 'successful person whose life – and this play does try to do, does try to show – whose life is essentially a failure in many ways. He failed to live his own personality,' whereas Wilde for him is 'this other man who crashed in flames … [whom] we now see, for perfectly obvious reasons, as being somewhat of a heroic figure and a successful person'.

For all their interest in intellectual life, indeed, you wonder whether Stoppard's plays aren't, ultimately, anti-intellectual; he loves to show – and audiences love to watch – brilliant, analytical minds humbled by messy, everyday emotions. (Stoppard has Housman cry out several times during the action of the play, 'Mo! Mo! I would have died for you but I never had the luck!') It's strange that a writer who presents himself – and is accepted as – an intellectual playwright shows so little real appreciation for 'affections' (as Housman called them) that originate above the neck; you'd never guess from Stoppard's presentation of Housman that the mind can be a passionate organ, too.

A speech that Stoppard has chosen not to quote in his play – the 1892 Inaugural – suggests a different picture of Housman. The poet-scholar declared that

> Existence is not itself a good thing, that we should
> spend a lifetime securing its necessaries: a life spent,
> however victoriously, in securing the necessaries of life
> is no more than an elaborate furnishing and decoration
> of apartments for the reception of a guest who is never
> to come. Our business here is not to live, but to live
> happily.

It hasn't occurred to Stoppard, or indeed to many of those writing about Housman, that although he never received Jackson as a full-time lodger in his life, Housman could actually have been, for the most part, happy. *Pace* Stoppard, Housman was no grim Stoic: 'I respect the Epicureans more than the Stoics,' he wrote. Stoppard's Frank Harris gets Housman all wrong when he grumbles that the point of *A Shropshire Lad* is that 'you're better off dead'. If you read beyond the melancholy and obsession with mortality, the point that emerges is, if anything, an Epicurean one: tomorrow we shall surely die, so today we must live – and be happy as best we know how. 'My troubles are two,' Housman wrote, and this troubled Housman is all *The Invention of Love* cares about; but what about 'My pleasures are plenty'?

During their climactic exchange at the close of *The Invention of Love*, Wilde mischievously tweaks Housman's famous devotion to scientific 'truth', a passion that pervades both his poetic and scholarly utterances. ('It is and it must in the long run be better for a man to see things as they are than to be ignorant of them,' he wrote in the UCL Inaugural; and in the penultimate poem of *A Shropshire Lad*, the narrator says of harsh poetic truths that they are worth having even 'if the smack is sour'.) Stoppard's Wilde is somewhat more sanguine about the relation between facts and truth, and shuns unpleasant realities. 'It's only fact,' he tells Housman, referring to a newspaper report about a young cadet who killed himself because he was a homosexual – the incident was the basis for one of the most searing and implicitly self-revealing of *A Shropshire Lad*'s poems ('Shot? So quick, so clean an ending?'). 'Truth', Wilde goes on, 'is quite another thing and is the work of the imagination.'

You're meant to applaud this line, which ultimately provides the explanation of the play's title. Wilde knows that Bosie is nothing more than a 'spoiled, vindictive, utterly selfish and not very talented' young man, but those are merely the boring 'facts'. The 'truth' is that for Wilde, Bosie is divine Hyacinthus. 'Before Plato could describe love,' Stoppard's Wilde says, 'the loved one had to be invented. We would never love anybody if we could see past our invention.' This exaltation of 'invention' over 'reality', of complaisant fantasy over unpleasant facts couldn't be further from Housman's hardheaded view of things. (He loathed Tennyson's 'In Memoriam', which he disdainfully summarized thus: 'Things must come right in the end, because it would be so very unpleasant if they did not.')

Of the cold realities of life, Housman got an early and bitter taste; his reaction was to abandon illusion, 'invention', and devote himself to laying bare reality as he saw it. If love, as Stoppard wants us to believe, lives in the province of the imagination – if it is, essentially, an invention – then Housman's handicap, we are meant to feel, was his limited, science-bound, fact-obsessed, philological mind. Even if you accept the dubious and disturbing proposition that we could never love people if we could see them for who they really are, Stoppard again isn't playing entirely fair here. Having erased all traces of Housman the poet, the amiable colleague, the warm and hilarious correspondent, there's nothing to stop the playwright from claiming that Housman wasn't a fully realized human being, wasn't capable of 'inventing'. This, in turn, allows him to deliver to his audience the always welcome news that scholars are dull and haven't got satisfying emotional lives, whereas other people live life to the hilt.

Had Stoppard dug deeper, been really interested in considering what the soul of a man who was both genuinely creative and rigorously intellectual might be like, he might have penetrated to the mystery of the 'two different people' that Housman was. With his playwright's imagination and presumed interest in the textures of human character, he wouldn't have had to dig very deep. Is the 'puzzle' of Housman's divided nature all that difficult to solve? To my mind, the fierceness of his scholarly invective is a mutation of the fierce protectiveness he felt for the beautiful lads he eulogized. *A Shropshire Lad* is a bitterly ironic antiwar poem: 'The saviours come not home to-night, / Themselves they could not save', goes a line from the sequence's first lyric, which refers to the thousands of young men fighting and dying in the Empire's wars, and which is set on the night of Victoria's Golden Jubilee, as choruses of 'God save the Queen' ring out into the bonfire-illuminated sky. Housman loves his young men, and hurts to think of them wounded ('lovely lads and dead and rotten,' he spits), and scorns those who would wound them. So too with his beloved texts: he loves them, and hurts to think of them wounded.

And surely the life-altering rejection by Jackson has much to do with the tone and character of Housman's two personae. The two emotions that underlay this hopeless, humiliating incident – desire (his for Jackson) and contempt (Jackson's, implicitly, for him and his world) – each found its own outlet: desire in the elegies for young men, contempt in the vituperative footnotes. (Housman wryly dedicated his magnum opus to Jackson the *contemptor harum litterarum* – 'the one who has contempt for these writings'.) Indeed, that contemptuous 'thousand-yard stare' seems all too clearly to have been a self-protective device, a way of distancing himself from the intense emotions that young men – students – could so easily arouse. For this we ourselves should feel sympathy, not contempt.

Desire, contempt; poetry, criticism. Housman's classical papers, abstruse as they may be, are filled with flashes of wit; they are also masterful examples of elegant and precise English. (Among his contributions to textual criticism was to make of what had been a truly dry-as-dust genre, characterized by terse, abbreviated notations, an almost literary one.) There's a strange moment in one of these, an early review of a new edition of Euripides' *Iphigenia Among the Taurians*, in which, during a discussion of textual matters, emotion suddenly kindles: Euripides' *Hippolytus*, the author fiercely writes, was 'by far the most faultless tragedy of Euripides, if not indeed the most fault-less of all Greek tragedies with the exception of the *Antigone* alone'. In Euripides' play, Hippolytus is portrayed as a proud and solitary youth who devoted himself to the austere cult of the virgin goddess Artemis; he perishes, as the indirect result of an unwanted erotic advance, because he would not break an oath of silence. Small wonder the play appealed so much to Housman, who in life had played not one but *both* of its great leading roles: the desire-maddened, rejected would-be seducer, and the solitary youth whose austere enthusiasms were a refuge from erotic confusions for which he claimed contempt.

As for Housman's exceedingly rarefied intellectual enthusiasms, we need not look to pathology to explain them. Of course it's tempting to think that there was, in his choice of Manilius as the object of his life's work, something deliberately perverse; it's as if, to punish the 'system' that had punished him, he chose to waste his awesome talents on someone wholly beneath him. (It wouldn't have been the first time.) In 1984, Professor Knox lamented about this waste in *The New York Review*:

> When I think of what Housman might have done
> for the improvement and elucidation of our texts
> of Aeschylus, Sophocles, and Euripides instead of
> devoting thirty years to the verses of an astrological
> hack, I am tempted to use his own words against him:
> 'The time lost, the tissues wasted … are in our brief
> irreparable life disheartening to think of.'

But even if there is some truth in the theory that Housman's choice of subject was deliberately perverse (after all, he had every reason to resent the system, and to want to subvert its needs and desires), to complain in this way is to inflict, as Housman might put it, the literary on the scientific. *We* may be interested in possessing the most accurate possible texts of the three great tragedians, but Housman's interest was to find corrupt texts and repair them – 'to strike your finger on the page and say, "Thou ailest here, and here."' It is important, too, to remember that among Manilius's previous editors were the great scholars Scaliger and Richard Bentley, whom Housman so revered. Whatever his modest refusal to be counted their equal, it would be inhuman to expect him to resist embarking on a project that, quite apart from its intellectual and technical appeal, would link his name permanently to theirs. And let us not forget that childhood fascination with astronomy. Why shouldn't Housman have had a Proustian motivation?

If Stoppard's interest in intellectuals and their lives and passions extended beyond his desire to use them as garnish for his essentially romantic vision – if, for instance, he'd taken more seriously, and investigated more closely, the contexts for and nuances of Housman's utterances about classical learning and the role of the scholar – he'd have found many things to admire. (And would have had to write a different play.) Not least of these would have been the very trait which, in this play, is too often an object for fun: his insistence on 'scientific' scrupulousness in dealing with ancient texts. 'The only reason to consider what the ancient philosopher meant about anything is if it's relevant to settling corrupt or disputed passages in the text,' AEH declares in Act One, as the audience, echoing Jowett – who also makes an appearance – sniggers knowingly. (How narrow he is, how horribly he has failed to see the glory that was Greece!) And again, toward the end of Act One, AEH is lecturing young Housman on the qualities of a good textual critic; among these was 'repression of self-will'. This also got a solid giggle on the night I saw the play, perhaps because people were making a connection – as I suspect Stoppard intends them to – between Housman's mania for intellectual 'repression' (by which he meant, of course, the effort to filter out the critic's own prejudices) and the alleged sexual and emotional repression for which, thanks to Auden and others, he is so well known.

Like many lines in this play, the one about self-repression is, in fact, a quotation from Housman, but Stoppard doesn't provide the idea with its proper context. In his Cambridge Inaugural Lecture of 1911, Housman argued passionately that scholars of ancient texts must repress their own tastes – what we today might call their cultural biases. He derides an appraisal of some lines by Horace as being 'exquisite':

> Exquisite to whom? Consider the mutations of
> opinion, the reversals of literary judgment, which
> this one small island has witnessed in the last 150
> years: what is the likelihood that your notions or your
> contemporaries' notions of the exquisite are those of
> a foreigner who wrote for foreigners two millenniums
> ago? And for what foreigners? For the Romans, for men
> whose religion you disbelieve, whose chief institution
> you abominate, whose manners you do not like to talk
> about, but whose literary tastes, you flatter yourself,
> were identical with yours ... Our first task is to get rid
> of [our tastes], and to acquire, if we can, by humility
> and self-repression, the tastes of the classics.

In the context of the fuzzy Victorian romanticization of classical culture, this is shockingly refreshing. The past thirty-five years of classical scholarship have, in fact, been devoted to stripping away our cultural preconceptions about and woolly idealization of the Greeks and Romans and trying to see them 'cold', for what and who they were – which was, as often as not, strange and off-putting, despite our desire to make them into prototypes for ourselves, to 'invent' them as 'Hyacinths' when the 'facts' suggest otherwise. Stoppard has AEH recite most of this speech in his play, but you wonder whether he does so without being aware of its implications – without realizing how startlingly prescient and contemporary this musty old character was. Fact-loving, scientific Housman was unsentimental about the Greeks and Romans – and therefore, more modern by far, when all is said and done, than 'Hyacinth'-loving Wilde.

The back cover of the printed edition of *The Invention of Love*, like the play itself, is less interested in the two Housmans than in comparing Housman and Wilde; in doing so, it makes a little joke of A. E. Housman. On it, the publisher rhapsodizes about Wilde's superior allure, about the fact that although his life was short and tragic, he had, at least, lived: 'The author of *A Shropshire Lad* lived almost invisibly in the shadow of the flamboyant Oscar Wilde' – this, of course, isn't true; Housman was hugely popular – 'and died old and venerated – but whose passion was truly the fatal one?'

After seeing Stoppard's one-sided play about this fascinatingly two-sided figure, I was moved to ask a different question. Let's say that Stoppard's Wilde is right – let's say he did invent the 'new' twentieth century, mad as it is for everything new. And indeed, so much of what he was famous (and infamous) for inventing in the nineteenth century has become commonplace in the twentieth: media celebrity, and the celebrity trial; personality as a form of popular entertainment; glittering pronouncement as ideology; 'image' culture; the adulation and tireless pursuit of idealized, rather than real, love objects. So let's say that Wilde (or at least the Wilde of Stoppard's play), the one who preferred silvery, seductive, vaporous images to unappealingly humdrum 'facts' and unpleasant realities, invented that – gave us the world we now inhabit. And let's say that Housman, after failing – or refusing – to 'invent' the one he loved, chose to be unglamorous, to devote himself to facts, to reality, to the dull task of bringing to light hard truths unlikely to endear him to a public hungry – as Stoppard's public is – for sentimental fantasies. Let's give Wilde that much, and Housman that little. Who is the greater hero?

– *The New York Review of Books*, 10 August 2000

Bitter-Sweet

'A talent to amuse' or '*just* a talent to amuse'? Even before Noël Coward's death in 1973, the former phrase – a line from one of his songs – had become the standard celebratory summation of his contribution to popular culture during a half-century as a playwright, actor, songwriter, diarist, composer, autobiographer, novelist, and cabaret entertainer. *A Talent to Amuse* is the title of Sheridan Morley's admiring but judicious 1969 biography of Sir Noël; A Talent to Amuse is the epigraph that adorns the Westminster Abbey memorial stone dedicated to him (located – appropriately, you can't help thinking, for this master of light verse – not in, but just adjacent to, the Poet's Corner).

But 'a talent to amuse' is not what Coward actually wrote. Or at least, not all of what he wrote. The phrase that has come to summarize Coward was, in fact, snipped from its context in a song called 'If Love Were All' that Coward composed for his 1929 'operette' *Bitter-Sweet*. It's sung by a lovelorn café chanteuse after she's been reunited with a former lover who has since remarried. Here is the entire verse:

> Although when shadows fall
> I think if only –
> Somebody splendid really needed me,
> Someone affectionate and dear,

> Cares would be ended if I knew that he
> Wanted to have me near.
> But I believe that since my life began
> The most I've had is just
> A talent to amuse.

In its proper context, then, 'a talent to amuse' is not so much a self-celebration as it is something more wistful and self-ironic, and not a little sad. A talent, yes, but a talent for something relatively minor: *just* a talent to amuse. A gift, yes, but one with limited power: the *most* she can offer.

The elision of that 'just' over the years, the gradual loss of the phrase's original, piquant context, can be seen as a symbol of our increasing failure to understand just what 'amusement' meant for the author of those words. Noël Coward's distinctive sensibility, as both writer and performer, was, in fact, a particularly complex one. Shaped in his Edwardian boyhood but ripened in his Jazz Age youth, it owed much to the revues of the late 1910s and early 1920s, like those of his early producer André Charlot, with their swift shifts in mood and tone. It's a sensibility that's poised, we might say, on the fulcrum between 'a talent to amuse' and 'just a talent to amuse' – between self-assertion and self-deprecation, merriment and melancholy, sweet and bitter. This curious hybrid is difficult to sustain in the present era of popular entertainment, with its effortfully ironic tone, its brittle carapace of postmodern knowingness, and its omnipresent violence and explicitness. To us, Coward's light touch, like the 'light' genres at which he excelled – light comedy, light verse, the latter in particular nearly extinct today, both aiming above all to provide pleasure, gaiety, amusement – is bound to come off as trivial, un-hip.

As a result, we tend to get Coward wrong: we find the elements that appeal to us, and forget the rest. Coward tends to be played as camp these days; the brittleness of his dialogue appeals to our own desire to appear knowingly world-weary. But emphasizing the cold glitter leaves out the strong feelings that run just beneath the surface – the sentimentality that lurks in the background of the comic plays, and explodes into the foreground in the 1945 film *Brief Encounter*, based on one of his 1935 *Tonight at Eight-Thirty* sketches, or his patriotic paean *In Which We Serve* (1942).

Coward's estimation of his own talent to amuse was itself characterized by a mix of celebration and deprecation. On the one hand, he had the healthy self-regard of talented people who have achieved success through tremendous hard work. ('I am bursting with pride, which is why I have absolutely no vanity.') Born just before Christmas 1899 – hence the given name – to a lower-middle-class Teddington piano salesman and his strong-willed wife, he first stepped on a stage at the age of ten, and throughout his life he was proud to have been in the business of giving pleasure. When he described his five canonical comic masterpieces – *Hay Fever* (1924), *Private Lives* (1930), *Design for Living* (1932), *Present Laughter* (1939), and *Blithe Spirit* (1941) – as being 'important', it was because they gave 'a vast number of people a great deal of pleasure'.

He himself took unabashed pleasure in the success that his ability to amuse had brought him already at a very tender age. He composed that bittersweet lyric for *Bitter-Sweet* when he wasn't quite thirty; by then, he'd been an international celebrity for five years, having rocketed to stardom in 1923, at the age of twenty-four, with his sensational cocaine-addiction melodrama *The Vortex*, which was followed the next year by a solid comic hit in *Hay Fever*. 'The world has treated me very well – but then, I haven't treated it so badly either.'

Yet Coward's satisfaction in what he did so abundantly well (and so abundantly: sixty published plays, three hundred published songs, a multivolume autobiography, dozens of short stories, a novel) was balanced by a healthy lack of illusions about the nature of his gift. 'I don't write plays with the idea of giving some great thought to the world,' he wrote on the eve of his sixtieth birthday, 'and that isn't just coy modesty … If I wanted to write a play with a message, God forbid, it would undoubtedly be a comedy.' 'God forbid' reminds you of Coward's distrust of weighty messages, his fervent belief that amusement could have nuance and substance; and it explains why, even after the rise of John Osborne and the kitchen-sink drama, he went on insisting, with perhaps pardonable shrillness, that the theatre must above all amuse, must be what it surely seemed to him in his Edwardian boyhood, 'a house of strange enchantment, a temple of dreams'. 'Nowadays,' he wrote in his late fifties,

> a well constructed play is despised and a light comedy
> whose only purpose is to amuse is dismissed as 'trivial'
> and 'without significance'. Since when has laughter
> been so insignificant? No merriment apparently must
> scratch the set, grim patina of these dire times. We
> must all just sit and wait for death, or hurry it on,
> according to how we feel. To my mind, one of the most
> efficacious ways of hurrying it on is to sit in a theatre
> watching a verbose, humourless, ill-constructed play,
> acted with turgid intensity, which has received rave
> notices and is closing on Saturday.

His characterization of what makes a play bad reminds us of what makes his own best work so good: verbal precision and economy (he declared himself 'one of the few remaining guardians of the

English language'), merriment and humour, elegance of construction, all of them showcased by an acting style that is gossamer, playful, blithe – a technique that easily reflects the many colours that shimmer across the surfaces of his lines. ('The befeathered sheen of a pheasant's neck' is how Kenneth Tynan described Coward's dialogue.) A technique, that is to say, that understands that his plays consist of nothing *but* surfaces – and that takes their superficiality with, of course, the utmost seriousness.

The difficulty of getting just right Coward's many complexities – the paradoxical ways in which wistfulness can be entwined with glitter, and meaning can exist in surfaces – is all too evident in two new productions. One of them is easy enough to dismiss, since Coward himself dismissed it: the world premiere of *Long Island Sound*, a 1947 play whose value even as a curio is, however, marred by a vulgar, tasteless staging. The other is a shiny new production of *Private Lives*. The fact that the latter manages to make this finest of Coward's comedies seem verbose, humourless, and ill-constructed – to say nothing of the fact that it has received rave notices on both sides of the Atlantic – indicates how far from Coward we now are, and how fragile his legacy is.

'Fragile' is a very good way to describe *Private Lives*. Its plot is as thin as any that Coward concocted – the most tenuous of structures on which to hang his *mousseline* wit. In the first act, Elyot Chase, an elegant young man of 'about thirty, quite slim and pleasant-looking', is honeymooning at a luxe hotel in France with his second wife, Sybil, a pretty blonde of twenty-three. The adjoining suite, of course, turns out to be occupied by Elyot's firecracker of a first wife, Amanda, who's honeymooning with *her* new spouse, Victor Prynne. Storming onto the terrace after fights with their respective mates, Elyot and Amanda catch sight of each other, and in the course of some verbal sparring realize they're still mad about each other; and proceed to flee their nice if somewhat conventional new spouses. The second act, set a few days later in Amanda's Paris flat, suggests why Elyot and Amanda divorced in the first place: tart-tongued, volatile, inventive, restless, each is the other's best audience – but who wants to live on stage? The third act, typical of Coward's finales, is less a resolution than an escape: Victor and Sybil catch up with their wayward mates, growing to loathe each other into the bargain, and during a furious breakfast-time fracas Elyot and Amanda laughingly sneak off together as Victor and Sybil start hammering away at each other. How they will actually live together is of no concern.

Typically, Coward had few illusions about the weightiness of this work, which was written in four frantic days in Shanghai after a vision of his acting partner and beloved friend Gertrude Lawrence 'in a white Molyneux dress on a terrace in the South of France' came to him as he readied himself for bed. (He'd promised to write a play for her while he was travelling in the Far East; leaving nothing to chance, Lawrence slipped a photograph of herself into the Cartier desk set that she'd given him as a going-away present.) In the first volume of his autobiography, *Present Indicative*, which he published at the tender age of thirty-seven, the playwright, with his usual blend of self-deprecation and self-celebration, characterized his creation as 'a reasonably well-constructed duologue for two experienced performers ... As a complete play, it leaves a lot to be desired ... From the playwright's point of view, [it] may or may not be considered interesting, but at any rate, from the point of view of technical acting, it is very interesting indeed.' And again, later: 'a shrewd and witty comedy, well-constructed on the whole, but psychologically unstable; however, its entertainment value seemed obvious enough, and its acting opportunities for Gertie and me admirable ...'

It's significant that Coward always rates the work's 'entertainment value' and, particularly, its 'acting opportunities' more highly than he does its structural or psychological coherence. The real hero of Coward's best comedies is, after all, Coward himself; a lot, if not most, of his *oeuvre* was composed with himself in mind as the male lead. (You'd think that this would alert directors to the fact that an appreciation of Coward's performance style is likely to be crucial to the success of his plays.) The repeated characterization of his plays as vehicles for interesting acting is one of the many things that distinguish Coward from Oscar Wilde, that other homosexual British master of crisp wit, to whom Coward is often, and for the most part inaccurately, compared. Wilde's plays are the creations of a playwright; Coward's are those of a performer. If the former's work achieves a hermetic perfection of structure that Coward's never does, it's because Coward is ultimately more interested in the performance than in the play.

And yet Coward's shrewd spotlighting of entertainers was more than a matter of giving himself work; it goes to the heart of what his plays are about. If he couldn't imagine writing plays with a weighty underlying 'message', it was because in his plays, the medium was the message: entertainment, amusement are our weapons against the vagaries of life. 'Laugh at everything,' Elyot tells Amanda, as they plot to abandon their brand-new spouses. 'We're figures of fun …' In part, this emphasis on laughter and fun reflected the outlook of a well-balanced person who had an agreeably optimistic view of life. (Of his longtime acquaintance Somerset Maugham, Coward wrote that 'he believed, rather proudly, I think, that he had no illusions about people but in fact he had one major one and that was that they were no good'.) But the omnipresent self-consciousness about fun and laughter in his work – his characters' amused awareness of being performers in a delicious play – was also his 'message': his serious response, as a popular entertainer (and no doubt as a homosexual, too) to what Elyot calls 'all the futile moralists who try to make life unbearable'.

The sense that Coward's favourite characters are performers in some way or another is particularly strong in *Private Lives*. Anomalously among this playwright's characters, neither Elyot nor Amanda has a career, and yet there is a strong sense throughout the play that the core of their enjoyment of each other (when they're not fighting) is their dramatic and verbal fantasy. They're writers, or perhaps playwrights, *manqués*, and they can't be together for two minutes without launching into a decidedly theatrical playfulness. Snuggling in Amanda's Paris flat in Act Two, Elyot starts the gramophone and asks Amanda to dance, and they're immediately off and running:

> ELYOT: Are you engaged for this dance?
> AMANDA: Funnily enough I was, but my partner was
>   suddenly taken ill.
> ELYOT: It's this damned smallpox epidemic.
> AMANDA: No, as a matter of fact it was kidney trouble.
>
> …
>
> AMANDA: Is that the Grand Duchess Olga lying under
>   the piano?
> ELYOT: Yes, her husband died a few weeks ago, you
>   know, on his way back from Pulborough. So sad.
> AMANDA: What on earth was he doing in Pulborough?
> ELYOT: Nobody knows exactly, but there have been the
>   usual stories.

By contrast, the perfectly nice Sybil and Victor have no 'usual stories' – indeed, have no stories at all. The extent of their fantasy is the awful little nicknames they've given their new spouses ('Elli' and 'Mandy'). It's this lack of imaginative élan that makes them losers in Coward's eyes. If what distinguishes the exchanges between Amanda and Elyot is the way in which they so readily pick up each other's cues, what alerts us to the unsuitability of Sybil and Victor to their respective mates is their flat-footed inability to recognize good cues when they see them. At the beginning of Elyot's first-act spat with Sybil – he's just caught sight of Amanda on the next balcony, and desperately tries to convince his new wife that they should leave the hotel at once – Elyot roars at his uncomprehending young bride that 'if there's one thing in the world that infuriates me, it's sheer wanton stubbornness'. Then, the characteristic, deliciously deadpan Cowardian gearshift: 'I should like to cut off your head with a meat axe.' To which Sybil can only respond, 'How dare you talk to me like that, on our honeymoon night.' This is clearly not a marriage made in Coward heaven.

The marriage between Noël Coward and Howard Davies, the director of the new Broadway *Private Lives*, isn't so great either. Davies's problem is that he doesn't trust Coward's belief in the fundamental seriousness of play; instead, he just goes for seriousness. The result is about as interesting as Sybil.

The irony is that Davies's heart is in the right place. Too often, *Private Lives* has been the vehicle for some good-natured camping on the part of middle-aged actresses eager for an adorable vehicle. (The last major Broadway revival was in 1992, featuring Joan Collins; before that, it was Elizabeth Taylor, in 1982, and long before that, Tallulah Bankhead, in 1948.) Coward himself deplored this approach to his work. As early as 1949, he expressed dismay at a revival of *Fallen Angels* (1925) that was done as camp self-parody, and he elsewhere denounced a production of *Present Laughter* in which the lead role, a famous, Cowardesque actor, was portrayed as being vicious. And a young actress performing Amanda in what she thought was the approved Coward style he dismissed as 'too piss-elegant by half'.

It's easy to see why he was so annoyed. Such interpretations fail to see that there are feelings in Coward's work; they miss the side of Coward that the playwright himself cherished as 'the romantic quality, tender and alluring', which Gertrude Lawrence brought to Amanda. They make impossible anything like what Coward's close friend and biographer Cole Lesley records in his description of Coward's and Lawrence's original performance of the play: 'They played the balcony scene so magically, lightly, tenderly that one was for those fleeting moments brought near to tears by the underlying vulnerability, the evanescence of their love.'

But in his quest to get the feeling back into *Private Lives*, Davies has grossly miscalculated; he fails to understand just where the feelings are. No doubt there was a superficial allure to the idea of reuniting Lindsay Duncan and Alan Rickman, the stars of the 1987 *Dangerous Liaisons* that he'd directed, as his Amanda and Elyot: the vicious, big-cat murderousness of the Marquise de Merteuil and the Vicomte de Valmont is a distant ancestor of what Coward's leads, 'biting and scratching like panthers', do to each other. Yet Davies doesn't even let his actors have that feline fun, because he's too busy having them emote – stretching out their lines, and the spaces between them, with long pauses, giving each other burning glances, and in every other way apparently trying to get behind the characters' witty repartee and excavate their true feelings.

In an interview with *The New York Times*, Rickman and Duncan revealed why. Davies, who'd never read the play until he got this job, wanted them to say the lines 'without any of the usual stuff that comes with Noël Coward' – to 'make these people real'. The problem is that there's nothing 'real' about them. In the stagey worlds of Coward's comedies, the witty repartee isn't a cover for feelings, as Davies seems to have felt; it *is* the feelings, or rather the vehicle for expressing them. In their recordings of *Private Lives*, Coward and Lawrence delight in their dialogue as if it were a tennis match, speaking briskly, each capping the other's lines; Rickman and Duncan, by contrast, took so much time delivering their volleys that it sometimes seemed as if they were hoping a 'message' would pop up in the pauses, if they could only make them big enough.

One result was to throw the play's delicate dynamics off-kilter. By making Amanda and Elyot comparatively normal (well, neurotically normal), their mates come off looking like morons, whereas they're just nice people unlucky enough to have drawn too close to the leopards' cage. (Preparing to revive the play, John Gielgud hoped to find a Sybil and Victor as *nice* as Adrianne Allen and Laurence Olivier, who'd created the roles.) What should fascinate us is the leopards: their danger, their beauty, the way they're lethal to others but necessary to each other.

The other result was what must be the longest *Private Lives* on record: Act One alone took nearly an hour. No wonder people asked Duncan if the play had been rewritten.

Deprived of Coward's fizzy pacing, *Private Lives* does just what an early reviewer of the play, for whom it 'hardly mov[ed] farther below the surface than a paper boat in a bathtub', feared it all too easily could do: become 'a shapeless, sodden mass'. (That, incidentally, is a good way to describe Louise, the hapless French maid to whom Davies, presumably out of desperation, gives a distracting series of vulgar pratfalls, as if to compensate for the lack of laughs elsewhere.) Part of the way in which Coward kept his little boats afloat was, in fact, to juxtapose, with giddy hilarity, his characters' fantasy with soggy everyday 'reality' (which is what Davies is interested in). There's a wonderful moment in the play, during the extended second-act love interlude, when Elyot starts getting frisky and Amanda rebuffs his advances on the grounds that it's 'so soon after dinner'. Angrily, Elyot accuses Amanda of having 'no sense of glamour, no sense of glamour at all'. For all its ravishing decor, this *Private Lives* is devoid of glamour; it's so suspicious of camp style that it ends up having no style at all. 'I see you're determined to make me serious, whether I like it or not,' Amanda sulks at Victor toward the end of the play. It's a line Coward might well address to Davies, if only he were here. That he isn't is all too obvious.

If Davies's Coward is rather stodgy and Victorish, the world premiere performance of *Long Island Sound*, based on an early short story called 'What Mad Pursuit?', reminds you of no one so much as poor, slapstick Louise. After his friends gave a reading of the new farce a cool reception, Coward had the good sense not to try to get it produced. No wonder: the story of a debonair English writer's hapless visit to a Long Island country house peopled by vulgar American *nouveaux riches* and their famous friends is all situation and no plot, and – not least because it assigns all the eccentricities to the frenetic Americans in order to make its victimized British hero, Evan Lorrimer, the 'good guy' – inverts the normal and usually successful structure of Coward's best comedies. (The writer's own home life was surprisingly domestic and, as his longtime companion Graham Payn recalled, '*simple*': but that simplicity, like the 'reality' that Davies wants, isn't a fruitful object of Coward's dramatic sensibility.) Even so, the play surely deserves better than the crude treatment it gets from Scot Alan Evans, whose idea of Coward style is to have men's faces shoved into women's bosoms and to allow the actor playing Don Lucas, Evan's temporary roommate, to flounce around in a dressing gown emitting high-pitched laughs – and giving a nonplussed Evan a kiss on the mouth.

In response to the first production of *Private Lives* in 1930, Ivor Brown surmised that 'within a few years, the student of drama will be sitting in complete bewilderment before the text of *Private Lives*, wondering what on earth these fellows in 1930 saw in so flimsy a trifle'. Stagings such as Davies's and Evans's, alas, produce just that sense of bewilderment. They remind us in an unfortunate way just how much Coward's texts were fragile armatures for a very specific sensibility, and in the absence of an appreciation for that sensibility, the student of drama cannot be blamed for wondering what everyone saw in Coward – why we thought him so damned amusing.

Assuming, that is, that the student of drama even knows who he is; and how should he? 'Even the youngest of us will know, in fifty years' time, exactly what we mean by "a very Noël Coward sort of person",' Kenneth Tynan confidently predicted in 1953. Fifty years later, I asked a student of mine what he thought 'a very Noël Coward person' was. The student, a Princeton undergraduate who's very involved in campus theatricals as both a performer and writer, cocked his head and gave it some thought. 'Wait,' he said. 'Noël Coward – weren't there two of him? And one was a songwriter?' Talk about bittersweet.

– *The New York Review of Books*, 27 June 2002

The Collector

It is somehow appropriate that the voice of deep and anguished ambivalence that speaks at the beginning of *Reborn*, the new volume of Susan Sontag's early journals and notebooks, does not belong to Susan Sontag. Self-doubt was not a quality you generally associated with her. From the moment she burst onto the literary scene nearly fifty years ago, with the publication of the essays subsequently collected as *Against Interpretation* – a cultural-critical Athena, armoured with a vast erudition, bristling with epigrams – Sontag exhibited a preternatural self-assurance in matters of art and culture, an unwavering belief in her own judgments and tastes that, as these early private papers now make clear, she possessed already in her early teens. (The first of a projected three volumes of Sontag's journals, this one takes her to the age of thirty; fully one-third of it is a record of her teenage years.)

The embarrassment with which *Reborn* begins belongs, rather, to her son, the writer David Rieff, who edited his mother's journals. In a preface, Rieff describes how he uneasily consented to publish this 'raw' and 'unvarnished' sampling of Sontag's adolescent effusions about life and her early perceptions about art; he shows a marked queasiness about 'the literary dangers and moral hazards of such an enterprise'. The anxiety stems from two sources. The first was ethical and, so to speak, generic: although his mother, in one of her final illnesses, was anxious for him to know where the journals were kept, there was no indication that Sontag would have wanted the contents of these papers to be made public. 'The diaries', Rieff notes, 'were written solely for herself ... She had never permitted a line from them to be published, nor, unlike some diarists, did she read from them to friends.'

Rieff's second scruple, more personal and more revealing, suggests the reason for the first:

> To say that these diaries are self-revelatory is a drastic
> understatement ... One of the principal dilemmas
> in all this has been that, at least in her later life, my
> mother was not in any way a self-revealing person.
> In particular, she avoided to the extent that she
> could, without denying it, any discussion of her own
> homosexuality or any acknowledgment of her own
> ambition.

Sexuality and ambition are, of course, the reason that many people read the private journals of public figures; in Sontag's case, the inevitable interest in the raw passions corresponding to 'homosexuality' and 'ambition' is bound to be particularly strong, because her highly polished public and literary persona seemed designed to quash interest in precisely those two things. On the one hand, there was the famous reticence about her lesbianism, despite the fact that it was, as she awkwardly admitted late in life, an 'open secret'. On the other, there was the cool Artemis-like glamour (that silver streak), the sense she projected of being the high priestess of High Culture (a sense heightened by her penchant for gnomic utterances: 'In place of a hermeneutics we need an erotics of art'; 'New York: all sensuality is converted to sexuality'). All of this conferred upon her an aura of intellectual invulnerability, of an authority that, rather than having been earned, or having evolved, she somehow had always possessed complete.

It is unlikely that readers who are motivated by prurience will be satisfied by the strangely scattered document that has resulted from Rieff's editing. (The volume has a jittery, disjointed feel; it isn't clear whether this is how the journals were written or if the published version of them was shaped to accord with Sontag's trademark aphoristic style.) What's fascinating – and, in the end, extremely suggestive – is that the journal reveals an adolescent and, later, a young woman, in whom 'ambition' – in this case, an overpowering yearning to be surrounded by and immersed in literature and culture – vastly outweighed, and seems ultimately to have overpowered, 'sexuality'. That disproportion explains a great deal about the strange career – its achievements and its fail-ures – of a writer who, as her son wrenchingly writes, 'was as uncomfortable with her body as she was serene about her mind'. Or for whom, as she herself puts it in the last entry of this journal, 'intellectual wanting' was the equal of 'sexual wanting'.

The erotic element about which David Rieff worries in his preface is, indeed, the least memorable part of Sontag's private writings, at least in this first volume. There is, to be sure, a good deal of emoting, particularly in the early entries, which are dominated by the usual sorts of adolescent anxieties. 'How easy it would be to convince myself of the plausibility of my parents' life!' she writes in 1947, at the age of fourteen, already showing the impatience with the petit-bourgeois assimilated Jewish-American back-ground into which she was born, and at which she would never look back – the impatience that would later drive her to Berkeley, then to the University of Chicago, and then to New York, where she lived for the rest of her life. 'I am in love with being in love!' she writes the next year, in one of the many girlish effusions about her already precocious erotic life that are sprinkled through the journals. (She understood that she was a lesbian very early on, and started having serious affairs as a teenager.)

Much of the material about the diarist's sentimental life constitutes a fairly typical *Bildungsgeschichte*, the record of a young person's initiation into the mysteries of adulthood. The only real surprise here is that, intriguingly for a woman of her class, culture (provincial: she grew up in Arizona), and era (she was born in 1933), Sontag did not express a great deal of anguish about homosexuality itself. The pain that she records in these pages – the journal chronicles two major lesbian relationships – is the pain that comes with any love affair, but the insights are no more illuminating, finally, than the confidences to be found in any number of such documents, straight or gay. ('Lesson: not to surrender one's heart when it's not wanted.') This is also true of the more explicit ruminations about sex itself, which are both infrequent and wholly conventional. ('Fucking vs. being fucked. The deeper experience – more gone – is being fucked.')

What you do want – what would, perhaps, be illuminating about Sontag's hitherto hidden emotional life – you don't get, at least in the text that has been published. There is almost no comment whatsoever on a notorious enigma of Sontag's early biography: her engagement, at the age of sixteen, to the sociologist Philip Rieff after a ten-day acquaintance – a decision about which this journal's near-total silence may, in the end, be more eloquent than words. As for the aftermath of that bizarre decision, there is much here about a bad marriage that, *pace* Tolstoy, seems to have been a lot like many other bad marriages, although Sontag can bring to her account of its collapse the same crisp intelligence that would make her criticism so satisfying. 'Whoever invented marriage was an ingenious tormentor,' she wrote in 1956, after nine years with Rieff. 'It is an institution committed to the dulling of feelings. The whole point of marriage is repetition. The best it aims for is the creation of strong, mutual dependencies.' She left Rieff in 1957.

So the sex isn't that good. That leaves ambition. That Sontag – the critic who emerged in the early 1960s as a Wildean champion of style wherever it could be found (camp, Godard, theatre, 'happenings', science-fiction movies, pornography), even as she brandished a formidable familiarity with the classics of the canon – was completely omnivorous and always hungry for something new, you understood from the work itself. What the early journals reveal, and what ends up, curiously, being far more moving than the material about her emotional life, is the intensity and the scope of a remarkable intellectual ambition that was present from the start: the astonishing avidity for culture, for aesthetic stimulation, that more than anything mark Sontag as a writer and a public figure. (Members of a certain generation of writers can invariably recall the play, or opera, or ballet, or opening, or reading at which they first saw Sontag: she seemed to be everywhere.) At the age of fifteen she already had an unwavering conviction of what she wanted to do and where she needed to be: 'I want to write – I want to live in an intellectual atmosphere ... I want to live in a cultural centre.' And then, later: 'I intend to do everything.'

Much of *Reborn* – and, according to Rieff's occasional interpolated commentaries, a great deal more of the original documents – consists simply of lists of 'everything': books that Sontag was determined to read, movies she had to see, poets and playwrights she had to know. An entry from 1948, when she was fifteen, looks like this:

Gide
Sherwood Anderson
Ludwig Lewisohn
Faulkner
George Moore
Dostoyevsky
Huysmans
Bourget
Arsybashev
Trumbo
Galsworthy
Meredith

poems of Dante, Ariosto, Tasso, Tibullus, Heine,
    Pushkin, Rimbaud, Verlaine, Apollinaire

plays of Synge, O'Neill, Calderon, Shaw, Hellman

In an italicized note to this passage, Rieff indicates that the list goes on for another five pages in the original.

As the years pass and the journal continues, this particular passion, at least, never abates. What strikes you is how you encounter less and less the kind of emotions most people confide to their diaries – tenderness, vulnerability, and so on. One list that is genuinely affecting, because it gives a rare glimpse of that kind of awkward vulnerability, is the one that the young woman drew up before her first trip to Paris in 1957, which reveals how nervously the already deeply francophile writer studied for her transatlantic debut:

cafe creme – white coffee after dinner
cafe au lait – breakfast coffee
une fine (brandy)
un Pernod (as many Pernods as colas in the US)

It's hard to avoid the impression that the outsized cultural avidity, the literary ambition to which these pages bear witness, seems eventually to have occluded the more tender feelings. Not the least of these was the maternal. It cannot have been easy for Rieff to come across lines such as 'I hardly ever dream of David, and don't think of him much. He has made few inroads on my fanta-sy-life.' Most editors aren't called upon for, and don't demon-strate, such probity.

Indeed, there is a strange, sometimes even shocking froideur in evidence here about subjects that most of us find hot: it is startling to grasp the extent to which Sontag brought to her own life the chilly assessing gaze that made her such a brilliant critic, such an expert looker. In one passage toward the end of the book (she is in her late twenties) she muses that 'sex as a cognitive act would be, practically, a helpful attitude for me to have, to keep my eyes open, my head up – where the point is not to show sexual excitement as long as you can. (No pelvic spasms, no hard breathing, no words, etc.)' 'Practical' and 'helpful' do not, for most of us, belong to the linguistic register that we bring to our understanding of a roll in the hay. And later on Sontag again returns to this wish 'to make sex cognitive' – and 'to correct the imbalance now'.

It isn't at all clear that the balancing act was a great success. If anything, the journal reveals a person for whom, however much she saw herself as a sensualist, the cognitive and the analytical invariably dominated the erotic and the affective. ('Emotionally, I wanted to stay,' Sontag wrote of her decision to leave home and family in Los Angeles for Berkeley. 'Intellectually, I wanted to leave.' She left.) The inevitable triumph of the head over the heart in these pages defies, I think, a description of his mother that Rieff gives in his preface: in speaking of Sontag's extraordinary literary ambition, he compares her to Balzac's Lucien de Rubempré, the hero of *Lost Illusions*, the talented youth who comes from the provinces to find literary fame in Paris. Rieff goes on to conclude with a summary characterization of Sontag as a 'nineteenth-century consciousness' – a judgment, you suspect, that Sontag, with her insatiable avidity for experience and her penchant for the continental novel as model of the highest form of literary activity, would have welcomed.

And yet when you survey her career with an eye as coolly dispassionate as the one she trained on so many objects, it becomes obvious that, temperamentally, she belonged to another century entirely. Her failure to understand just which century it was accounts for the sense you often get, taking the work as a whole, of aspirations that were at odds with her temperament and her talent; and it explains a great deal about both the strengths and the weaknesses of her work, and the strange fascination that she exerted.

If you looked closely enough, this uneasy, even riven quality was there from the start, in the breathtakingly authoritative critical pieces with which she made her reputation in the early 1960s. But as would often happen with this remarkable personality, the sheer force and stylishness of her utterances overwhelmed whatever doubts there might have been. The essays in *Against Interpretation* (1961) and in *Styles of Radical Will* (1966) may champion, famously, the need not for 'a hermeneutics but an erotics of Art', but what is so striking is that there is not anything very erotic about them; they are, in fact, all hermeneutics. In the criticism, as in the journals, the eros is all from the neck up.

The heat, if anything, tended to be generated by the objects of Sontag's interest, rather than by her investigation of them. The early forays into cultural criticism often derive their power precisely from the tension between the iciness of Sontag's Olympian gaze and the unexpectedly funky, roiling, popular objects at which she levels it: porn, movies, sci-fi, camp. There was a deep pleasure, a thrill even, in seeing how she used a formidably broad and deep learning, and the traditional tools of formal literary analysis, to turn cultural sows' ears into critical silk purses. In demonstrating the deeper cultural significance of phenomena that nobody else had thought to take seriously ('camp is the answer to the problem: how to be a dandy in the age of mass culture ... camp taste transcends the nausea of the replica'), she anticipated by a generation the belated adolescence of the American academy – all those Comp Lit and Cultural Studies dissertations, in the late 1980s and early 1990s, on Madonna and Boy George. This willingness to see the value in material disdained by 'high' culture – something for which Pauline Kael would later become famous, after Sontag's tastes ossified – was an important and satisfying part of Sontag's rhetorical persona, and went a long way toward giving her the iconoclastic allure that would cling to her for the rest of her life, however conservative her tastes were to become.

And yet this astoundingly gifted interpreter, so naturally skilled at peeling away trivial-seeming exteriors to reveal deeper cultural meanings – skilled, too, at teasing out the significance of surface features to which you might not have given much attention ('people run beautifully in Godard movies') – fought mightily to affect an 'aesthetic' disdain for content. Again and again, the essays themselves give the lie to her agenda of devaluing interpretation: even as she appears to swoon over 'the untranslatable, sensuous immediacy' of, say, *Last Year in Marienbad*, you can't help noticing that there is not a single sensuous surface that she does not try to translate into something abstract and rarefied, that is not subject to the flashing scalpel of her critical intellect. While this championing of form and especially 'style' at the expense of content and 'meaning' is hardly original – it is re-heated Wilde – what's so striking in Sontag's case is her furious insistence that it be true, her desperate need to believe the rhetorical claim that her own writing subverts.

There is an odd quality of protesting too much to these gestures, to the booming opening salvos against contemporary intellectual culture's 'hypertrophy of the intellect at the expense of energy and sensual capability', and of interpretation as 'the revenge of the intellect upon art'. As you make your way through these exercises in interpretative finesse, with their flourishes of epigrammatic bravura ('the greatest artists attain a sublime neutrality'), you wonder who is taking revenge on whom, exactly. Here again you feel the presence of an underlying conflict: Sontag the natural analyst against Sontag the struggling sensualist. You don't doubt that she genuinely wished to experience works of art purely with the senses and the emotions, but the author of these celebrated essays is quite plainly the grown-up version of the young girl who, at fifteen, declared her preference for 'virtuosity ... technique, organization ... the cruelly realistic comment (Huxley, Rochefoucauld), the mocking caricature'. Technique, virtuosity, raillery, cruelty even: all this, capped by the reference to Rochefoucauld, reminds you that, whatever her Balzacian yearnings, Sontag's young tastes were far more in line with French classicism than with Romantic passion.

*

Sontga's career as a novelist is simarly marked by a strange misapprehension of her own gifts and nature. Everything that makes her an extraordinary critic – the extreme analytical self-consciousness, the way in which she can't help but train the cool and assessing eye on every available object, the thirst for learning all the relevant and arcane details, the inability to resist any opportunity to interpret and to explain – makes her an inept novelist. There is a jarring contrast between the thrilling vividness of her critical writing and the almost total inertness of her fiction. And yet, she clung stubbornly to a view of herself as essentially a writer of novels and stories, from her claim in the preface to *Against Interpretation* that her critical essays were largely ancillary to her fiction, helping her to 'radically change' her 'conception of [her] task as a novelist', to her pronouncement, in a speech she gave on accepting a prize in Germany in 2003, that 'I am a storyteller.'

Her fiction suggests otherwise – from the strained exercise in francophilia that was *The Benefactor* in 1963, replete with the kind of archness and striving for effect that so often result when critics aspire to fiction ('he always spoke across the unbesiegeable moat of his own chastity') to *The Volcano Lover*, in 1992, and *In America*, in 2000. In all of these, the critic's analytical and self-examining eye dominates, explaining too much, getting in the way. In both *The Volcano Lover*, a kind of intellectual recasting of *That Hamilton Woman*, and *In America*, a highly self-referential fictionalization of the career of the nineteenth-century Polish actress Helena Modjeska, Sontag herself, in the form of a disembodied narrator's voice, hovers intrusively over the story that she claims to want to tell, commenting on the action, distracting your attention from the story by reminding us that this is a Susan Sontag production. 'Appalled by the lethal upsurge of nationalist and tribal feelings in my own time,' the narrator of *In America* says, apropos of some ruminations about her Polish characters' national history, 'I'd spent a good part of three years in besieged Sarajevo.' There is no aesthetic reason, nothing in the form or the narrative, for the reader to have this information. Sontag just can't get out of the way. You suspect that this arch carrying on was meant to be justified as a playful, even chicly postmodern device, but Sontag was too solemn and self-serious a writer to get away with such tricks, and the intrusions come off as merely pretentious.

The Sontag that the author of the later fiction seems to think we want is not even Sontag the great critic: it's just 'Sontag', the celebrated public figure. Already in *The Volcano Lover*, but particularly in the unbearably laboured and self-conscious *In America*, the authorial interventions feel not only self-referential but also self-congratulatory. Even the true believers who felt that *In America* deserved the acclaim it received must have stumbled over passages such as the following one, in which, as the novel opens, the hovering Sontag-narrator explains how she manages to understand the conversation of the Polish characters she mysteriously finds herself observing at the beginning of her tale:

> But I, with my command only of Romance languages
> (I dabble in German, know the names of twenty kinds
> of fish in Japanese, have soaked up a splash of Bosnian,
> and understand barely a word of the language of the
> country in which this room is to be found), I, as I've
> said, somehow did manage to understand most of what
> they were saying.

The command 'only' of Romance languages; the pompous advertisement for what we understand to be her sophisticated appreciation of sushi and sashimi – stuff like this, and there is a lot of it, makes you wish that Sontag had hoped more fervently for herself what, as the narrator of *In America*, she 'hoped' for her protagonist: that 'she hadn't been made less of an artist by high-minded-ness. Or by self-regard.'

The great irony of her career is that her apparent conviction, derived from her early immersion in nineteenth-century European literature, that to be a significant literary figure you had to be a novelist, paradoxically blinded her to what already made her a significant literary figure. There's a passage in *Regarding the Pain of Others*, a slender critical work published in 2003, in which, making a case about the special rhetorical quality of photography, she observes that 'photographs [are] both objective record and personal testimony, both a faithful copy or transcription of an actual moment of reality and an interpretation of that reality – a feat literature has long aspired to, but could never attain in this literal sense'. But of course literature does possess a genre that strives to be both objective and personal, an accurate record and a subjective testimony, a representation and an interpretation at the same time, and it's the genre at which Sontag really excelled: criticism. That she could write such a passage – that it never occurred to her to think of her own métier when thinking about what literature could do – is more wrenching than anything she ever wrote in her fiction.

The contrast between the pointed effectiveness and verbal élan of Sontag's critical writing and the bloated grandiosities of her fiction makes it that much more regrettable that, as time passed, the criticism itself seemed to metamorphose, to change direction and tone.

Like Wilde, whose arguments and aphoristic dazzle she appro-priated, Sontag achieved considerable fame and authority early on by rebelling against staid, academic, old-fashioned intellectual culture. And like Wilde, she paradoxically used the tools provided by a formidable traditional education (he as a classicist, she as a student of philosophy and a precocious autodidact) to reject the academy, carving out a career for herself instead as a popular literary figure – a move that surely accounts for the cult-like status that she, like Wilde, enjoyed. Both were intellectuals who made good, who achieved glamour in the great world. And yet, once she had made her name with those extraordinarily cunning and excitingly fresh validations of popular American culture, Sontag went on to spend the rest of her career as a tireless cheerleader for the canon, for what she referred to, with telling frequency, as 'greatness' – a quality that, strikingly, she seemed increasingly to find only in the works of middle-aged, white, European men.

This is most apparent in the later essays, such as those collected in *Where the Stress Falls* (2001). These pieces were written in the years after she published the last of her significant works of cultural criticism, *Illness as Metaphor* and *AIDS and Its Metaphors* – texts in which she brilliantly brings a calm philological eye to reveal the cultural anxieties and prejudices that lie beneath the overwrought diction of pop epidemiology and professional medicine. The problem with *Where the Stress Falls* is, in fact, that there is not a whole lot of stress in evidence. There is a played-out feel about the book, whose serious critical reflections are increasingly rambling and diffuse, and whose many incidental pieces seem, more than anything, like advertisements for Sontag's status as a cultural icon: answers to French questionnaires about the role of intellectuals, for example, and self-flattering ruminations on being translated. ('You might say I'm obsessed with translations. I think I'm just obsessed with language.' What writer isn't?)

This exhaustion is even more marked in the collection published after Sontag died in 2004, called *At the Same Time*, which includes the now-notorious speech in which she seems to have plagiarized her observations about hypertext: the ultimate mark of creative exhaustion. But a critical tendency does emerge. The vast majority of these late and ostensibly critical pieces are encomia to (and sometimes eulogies for) a long list of European (preferably *Mittel-*) men: Victor Serge, W. G. Sebald, Robert Walser, Danilo Kis, Joseph Brodsky, Witold Gombrowicz, Adam Zagajewski. The essays are curiously shorter and more desultory than the early pieces; there is a restless quality even to the project of praise, which Sontag very early on saw as her speciality. ('I don't, ultimately, care for handing out grades to works of art,' she wrote in a later preface to *Against Interpretation*. 'I wrote as an enthusiast and a partisan.') Walser, for whom she professes to want to perform her signal service and thereby 'bring [him] to the attention of a public that has not yet discovered him', gets a scant two pages, which end with the kind of banal encomium, a blurb really, that you expect from the harried reviewers in the dailies: 'a truly wonderful writer'.

Compare all this to the forty-two densely packed pages of her thrillingly brilliant 1968 dissection of Godard, for whose reputation she set out to perform a similar service. In that instance Sontag was providing a rigorous and wholly original way of thinking about the complex work of a major young contemporary artist; it was an essay that felt like part of something vital that was happening in the arts. In the Walser piece, by contrast, you get a whiff of Lemon Pledge: she's dusting off a forgotten tchotchke and putting it back on the very high shelf from which it had fallen. The style, too, is diminished, wearied. The surgical gleam and 'aphoristic glitter' – Sontag's admiring description of Glenway Wescott's style in *The Pilgrim Hawk* – of the strong youthful pieces come more and more to be replaced here by expressions of anxious concern for the safety of High Culture. 'Is literary greatness still possible?' she frets in the slim essay on Sebald.

All this suggests, in the end, a certain melancholy fulfilment of a prophecy that Sontag made in her journals when she was in her early twenties. Not long before her twenty-fourth birthday, she wondered to herself which of two roads she might take, and the question she posed suggests that she understood more, then, about the divided nature of both her gifts and her ambitions – the struggle, not least, between genuine innovation and intelligent adulation – than some of her later pronouncements, and projects, might indicate. The answer, too, was prescient. 'To philosophize, or to be a culture-conserver?' she wondered in October, 1956. 'I had never thought of being anything other than the latter.'

Anyway, what had 'greatness' come to mean for Sontag? It was, for a start, almost exclusively identified with Europe. In his preface Rieff acknowledges that for his mother 'American literature was a suburb of the great literatures of Europe,' and he is right: Sontag devoted none of her remarkable interpretative energies to significant American writers, either of an earlier time or of her own. The most effusive of her literary encomia, indeed, often come at the expense of the Anglo-American tradition. 'When has one heard in English a voice of such confidence and precision, so direct in its expression of feeling, yet so respectfully devoted to recording "the real"?' she asks in her piece on Sebald, the last in the string of German novelists whom she exalted, an adulation that started with her life-altering reading of *The Magic Mountain* as a teenager. (In *Reborn* Sontag records her meeting with Mann when she was fourteen and he seventy-two, and both were living in Los Angeles; rather typically, she expresses disappointment that the flesh and blood person failed to live up to the books.) And, as the list of writers whom Sontag does choose to exalt in collections such as *Where the Stress Falls* also suggests, 'greatness' seems to be largely the property of men, and is most likely to be achieved through the writing of novels. And so, in the end, Sontag became a genuine traditionalist – not only a conserver but also, at least in matters of culture, a conservative.

This desire to be associated with 'greatness' of a kind that is, when all is said and done, exceedingly old-fashioned, brings you back to the Sontag of the early journals – to the 'ambition', to the starry-eyed lover of books who reminds Rieff of Lucien de Rubempré. Lucien's real name is the comically plebeian Chardon, or 'thistle': he has to shake the family tree a bit before the surname that he eventually adopts, with its glamorous aristocratic 'de', falls out. The desire not merely for self-transformation, but for a kind of validation that only an association with the highest echelons of culture can bring, is one to which *Reborn* bears ample witness. As his name change indicates, Lucien's aspirations were social as well as artistic; Sontag, to her great credit, was purely intellectual and cultural in her ambitions. Her desire, twice articulated in these pages, to be 'reborn' itself testifies to the fervour of her belief that it was necessary to abandon where she came from in order to get where she wanted to be – an impetus that may well never have found an end point, and that itself may have seemed to her a mark of 'greatness'.

The obsession with 'greatness' also has other implications. There is, you realize, something odd about the list of qualities that she herself associated with literary greatness: it is a list of things that Sontag was not. The sense you get here of a profoundly divided identity is, for Rieff, entirely consonant with his mother's taste for transformation, the lifelong effort to 'remake herself'. Anticipating the questions about self-knowledge and identity that such efforts inevitably raise about people, he hints that what in other people could be seen as embarrassment, a kind of covering up, was in Sontag's case exemplary. Casting her strenuous 'jettisoning' of her middle-class, American, Jewish roots ('her social and ethnic context', as he puts it) as a heroic nineteenth-century, and even somewhat Nietzschean, affair – the achievement of a titanic 'will' – he cites Fitzgerald on second acts in American lives, a nice way of suggesting that Sontag's increasing dissociation from things American was the most American thing about her.

But this pervasive irresolution and desperate desire for transformation can also be ascribed to another factor, to the other of the two strands that unspool in *Reborn* – not to ambition, but to sexuality. In this case, the instability had a marked effect on Sontag's engagement with politics. I am referring to the issue of the writer's homosexuality, which she discussed forthrightly enough in her private musings, but about which she remained curiously reticent even when such reticence was no longer expected of important left-wing intellectuals – indeed, when to come out of the closet would have been an affirmation of a certain kind of cultural bona fides.

It is a measure of the intimidating power of Sontag's mystique that comparatively little has been made over the years of the refusal by this, the most public of public intellectuals, to engage – in her speeches and her essays – with the pressing issues raised particularly by the AIDS crisis and the political and cultural controversies that it generated throughout the 1980s and 1990s. It says something that when Sontag did write about homosexuality, it was in a work of fiction: the now-famous short story 'The Way We Live Now', first published in the *New Yorker* in November, 1986. (It is a story about men, about male homosexuals and their experience: a suggestive displacement.) Any notion that she might have connected the dots between her sexual nature and her public utterances on power and justice tended to be cast as a vulgar parochialization, a crass infringement upon her citizenship in the wider republic of letters. Rieff, as we know, acknowledged that his mother 'avoided to the extent that she could, without denying it, any discussion of her own homosexuality'. Much depends on that 'without denying it'. Sontag's passivity in this regard may have been the only feeble thing about her; she was, after all, no stranger to controversy. She herself was almost touchingly forthright about her ambiguity, in remarks she made late in life to the editor of *Out* magazine:

> I grew up in a time when the modus operandi was the 'open secret.' I'm used to that, and quite OK with it. Intellectually, I know why I haven't spoken more about my sexuality, but I do wonder if I haven't repressed something there to my detriment. Maybe I could have given comfort to some people if I had dealt with the subject of my private sexuality more, but it's never been my prime mission to give comfort, unless somebody's in drastic need. I'd rather give pleasure, or shake things up.

The passage is wholly typical. Apart from the characteristic tension between the mind ('intellectually, I know why') and the heart, and a certain awkwardness reflected in the stiffness and the circuitousness of the language ('I do wonder if I haven't repressed something there'), the statement represents yet another triumph of that ferocious intellect at the expense of the realm of feelings. Note the reflexively disdainful dismissal of any possibility that she might have spoken publicly about issues relating to homosexuality as a merely sentimental gesture, a treacly project of 'giving comfort'.

But as we know, Sontag certainly wasn't above giving comfort to groups that she saw as oppressed, and she didn't disdain making large and dramatic public gestures meant to validate the rights, and the humanity, of certain minorities. About the citizens of

Bosnia, that province of Mitteleuropa that became one of her intellectual homelands, about Europe and its political outrages, Sontag never ceased to speak, with her usual crispness and a smart, outraged passion. All this was deeply admirable. But finally there was something familiar about the way in which she championed the foreign over the domestic, the idealized identity rather than the core identity. *Intellectually I wanted to go.* As we know, she went; and to be sure, there is a kind of touching grandeur to the famous *folie* of her producing *Waiting for Godot* in Sarajevo under siege, which, whatever else it may have achieved, certainly gave comfort.

My point is not to correct Sontag politically; nor do I want to denigrate the significant positive effects of her political arguments and activities. Everyone, after all, is self-interpreting and self-inventing – writers and artists more than most. Sontag was a true cosmopolitan, and that is an achievement not only of morality but also of imagination. But cosmopolitanism, too, is a set of choices, and Sontag's choices in the realm of politics strikingly resemble her choices in the realm of literature and culture. At a certain point you have to ask why there was this unquenchable need to comfort, this limitless sympathy, for Bosnians, but not for lesbians.

In the end, it was Sontag herself who gave us the most useful metaphor for understanding her. The key is to be found in *The Volcano Lover*, a work whose ambivalent seesawing between two crucial centuries, between two irreconcilable world-views, tells us more than anything else she wrote about the uneasy divisions in Sontag herself.

The novel is an unusual take on a famous story: the love affair between Emma Hamilton and Admiral Nelson. It is told primarily through the eyes of Emma's cuckolded husband, Sir William Hamilton, the great collector of classical antiquities who, as British envoy to the Kingdom of the Two Sicilies, in Naples, had the pick of the splendid works that emerged from the excavations at Pompeii and Herculaneum; these helped to create the great craving for all things classical (and neo-classical) that marked the end of the eighteenth century. A good deal of the book is devoted to brilliant ruminations on the nature and the psychology of collecting, a passion apparently shared by the Sontag-like narrator who, like the narrator of *In America*, hovers obtrusively over the opening of the novel. 'I'm seeing,' this disembodied voice says, during a visit to what seems to be a flea market,

> I'm checking on what's in the world. What's left.
> What's discarded. What's no longer cherished. What
> had to be sacrificed. What someone thought might
> interest someone else … there may be something
> valuable, there. Not valuable, exactly. But something I
> would want. Want to rescue. Something that speaks to
> me. To my longings.

As we know, a taste for 'checking on what's in the world', to say nothing of aesthetic rescue missions, constituted a significant part of Sontag's critical project. Hamilton's own characterization of the point of his activities – 'To surround oneself with enchanting and stimulating objects, a superfluity of objects, to ensure that the sense will never be unoccupied, nor the faculty of imagination left unexercised' – reminds you even more strongly of the author, with her frenetic desire to be aesthetically stimulated, occupied, exercised. The sense of a strong identification is palpable. Not surprisingly, this novel was the closest to a real literary success that her fiction ever achieved.

The metaphor of the collector is the perfect one for Sontag. Her impressive sympathy for Hamilton, with his great hunger for inanimate objects, explains so much about her – the unbelievable avidity, the impossibility of satiety, the need to possess it all, to know 'everything'. And it provides, too, another explanation for her incessant promotion, toward the end of her career, of 'greatness': like all good collectors, she wanted you to know how precious her objects were, how much they were worth. Small wonder that some of her most intense aesthetic enthusiasms were inspired by collectors – William Hamilton; Walter Benjamin, in his library and in the arcades; Godard. She wrote feelingly about the latter's 'hypertrophy of appetite for culture (though often more avid for cultural debris than for museum-consecrated achievements); they proceed by voraciously scavenging in culture, proclaiming that nothing is alien to their art'. It would be hard to think of a better description of Sontag herself.

As it proceeds, *The Volcano Lover* moves away from the eighteenth century, from the cool acquisitive gaze of the Enlightenment, to the grand passions of the Romantic century that followed. (The book's coy subtitle is 'A Romance'.) In the novel, headlong passions are represented by two narrative threads, one 'personal' and one 'political', that become intertwined. The first is the adulterous love of Nelson and Emma (who abandons, you might say, the love of the old for the love of the new – the elderly Hamilton for the war hero Nelson), and the second is an ongoing series of references to the violent revolutions with which the eighteenth century ended – in particular, the brief republican revolution in Naples in 1799, which resulted in the short-lived overthrow of the Bourbon monarchy. Nelson, on orders from London, gave military support, as Hamilton gave diplomatic support. (Emma, for her part, was the bosom friend of the queen, Maria Carolina, sister of Marie-Antoinette.) With Nelson's aid, the republic was soon overthrown and the repressive monarchy was re-established.

But if the novel moves you, it is – as sometimes occurs in Sontag's writing – because of something that is happening between the lines. Everything about Hamilton, about the collector, is wonderful: the evocation of what it is like to live a life given to intellectual and aesthetic pursuits, the rich sense that Sontag gives of what it's like to 'discover what is beautiful and to share that with others', an activity that Hamilton passionately defends as 'also a worthy employment for a life'. And yet, against all narrative and logical expectation, Sontag ends by wrenching the novel (and the reader's sympathy) away from Hamilton who, we perceive, will not be the hero. That role, it turns out, is given to a person who comes late on the scene: another historical figure, Eleonora de Fonseca Pimentel, a Neapolitan aristocrat and poet who sided with the republican rebels and was executed by the restored Bourbons as the exhausted century ended, in August 1799. The book ends with her musings at the moment of her death – reflections that comprise a stunning rejection of the character, and indeed the values, that Sontag has so feelingly evoked throughout the book. 'Did he ever have an original thought,' Pimentel furiously wonders about Hamilton,

> or subject himself to the discipline of writing a poem,
> or discover or invent something useful to humanity, or
> burn with zeal for anything except his own pleasures
> and the privileges annexed to his station? He knew
> enough to appreciate what the picturesque natives
> had left in the way of art and ruins, lying about the
> ground …

And the novel's last lines make a final overt allusion to Sontag herself, one that suggests that she saw her political engagement as an expression of this 'romantic' side:

> Sometimes I had to forget that I was a woman to
> accomplish the best of which I was capable. Or I
> would lie to myself about how complicated it is to be
> a woman. Thus do all women, including the author
> of this book. But I cannot forgive those who did not
> care about more than their own glory or wellbeing.
> They thought they were civilized. They were despicable.
> Damn them all.

Anyone who has considered Sontag's career will find that 'damn them all' profoundly affecting; it expresses, yet again, her desire to forsake who she was in favour of a romantic dream. *The Volcano Lover* makes it clear that Sontag's sensibility was the eighteenth-century one that she so successfully evoked in the character of Hamilton, whom she ends by damning. And yet this aesthete and accumulator of experience nonetheless yearned all her life – because she was so taught by the kind of novels that she ingested but could not, in the end, ever write – to inhabit the century to which her son touchingly assigns her, the nineteenth, with its grand passions and its Romantic energies. Emotionally, she thought she was the one; intellectually, she was the other. This confusion helps to account for so much about her life and her work: the strange analytical coldness about normal human passions – that desire to make sex 'cognitive' – and the remarkably hot passion for the stimulation of books, theatre, films; the initial embrace of the importance of the daringly new, the avant garde, the louche and outré, followed by the retreat into the conventional (the historical novel!), the canonical, the established, the 'great'; the wobbly relationship between the criticism, which was her calling, and the fiction, which was not.

This lifelong struggle to find a place between these various poles – extremities nicely summed up, in *The Volcano Lover*, during an amusing encounter between Hamilton and Goethe, as 'beauty' and 'transformation' – gives Sontag a certain novelistic allure of her own. But here again the character whom she calls to mind is a decidedly pre-Romantic figure. In one of the shortest literary essays that she ever wrote, Sontag ruminated on a favourite novel, and her description of its hero suggests a strong affinity between the critic and the character:

> With Don Quixote, a hero of excess, the problem is not
> so much that the books are bad; it is the sheer quantity
> of his reading. Reading has not merely deformed his
> imagination; it has kidnapped it. He thinks the world
> is the inside of a book … Bookishness makes him,
> in contrast to Emma Bovary, beyond compromise or
> corruption. It makes him mad; it makes him profound,
> heroic, genuinely noble.

Thanks to her son's nervous but rewarding decision, Sontag herself has finally achieved a kind of resolution. For she has made the translation that, you sometimes feel, she had always yearned for and so long awaited. Now others must do the interpreting; she herself, beyond compromise and corruption, no madder than most and more noble, too, has become the text. Infinitely interpretable, she has at last ended up on the inside of a book.

The End of the Road

'We shall never get to Constantinople like this.' This rueful aside, which comes toward the end of the first of the three books that the late Patrick Leigh Fermor devoted to his youthful travels on foot across Europe in the early 1930s, was to prove prophetic. 'Like this' ostensibly refers to the author's weakness for detours. By this point in *A Time of Gifts* – written some four decades after that remarkable journey and first published in 1977 – it is late in 1933, and the high-spirited, precocious, poetry-spouting eighteen-year-old, long since expelled from school ('a dangerous mixture of sophistication and recklessness', a housemaster clucked), weary of England, and hungry for adventure, finds himself in Czechoslovakia, having walked from the Hook of Holland through the Low Countries, southern Germany, and Austria, his battered copies of *The Oxford Book of English Verse* and Horace's *Odes* firmly, famously in hand.

His plan at this point was to follow the Danube all the way to the Black Sea, whence he would head south to Constantinople – the name by which the romantic-minded youth, his head brimming with memorized verse, insisted on calling Istanbul. But in Bratislava, with Hungary and the continuation of his southeasterly route shimmering just across the great river, he finds himself unable to resist a Czech friend's invitation to go north to see Prague, that 'bewildering and captivating town'.

Here, as often with this erudite and garrulous author – the dashing autodidact and Second World War hero, considered by some to be the greatest travel writer of the twentieth century – the geographical digression becomes a narrative one. As the impecunious Leigh Fermor zigzags around the city, the guest of his better-heeled and well-connected friend (the blithe sponging off obliging students, postmistresses, madams, diplomats, and aristocrats is an amusing leitmotif of his travels), goggling at the castles and bridges, the relics and the nightclubs, the text goggles and zigzags, too. And so we carom from the murder of the tenth-century Bohemian leader we know as 'Good King Wenceslas' (actually, a duke; later a saint) to the brief *Mitteleuropäisch* reign of James I's daughter, the so-called Winter Queen; from swoony evocations of medieval architectural details ('in King Vladislav's vast Hall of Homage the ribs of the vaulting had further to travel, higher to soar') to the tale of the Defenestration of Prague in 1618; from Kabala, Rosicrucians, the 'sad charm' of the Habsburgs, and the tomb of the creator of the Golem to a triumphant conclusion (via an offhand rumination about the identity of Shakespeare's Mr W. H.) in which the teenaged narrator believes he has solved the mystery of where the mysterious 'coast of Bohemia' in *The Winter's Tale* could possibly have been. It is only after all this that the Leigh Fermor of 1933 heads south once again, to the Danube and his planned itinerary.

So it is possible to take 'we shall never get to Constantinople like this' as a humorous acknowledgment by the author of a helpless penchant for digressions literal and figurative, one that will be familiar to anyone who has read even a few pages of Leigh Fermor's books: the early one about the Caribbean, *The Traveller's Tree* (1950); a slender volume called *A Time to Keep Silence* (1957), about his visits to three monastic communities; *Mani* (1958) and *Roumeli* (1966), his two lively and impassioned books about Greece, the country he loved best and where he ended up living part-time; and of course the trilogy of his walk across Europe – *A Time of Gifts* and its sequel, *Between the Woods and the Water* (1986), the first two instalments, now completed by the posthumous publication last year of an unfinished final volume, *The Broken Road*.

The author's chattiness, his inexhaustible willingness to be distracted, his susceptibility to geographical, intellectual, aesthetic, and occasionally amorous detours, constitute, if anything, an essential and self-conscious component of the style that has won him such an avid following. It has more than a little in common with the 'centrifugal lambency and recoil' he found in Central European design, the 'swashbuckling, exuberant and preposterous' aesthetic that he so extravagantly admired in a picture of Maximilian I's knights, which he came across one night while leafing through a book on German history in the luxurious apartment of a charming girl he met and ended up staying with in Stuttgart. (The strange new city, the chance meeting, the aesthetic reverie, the hints of money and eros: this would prove to be the pattern of the young man's progress across the continent.)

It is indeed odd that, among the many classical authors to whom Leigh Fermor refers in his writing (none more famously than Horace, verses of whose 'Soracte Ode' the author found himself swapping, in Latin, with a German general he had kidnapped on Crete during the Second World War, a famous incident that was later turned into a film starring Dirk Bogarde), Herodotus does not figure more prominently. There is no ancient writer whose technique Leigh Fermor's more closely resembles. Expansive, meandering, circular, it allows him to weave what is, after all, a relatively straightforward tale of a youthful backpacking hike into a vast and highly coloured tapestry, embroidered

with observations, insights, and lessons about the whole pano-
rama of European history, society, architecture, religion, and art.

And yet the author's charming and useful tendency to lose
track of his destination became a serious real-life problem in the
case of the books about the walk across Europe – the most beloved
of his works, which have achieved the status of cult classics
particularly among adventure-bent youth. ('Those bibles of
backpacking seekers everywhere': so Joshua Jelly-Schapiro, a
young California-based writer and geographer who wrote the
preface to a recent reissue of *The Traveller's Tree* by New York
Review Books, which has now republished nearly all of the
author's work.) However many the detours, Leigh Fermor's
youthful journey did have a destination, which the author finally
reached: he got to 'Constantinople' on New Year's Eve, 1935, a
little shy of his twenty-first birthday.

The two instalments he eventually published committed him
inexorably to writing about that climactic arrival. *A Time of Gifts*,
which ends with Leigh Fermor arriving at last in Hungary – he
crosses the Danube from Slovakia in the spring, just in time to
witness a magnificent Easter service at the Basilica of Estergom
– closes with the legend 'TO BE CONTINUED'. *Between the Woods
and the Water* concludes in much the same way. Having followed
its young hero through many a Hungarian and Yugoslavian
castle's 'antlered corridor', the narrative of this second volume
brings him at last to the Iron Gates, the gorge on the Danube that
forms the boundary between Serbia and Romania. It is the Feast
of the Dormition of the Virgin, Leigh Fermor is in his nineteenth
summer, and the book bids him farewell with an all-caps promise:
'TO BE CONCLUDED'. (That the climaxes of both works are
marked by great religious events is not accidental: the *mondain*
and sensual Leigh Fermor, who always knew how to find his way
into a count's castle or a duchess's good graces – Somerset

Maugham once dismissed him as a 'middle-class gigolo for upper-class women' – was beguiled by religious ceremonials; and, perhaps not so paradoxically, by intense religious feeling.)

But the conclusion never came. When Leigh Fermor died in 2011, at ninety-six, he had been afflicted by a writer's block that had lasted a quarter of a century. Soon after the publication of *Between the Woods and the Water* in the 1980s, he was already worried that the subject was, in the words of his friend and biographer Artemis Cooper, 'stale' and 'written out'. In the early 1990s, his wife Joan wrote to a friend that he was 'sadly stuck'; not long after, Charlotte Mosley, who at the time was editing a volume of Leigh Fermor's correspondence with the Duchess of Devonshire (another distraction), observed that 'it takes his mind off Vol III which is clearly never going to appear'. Given his predilection for wandering, invention, and improvisation, it may well be that the mounting expectations about the final volume had caused a kind of creative paralysis. The feverish anticipation wasn't limited to his friends. When Leigh Fermor's name appeared on the 2004 Honours List, a fan wrote a letter to the *Daily Telegraph* declaring that the knighthood should be conditional on finishing the trilogy.

It now turns out that the work was, in a way, already complete. As you learn from the preface to *The Broken Road* (edited by Artemis Cooper and the novelist and travel writer Colin Thubron), a preliminary draft describing the last leg of his European adventure had been composed long before, in fact when the idea for the books about the walking tour first germinated. In the early 1960s, Leigh Fermor was invited by the editor of *Holiday* to write an article on the 'pleasures of walking'. As he began to write about his youthful journey, the floodgates of memory opened; he wrote to his longtime publisher and friend John Murray that the article had soon 'ripened out of all recognition'. After nearly seventy manuscript pages he'd only got as far as the Iron Gates – at which point, frustrated by the need for compression, he began to write at the more expansive, elaborated pace he preferred, bringing his narrative as far as his arrival at the shores of the Black Sea.

This manuscript, tentatively known as 'A Youthful Journey', eventually formed the basis for the whole trilogy. After setting the pages aside for a decade (during which time he published *Roumeli* and built a fabulous house for himself in the Mani, the Wild West-ish tip of the southern Peloponnese, about which he also wrote: more distractions), the author went back to the beginning, expanding those compressed first seventy pages into what became the richly wrought narratives of *A Time of Gifts* and *Between the Woods and the Water*.

It was only when he was in his early nineties that Leigh Fermor finally summoned the will to confront the decades-old pages covering the final third of his journey, from the Iron Gates to the Black Sea – the part he'd slowed down to treat at greater length in the original manuscript – and painstakingly set about elaborating them in his inimitable style.

The text he was working on at his death, along with excerpts from his original travel journal – brief entries covering his stay in Istanbul and a much longer narrative about his visit to the monasteries of Mount Athos – make up *The Broken Road*: the long-awaited 'Vol. III'. Precisely because its author didn't have time to bring his text to its usual level of high and brilliant polish, this final work – plainer, more straightforward, less elaborate, and more frank than its predecessors – provides some intriguing retrospective insights into Leigh Fermor's distinctive tics and mannerisms, strengths and weaknesses.

*

In a review of *Mani* that appeared when the book was first published, Lawrence Durrell referred to the 'truffled style and dense plumage' of Leigh Fermor's prose. What you think of his writing, and indeed what you make of the final instalment of his most beloved work, depends on your taste for truffles and feathers.

Structural rigour was, as we know, never Leigh Fermor's strong point – inevitably, perhaps, in the case of narratives that follow a real-life itinerary. The two walking-tour books published during his lifetime have a fortuitous coherence – he is, after all, heading *somewhere* – but what holds the others together are the intensity of the author's curiosity about whatever happens to (literally) cross his path, and the brilliance of his talk about them: the 'saga boys' of Trinidad in their wildly patterned shirts, 'worn with a flaunting ease and a grace of deportment that compels nothing but admiration'; the nomadic Sarakatsáns of the northern Greek region called Roumeli (*Roumeli* opens with a dazzling set piece about a Sarakatsán wedding); the *miroloyia* or funeral dirges that are the only poetry prevalent in the Mani; Jewish lumbermen in Romania; the Uniotes of Eastern Europe, who observe the Eastern Rite while submitting to the authority of Rome (a recurrent object of fascination).

Small wonder that a salient feature of Leigh Fermor's style is the long list, that most unconstructed of devices. His penchant for lengthy enumerations confirms your sense that what delights this writer most is the sheer abundance in the world of things for him to look at and learn about. *Mani* memorably opens with one such enumeration, in this case of the varieties of Greek communities throughout the world (to which the author hopes to add a group of Jews who, he has heard, live in the Mani):

I thought of the abundance of strange communities:
the scattered Bektashi and the Rufayan, the Mevlevi
dervishes of the Tower of the Winds, the Liaps of
Souli, the Pomaks of the Rhodope, the Kizilbashi near
Kechro, the Fire-Walkers of Mavrolevki, the Lazi from
the Pontic shores ... the phallus-wielding Bounariots
of Tyrnavos, the Karamandlides of Cappadocia, the
Tzakones of the Argolic gulf ... the Basilian Monks
... both Idiorrhythmic and Cenobitic, the anchorites
of Mt Athos, the Chiots of Bayswater and the Guards'
Club ... the Shqip-speaking Atticans of Sfax ...
the exaggerators and the ghosts of Mykonos, the
Karagounides of the Thessalian plain ... the princes
and boyars of Moldowallachia, the Ralli Brothers of
India ... the lepers of Spinalonga – if all these, to name
a few, why not the crypto-Jews of the Taygetus?

There is an incantatory charm about such accumulations that, among other things, neutralizes the critical faculty. I have read this book three times – it is by far his best, a work in which the author's high style finds an appropriate correlative in the piratical dash of his favourite region's inhabitants – and have still never bothered to find out just who the 'exaggerators of Mykonos' might be. Such stylistic prestidigitation is an advantage when you are a fabulist like Leigh Fermor, who admitted late in life to having distorted and elaborated his ostensibly nonfiction works.

A related stylistic tic, born of the author's resistance to the strictures of factuality and his relish for long concatenations of chewy words, is the occasional flights of prose in which he indulges in extended imaginative riffs that allow him to leave, briefly, whatever scene he happens to find himself in and provide a bird's-eye view of some bit of geography or history. Some of these, like the one in *Mani* in which the cock-a-doodle-doo of an Athenian rooster is picked up, from bird to bird, until it spreads around the world ('swelling now, sweeping south across the pampas, the Gran Chaco, the Rio Grande … to the maelstroms and the tempests, the hail and the darkness and the battering waves of Cape Horn'), are little more than self-indulgences.

But others can be deliciously pointed. In the same book, the author excitedly pays a call on a humble fisherman named Strati who, he has heard, is a remote descendant of an imperial Byzantine dynasty. As the kindly man tediously recounts the story of a near disaster at sea, Leigh Fermor sits across from him, constructing a private fantasy in which this last scion of the Paleologues is whisked to Istanbul to be crowned at Hagia Sophia as the emperor of a restored Byzantium. The increasingly funny oscillation between the two narratives and two narrative styles – one bejewelled ('Semantra hammered and cannon thundered as the Emperor stepped ashore; then, with a sudden reek of naphtha, Greek fire roared saluting in a hundred blood-red parabolas from the warships' brazen beaks'), the other plainspoken ('I was never in a worse situation! … There I was, on all fours in the bilge water, baling for life') – becomes a tart vehicle for ruminating about the special burden of history that contemporary Greece has to deal with.

A drawback of these predilections is that the books can sometimes feel like agglomerations of showy set pieces. (In her biography, Artemis Cooper describes Leigh Fermor's mother, a bright and talented woman who found herself married to a dour geologist, as someone who 'sparkled a little too brightly'; the son could be like that, too.) *Roumeli*, in particular, is a stew in which the ingredients, delicious as many are, never quite blend. At one point the author gets so bored with the book's nominal subject that he writes at length about his years in Crete, which clearly he felt more passionately about. John Murray once observed, as Leigh Fermor was preparing to write his first book, that 'there is no doubt that he can write though sometimes rather incoherently'; the problem, he went on, was to give the book 'a sense of purpose'. It would remain a problem.

A certain narrative purposefulness, an organic shape, might, in other hands, have derived from the autobiographical impulse: the tale of a young man's walk across Europe in the years just before World War II could, indeed, have made an ideal vehicle for a stirring *Bildung* narrative. But between his British distaste for public introspection and his magpie's curiosity, Leigh Fermor is at his best when he avoids emotions and hews to the bright surfaces of things. He's fascinated by, and knows an astonishing amount about, the glamour of history, the glitter of ceremonial, the gilt on a reliquary; and he knows how to make them gleam for us, too.

Leigh Fermor's travel books are the works of a great talker, and his strong points are those of the best conversationalists. He has, to begin with, a memorably vivid turn of phrase. Turkish loan-words in modern Greek are like 'a wipe of garlic round a salad bowl'; Armenians whom he encounters in Sofia are 'grouped, their eyes bright with acumen on either side of their wonderful noses, in the doors of their shops, like confabulating toucans'. His deep affection and admiration for the Greeks are reflected in particularly colourful and suggestive writing. There is a passage in *Mani* in which the letters of the Greek alphabet become characters in a little drama meant to suggest the intensity of that people's passion for disputation:

> I often have the impression, listening to a Greek
> argument, that I can actually see the words spin from
> their mouths like the long balloons in comic strips ...
> the perverse triple loop of Xi, the twin concavity of
> Omega ... Phi like a circle transfixed by a spear ... At
> its climax it is as though these complex shapes were
> flying from the speaker's mouth like flung furniture and
> household goods, from the upper window of a house
> on fire.

He also has the born teacher's gift for bringing to arresting life the remote and complicated histories that lurk beneath the landscapes, architecture, and artefacts he encounters. Early in *The Broken Road* we find him in Bulgaria, where for the first time he gets a glimpse of a substantial number of Turks – 'the westernmost remnants' of the 'astonishing race' that had forged a mighty Asiatic empire and come close to overrunning Europe. This remarkable fact, which (he implies) Europeans themselves have lost track of, is vividly present to Leigh Fermor:

> When we remember that the Moors of Spain were only
> halted at Tours, on the Loire, it seems, at moments,
> something of a fluke that St Peter's and Notre
> Dame and Westminster Abbey are not today three
> celebrated mosques, kindred fanes to Haghia Sophia in
> Constantinople.

He is, too, a master of the illuminating aperçu. Italian statues of the Virgin Mary, he remarks in the course of a terrific excursus in *Roumeli* about Byzantine icons, 'woo her devotees', but 'the expression of the Panayia, even at the foot of the Cross, says "No comment"'. And he knows how to leaven his legendary and occasionally irritating penchant for ostensibly offhand pedantic display ('What figure could seem more remote than Swiatopluk, Kral of the brittle Moravian realm?' he wonders aloud at one point in *Between the Woods and the Water*) with exclamations of disarmingly ingenuous charm. 'With what ease populations moved about in ancient Greek lands, in the world conquered and Hellenized by Alexander, the wide elbow room of Rome and the Byzantine Empire!'

Wide elbow room. Not the least part of Leigh Fermor's appeal to us is his concrete sense, however romanticized it may have been, of the past as a kind of mythic outback, the habitation of grander, more authentic, more liberated men than we can hope to be today. Small wonder that the people Leigh Fermor admires the most are those canny and swashbuckling Maniots, with whom he clearly identified. His worshipful description of a famous Maniot leader in the Greek war of independence is, you suspect, a fantasy that the womanizing, hard-drinking writer had of an idealized self:

> His fine looks and dignity and gracious
> manners were the outward signs of an upright
> and honourable nature, high intelligence, diplomatic
> skill, generosity, patriotism, unshakable courage
> and strength of will: qualities suitably leavened by
> ambition and family pride and occasionally marred by
> cruelty.

Certainly his need to sparkle at all costs could cause him to be cruel: at least a small part of Somerset Maugham's hostility can be attributed to an evening during which Leigh Fermor, a guest at the older writer's table, entertained the company by making fun of his host's stutter.

The narcissistic glitter, the aversion to introspection, can hinder some of the books from being all they might have been. There is, among other things, a startling lack of interest in the politics that were seething beneath the landscapes he so loved to describe. *A Time of Gifts* covers his walk through Germany in 1933 – a setting that, you'd think, would inspire some broader ruminations and deep thinking in a youth so fervently interested in history. But the young author – as his older self, to his credit, would acknowledge – 'didn't care a damn'; he thrilled to the dramas of the past, without seeming to care a great deal about their import for the present. 'The gloom didn't last longer than breakfast,' he blithely writes after the assassination of the Austrian chancellor Dollfuss in 1934.

The youthful apathy eventually ossified into a staunchly reflexive, monarchist conservatism. Leigh Fermor can summon outrage about the deprivations, during World War II and the Cold War, suffered by his aristocratic Hungarian and Romanian friends; but given his deep and clearly authentic love of Greece, it is disturbing to read, in Artemis Cooper's biography, that this extravagant philhellene – a friend of George Seferis, no less – never spoke out against the oppressive right-wing regime of the Colonels in the 1960s and 1970s.

His tendency to stick to the surfaces becomes a problem even when politics isn't an issue – as, for instance, in the underpowered and, I think, overrated *A Time to Keep Silence*, about the Benedictine and Trappist monasteries where he spent some time in the 1950s in order to work quietly on his first couple of books, and about his visit to the abandoned cells of Orthodox Greek monks in Cappadocia. There's something amusing about the premise: the notoriously voluble and social author forced to be silent for the first time, an experience that gives him a fleeting, climactic appreciation of the outside world as an 'inferno of noise and vulgarity entirely populated by bounders and sluts and crooks' when he returns to it. But the aperçus feel generic and the ostensibly humble insights hollow. Here as elsewhere, you feel that, whatever his apparent interest in religion and spiritual devotion, Leigh Fermor is finally far more comfortable flourishing his eruditions. ('The gulf between the cenobites of Rome and those of Byzantium was often in my mind.') It is hard to write profoundly about spirituality when you don't really like to talk about the inner life.

In *The Broken Road*, we get many of the things we love in Leigh Fermor. Here again, he goggles and zigzags, flirts and pontificates. There are the vivid descriptions and the donnish asides; a touching near romance with a Greek girl – his first exposure to the people who would capture his imagination later – and a fantastical encounter with dancing fishermen in a cave, which affords the elderly author a chance to discourse on Greek folk choreography in a way his younger self couldn't possibly have done. ('The other great dancers of the *hasapiko* and the *tzeibekiko*, as the two forms of *rebetiko* dances are severally called …')

One of the most arresting revelations afforded by the new book is that the high style of later years was already more or less fully formed by the end of his great walking tour. The latter part of *The Broken Road* consists of transcribed entries from the journal he was keeping during his voyage to Mount Athos after he left Istanbul. (Ironically, all we have of the long-awaited sojourn in the historic capital city are terse and colourless notes.) The prose here already bristles with the flights of invention and erudite riffs we know so well from the finished books:

> I thought of the triremes of all the empires that have
> sailed these same waters, and called to mind the tales
> about Perseus, Jason and Odysseus, and the Tyrants of
> the Archipelago; the piracy of Mithridate …

In other important ways, the Leigh Fermor of this final book of the trilogy – which, as we know, was in fact the first instalment to be written, and in many ways the freshest and least mediated by subsequent authorial fussing – isn't quite the person familiar from the earlier books. A gratifying new element is an emotional frankness, even vulnerability, that was edited out of the earlier books. Here, for the first time, you see the flip side of the blithe self-involvement and brash charm. ('Not for the first time, I concluded despondently, I have wounded somebody badly without meaning to; nor, alas, for the last. But I wish I knew exactly how.') Here you get the moments of terror that, you always felt reading the earlier books, must have been part of all that solitary wandering: 'Then my guts seemed to drain right out of me,' he writes at one point, 'and a fit of panic came, thoughts of passing the night there, without food in the rain.'

And whereas in *A Time of Gifts* and *Between the Woods and the Water* Leigh Fermor more than once draws attention to the 'ecstasy' he claims he always felt on realizing that nobody in the world knew where he was – an emotion that travellers today are unlikely ever to have, and that surely accounts for some of the nostalgic appeal of these volumes – here he admits, for the first time, to a paralysing homesickness:

> Outside now, the moon and stars are shining brightly
> on the snowy roofs, and making a silver track across
> the inky sea. I do so wonder what everyone is doing at
> home now.

I have said that Patrick Leigh Fermor's first two books about his great adventure lacked the satisfying structure of *Bildung* narratives. The irony of the publication of his final, posthumous work is that it creates, retrospectively and almost accidentally, something of that meaningful arc for the entire trilogy. By the end, the lacquered manner has dissolved, and a different, far more touching and sympathetic hero emerges. The whole thing couldn't have been better structured if the author had planned it this way all along. When you put down *The Broken Road* you may feel what he felt on leaving Mount Athos, another place of quiet that he eventually felt compelled to leave in the end in order to rejoin the noisy world: 'a great deal of regret'.

– *The New York Review of Books*, 19 June 2014

I, Knausgaard

Which would prevail – Scandinavian high literature or Meghan Markle?

This is the question that dogged me between May and August of this year, during which time I devoted myself to two cultural undertakings: reading all of *My Struggle* and watching all of *Suits*. *My Struggle*, as readers of this or any other literary publication will know, is the sometimes brilliant, sometimes tedious, intermittently frustrating and always genre-defying 3,600-page autobiographical novel by the Norwegian writer Karl Ove Knausgaard that became a phenomenon among Anglo-American literati when the translation of Book 1 appeared here, in 2012, and whose sixth and last volume appears this month.

Suits, as readers of pretty much every other publication will have known since Prince Harry of Wales became engaged last autumn to Markle, one of the show's stars, is a popular USA Network legal drama, currently in its eighth season – now of course *sans* Markle, who has abandoned fictional dramas forever, although whether being a member of the British royal family (currently the subject of another popular TV series) constitutes 'reality' is a question beyond the scope of this essay.

But it is within the scope of this essay to ponder some implications of the differences between the two fictions, as I found myself doing over the course of the four months during which I was wrapped up in both – not the least of those implications being questions about precisely what fiction is and how it relates to reality, and the extent to which traditional narrative can be a delivery vehicle for saying something true about life. These, as it happens, lie at the intellectual and aesthetic heart of Knausgaard's huge undertaking.

Both *My Struggle* and *Suits* are serial entertainments, with the difference that the TV show is a turbid middlebrow melodrama that places all of its aesthetic chips on plot – patently contrived story lines engineered to generate further incident. (The gimmick that sets the whole drama in motion is typically high concept. The brilliant young lawyer who is the show's hero never actually went to law school – a dire secret that motivates his, and eventually more and more of his colleagues', actions, as they go to increasingly desperate lengths to conceal his past.) *My Struggle*, by contrast, has no plot. Confidently bestriding the increasingly popular grey zone that lies between fiction and autobiography (the genre the French call 'autofiction'), it purports to be a minutely accurate reconstruction of the author's life from earliest childhood to the present, populated by characters who bear the names of, or are identifiable with, people he knows in real life, its meandering narrative dutifully reproducing events as they unfolded with few visible attempts to shape or edit their flow to suit expectations of 'story'. All this is an expression of the author's conviction, announced in Book 1, that 'our ludicrously inconsequential lives ... had a part in this world'.

The great technical ambition of this work is the attempt to reconstruct the rich inconsequentiality of our quotidian experience in prose stripped of the usual novelistic devices. Before embarking on *My Struggle*, Knausgaard had published two atmospheric novels – one an eccentric but rather beautiful recreation of Genesis in a Norwegian setting, complete with angels – and since then he's produced a series of four gossamer volumes, each named after a season and filled with artfully etched observations about everyday things and experiences. But in the magnum opus he claims to eschew any prettifying literary technique. Every object, every event, it seems, is reduced to its bare mechanical particulars: there's a reason that an account of teenagers trying to get some booze for a New Year's Eve party, which might have occupied a paragraph in another kind of novel, takes seventy pages. Where some authors might write 'He drove off', Knausgaard gives us 'Yngve plumped down in the seat beside me, inserted the key in the ignition, twisted it, craned his head and began to reverse down the little slope.'

Likewise, the volumes obey few of the laws of narrative structure; the most you can say for each is that it covers some phase of the author's life, although not necessarily in chronological order. Book 1 is set in motion by the death, in the late 1990s, of Knausgaard's schoolteacher father – by far the most powerful 'character' here, a grandiose alcoholic whose abusiveness is elliptically yet indelibly evoked in a series of long flashbacks to the author's childhood. These alternate with scenes set in the present, at the funeral home and the house where the father ended his days sordidly, sitting in his own excrement and surrounded by empty bottles. This first instalment is by far the most artful (many would say the most successful) of the six, not least because it self-consciously emulates Proust, to whose own multivolume autobiographical novel Knausgaard acknowledges his indebtedness. Some readers of Book 1 will feel as though they're on a treasure hunt for allusions to the French masterpiece: there are reflections on how different rooms feel, meditations on famous paintings, a preoccupation with a beloved grandmother, early fumblings with girls that result in premature ejaculations.

Through all this, the author's past is reconstituted at a level of detail so dense that you're persuaded of the narrative's factuality even as you're forced to acknowledge that it has to have been, at the least, greatly enhanced, however close to some emotional truth or memory an individual scene or stretch of dialogue may be. This technique raises – as Knausgaard wants it to – questions about the limits both of memory and of fictional representation. 'The fourteeen years I lived in Bergen', he writes at the beginning of Book 5, 'are long gone, no traces of them are left' – a sly claim, given that the 614 pages that follow constitute a seemingly 'factual' recreation of that very period.

This faux factuality is the hallmark of all six volumes. Book 2 begins in the 'present' of 2008, when Knausgaard, nearing forty, is living in Malmö, Sweden, with his wife, Linda, and their children, contemplating the novel that would become *My Struggle*. These scenes alternate with flashbacks to the period several years earlier when he had left Norway for Sweden; it is there, crippled by emotional and intellectual insecurities, that he arduously courts Linda, a poet with psychological troubles of her own. Book 3 leapfrogs back in time to provide an unexpected and often charming glimpse of his childhood and teenage years – the source of those awful insecurities (he describes his childhood as a 'ghetto-like state of incompleteness'); in this volume, the author's desire to recreate every aspect of the past extends to descriptions of his bowel movements. Book 4 finds the eighteen-year-old Karl Ove living in a tiny town in northern Norway, where he spends a year as a schoolteacher, struggling with an increasingly alarming drinking problem, his attraction to some of the underage girls in his class and his attempts to write serious fiction. Book 5 moves on to the author's twenties and early thirties – those fourteen years during which he lived in Bergen and experienced his first literary failures and successes, as well as an early marriage that collapsed in part because of his infidelity.

As this summary suggests, the life recounted here is one of unusually intense emotional extremes of the sort that can make for powerful writing. The childhood abuse, the alcoholism, the affairs and breakups are the stuff of many a memoir – a genre that, curiously, doesn't figure at all in the numerous digressions on literature that dot the landscape of intentional quotidian banality here, even though *My Struggle* has far more in common with memoir than it does with fiction. (I suspect that Knausgaard decided to call his work a novel because memoir continues to be seen as a 'soft' genre, and he's after bigger literary game.)

And yet, despite all the emotional drama, I was rarely moved by this vast and often impressive work. As with some blogs or soap operas, the ongoing narration, however tedious it often is, can be weirdly addictive, and the suggestive play with fact and fiction can be intriguing. But in the end, the books left me cold and, not infrequently, exasperated. *Suits*, on the other hand, was offering just about everything that *My Struggle* wasn't, and now and then even left me in tears – as artfully constructed narratives can do, propelling us toward emotions that flow naturally from certain kinds of situations. (There's a marvellous scene in Season 5 when the young lawyer, guilt-ridden over the way in which his secret has compromised his friends' and colleagues' integrity, finally breaks down – as you will, too.)

As it happens, the ability to evoke emotions through art is something the author of *My Struggle* worries about, too. Writing in Book 3 about his father once more, he acknowledges that 'even with the greatest effort of will I am unable to recreate the fear; the feelings I had for him'. But why not? Why, when to give the reader access to the emotions the writer wants to conjure is one of the great aims of any kind of writing, does Knausgaard make this strange confession of defeat? Why, if *Suits* can catch you up in its characters' often preposterous crises, can't *My Struggle*?

The answers to these questions become clear when you finally get to Book 6. In many ways, the final volume represents a continuation of the author's characteristic matter and method – with the addition of a hall-of-mirrors story line, since this climactic instalment is, in fact, about the publication and reception of the previous *My Struggle* books in Norway. It opens in autumn 2009, just as the first volume is about to appear, and closes two years later, at the moment the author finishes writing the very book you're reading. If the previous volumes track the narrator's evolution into a writer (the same arc traced in Proust's novel), this one shows him at the moment he grasps the golden ring.

For that reason, one recurrent theme of the preceding volumes – the difficulty of balancing life and writing – comes to dominate this final book. Earlier, the fine-grained narration of lived life occasionally blossomed into ruminations on art, literature, music and life. Here, the two strains seem to be in desperate competition, each demanding more and more space until the narrative literally breaks apart, its two autobiographical sections – the first 400 and final 300 pages – separated by a 440-page digression on literature and history. (One of the many literary models that Knausgaard cites in this extended reflection on art and life is James Joyce's *Ulysses*, which, he implies, inspired the structure of his own novel, observing that Joyce's epic contains a lengthy section, Molly Bloom's soliloquy, that in tone, content and style is nothing like the rest of the book.)

Perhaps because they have so much more to compete with, this volume's evocations of domestic life – fraught spats with Linda about who will mind the children in the apartment in

Malmö, gruelling family vacations, simmering irritation with the stridently politically correct parents of the kids' school friends, shopping for dinner parties – are not only exhaustive, but downright exhausting. Do we really need to know that his apartment building's elevator is 'the dark and narrow shaft that ran through the middle of the building'? It's as if the particular, the concrete reality of 'life' to which this author attaches so much importance, were trying to assert its claims in the face of the increasing preponderance of 'art': the metastasizing meditations on his method (writing must be 'raw, in the sense of unrefined, direct, without metaphors or other linguistic decoration'), the proliferating and often brilliant mini-disquisitions on works of art and literature. These range over everything from the paintings of Munch, Turner and Leonardo (the latter's canvases 'so perfect' that – a wonderful if jarring thought – they seem 'rather *lazy*'); to *Hamlet*, Francis Bacon and Kafka. At one point in his young manhood, Knausgaard writes in Book 5, he worried that he might end up as just a critic; there were moments when I wished he had.

The difficulty of balancing his private and literary lives erupts in scenes that have a refreshingly absurdist edge. Knausgaard is terrific on the disorientation that goes with being an author who has made his private life public: the way in which the interviews you give never quite sound like the real you, or the oddness of having total strangers approach you in airports to share their feelings about your children. Still, it occurs to you that, in the hands of another writer (David Sedaris? Michael Chabon?), these and other scenes in *My Struggle* could well have provided material for some comic relief amid the relentless self-seriousness.

There was certainly nothing funny about the event that hangs over this final book: the public controversy that accompanied the novels' publication in Norway. This volume's preoccupation with the meaning and methods of literature is, you realize, inevitable, given that the story it tells shows the devastating consequences of the author's decision to depict life 'raw' – to use real people, often with their real names. His father's brother, for instance, threatened to sue him and his publisher after reading the manuscript of Book 1, insisting that all 'errors of documentary fact' be removed – a demand that inevitably leads Knausgaard the *auteur* to ponder what a 'fact' of a remembered life might be. He later admits to a former girlfriend who appears in the novel that he doesn't remember 'exact details' but, rather, 'moods, that kind of thing'. Hmm.

Even more troubling is the account of the nervous breakdown that his bipolar wife suffered after the publication of the first few novels, which paint an intimate portrait of the couple's courtship, passions, quarrels and, increasingly, competitiveness. (Linda, too, is a writer.) Her mental collapse, to which the final 150 pages of the new novel are devoted, is evoked in the usual minute detail – which here, you feel, does in fact serve a strong narrative purpose, recreating Linda's torturous descent in a genuinely agonizing way. Knausgaard understands that this is a gruesomely high price to pay for his lofty literary aims. But for all his theorizing about literature and modernity, he's a true Romantic, in love with the sacrifices that must be made for Art – even when they're not his: 'And if you want to describe reality as it is, for the individual, and there is no other reality, you have to really go there, you can't be considerate.'

All this may well have you wondering just what kind of man this writer is, and it is to Knausgaard's credit that he struggles with precisely this question in the book's 450-page central section. This book-length excursus, representing a radical stylistic departure from the rest of the volume (this is the 'Molly Bloom' section), explains, at last, his work's strange and provocative title, which it shares with another famous book: Adolf Hitler's autobiography, *Mein Kampf*.

Until Book 6, and indeed through this volume's first long autobiographical section, you're tempted to take that title as a weak joke: What, after all, could the autobiography of one of history's greatest monsters have in common with that of a middle-class, middle-aged Norwegian writer with his trivial day-to-day doings? ('I donned my Ted Baker shirt, which stuck to my still-damp shoulder blades and would not hang straight at first, then I got into my Pour jeans with the diagonal pockets, which usually I didn't like, there was something so conventional about them.')

But Knausgaard wants to argue that any human life is, in the end, just that – a life. And it's here that his ideological commitment to minutely representing reality – or, rather, his fervent belief that the particulars of our lives, in their complexity and their vivifying incoherence, always trump any attempt to impose ideology on them – achieves a strange fulfilment.

The central section, entitled 'The Name and the Number', begins with a reflection on the fact that, owing to his uncle's threats, Knausgaard's father can never be named in the book over which he so memorably looms, a necessity that compels the author to ponder the strange power of names. This, in turn, leads to a thrilling – there is no other word – fifty-page explication of 'The Straitening', a poem by Paul Celan, a Holocaust survivor, in which the Holocaust is never named although it hovers over every word: another case in which presence and absence float in a kind of negative equilibrium.

All this, finally, brings us to the main event, by far the finest thing in this strange book and, in my experience, the best thing Knausgaard has written, marked by enormous intellectual panache and quite different from anything else in the novel (it's amazing how lively the writing suddenly is when he's not writing about himself): a nearly 400-page close reading of *Mein Kampf*, complete with detours through related texts, in which the author tries to recover and reproduce the lived experience of the frustrated, depressed and impoverished young man who would become the Nazi tyrant.

The life of that sad human being, as Knausgaard's far-ranging and brilliant analysis implies, bears more than a little resemblance to that of Knausgaard himself: the tyrannical father, the grandiose dreams of cultural achievement, the humiliations and the poverty. Yet Hitler became Hitler, and Knausgaard is just himself. A life is a life; that's the struggle. No life 'means' anything more than itself.

This powerful digression is ultimately joined to a sorrowful reflection on the July 2011 mass shooting on Norway's Utøya island, where sixty-nine people were shot by a sole gunman, Anders Behring Breivik, pretending to be a police officer. Here, Knausgaard uses the insights afforded by his reading of *Mein Kampf* to theorize about the similarities between Hitler and Breivik. What made the inhumanity of the two possible, he suggests, was the fact that their psyches embraced only the first and third grammatical persons: an 'I' (the grandiose perpetrator) and a 'they' (the dehumanized victims) but never a 'you' – the second person, who, in confronting us one-on-one, forces us to engage an 'other' as a human being.

This intriguing notion, however, forces you into an uncomfortable reconsideration of Knausgaard himself. As I closed the final volume of *My Struggle*, struck by how little this hugely ambitious artistic undertaking had moved me, I thought about the emotions that course through it and how they are presented. Like the grandiose figure he writes about in his masterly central section, Knausgaard, too, is always telling you *about* his feelings and how profound they are, his weeping, his lusts, his ambitions, his insecurities, his frustrations and regrets. But precisely because the feelings are reported rather than evoked, they belong only to the author; between him and his characters – 'I' and 'they' again – there is no room for 'you', the audience.

This poses a serious challenge for the reader – and, indeed, suggests a certain incoherence in the author's aesthetic ideology. At one point early on, Knausgaard writes about how moved he can be by certain pre-twentieth-century paintings – artworks, as he puts it, 'within the artistic paradigm that always retained some reference to visible reality'. But those works move us because the reality to which they refer is a shared reality (the world), whereas the overwhelming reality of *My Struggle* is Knausgaard himself. The books constitute a kind of genre novel in which the author himself has become the genre.

Hence their effect: if your experiences in life happen to overlap with the author's, you can find yourself stirred by certain passages; still others may leave you impressed by his intellectual dexterity, as in the dazzling analysis of *Mein Kampf*. But to be conscious of how the novel functions, of how it's designed to make you 'think' about the 'subject', means that you're in the presence of a work that is, in the end, less like the nineteenth-century paintings the author so admires than like a very current genre indeed: conceptual art, which invites you to nod in recognition when you 'get' how it generates its meanings, but rarely provokes large human feeling.

It is for this reason that *My Struggle* in fact bears so little resemblance to the work that the author himself so frequently refers to as an inspiration, and to which his magnum opus has so eagerly been compared by reviewers: Proust's *In Search of Lost Time*. In that novel, the life of the narrator, its arc from childhood to middle age, climaxing in his becoming a writer, functions as a prism through which virtually every aspect of the lived reality of the author's time – art, music, literature, sex, society, class, theatre, technology, science, history, war, memory, philosophy – is refracted, in a way that enlarges you, gives you a heightened sense of the world itself, its realities and possibilities.

Knausgaard's creation, for all its vastness and despite its serious intellectual aims and attainments, reduces the entire world to the size of the author. This is happening everywhere now – as the writer himself, with characteristic insight, recognizes in a long passage about the ways in which the internet and social media, by forcing us endlessly to perform our own lives, threaten to trivialize the very notion of selfhood: 'Our identities ... gradually recalibrate toward the expectation of an observing "everyone" or "all".' But, just as typically, he seems unaware of the extent to which he and his novel participate in the disturbing phenomenon that he so acutely analyses. What work more than his deserves to become the great new classic of the age of the blog?

– *The New York Times Book Review*, 24 September 2018

A Lot of Pain

The title of Hanya Yanagihara's second work of fiction stands in almost comical contrast to its length: at 720 pages, it's one of the biggest novels to be published this year. To this literal girth there has been added, since the book appeared in March, the meta-phorical weight of several prestigious award nominations – among them the Kirkus Prize, which Yanagihara won, the Man Booker, which she didn't, and the National Book Award, which will be conferred in mid-November. Both the size of *A Little Life* and the impact it has had on readers and critics alike – a bestseller, the book has received adulatory reviews in *The New Yorker*, *The Atlantic*, *The Wall Street Journal*, and other serious venues – reflect, in turn, the largeness of the novel's themes. These, as one of its four main characters, a group of talented and artistic friends whom Yanagihara traces from college days to their early middle age in and around New York City, puts it, are 'sex and food and sleep and friends and money and fame'.

The character who articulates these themes, a black artist on the cusp of success, has one great artistic ambition, which is to 'chronicle in pictures the drip of all their lives'. This is Yanagihara's ambition, too. 'Drip', indeed, suggests why the author thinks her big book deserves its 'little' title: eschewing the kind of frenetic plotting that has proved popular recently (as witness, say, Donna Tartt's *The Goldfinch*, the 2014 Pulitzer winner), *A Little Life* presents itself, at least at the beginning, as a modest chronicle of the way that life happens to a small group of people with some history in common; as a catalogue of the incremental accumulations that, almost without our noticing it, become the stuff of our lives – the jobs and apartments, the one-night stands and friendships and grudges, the furniture and clothes, lovers and spouses and houses.

In this respect, the book bears a superficial resemblance to a certain kind of 'woman's novel' of an earlier age – Mary McCarthy's 1963 bestseller *The Group*, say, which similarly traces the trajectories of a group of college friends over a span of time. But the objects of this particular woman novelist's scrutiny are men. Bound by friendships first formed at an unnamed liberal arts college in the Northeast of the United States, Yanagihara's cast is as carefully diversified as the crew in one of those 1940s wartime bomber movies, however twenty-first-century their anxieties may be. There is the black artist, JB, a gay man of Haitian descent who's been raised by a single mother; Malcolm, a biracial architect who rather comically 'comes out' as a straight man and frets guiltily over his parents' wealth; Willem, a handsome and amiable Midwestern actor who stumbles into stardom; and Jude, a brilliant, tormented litigator (he's also a talented amateur vocalist and *patissier*) with no identifiable ethnicity and a dark secret that shadows his and his friends' lives.

As contrived as this setup can feel, it has the makings of an interesting novel about a subject that is too rarely explored in contemporary letters: nonsexual friendship among adult men. In an interview that she gave to the publishing industry magazine *Kirkus Reviews*, Yanagihara described her fascination with male friendship – particularly since, she asserted to the interviewer, men are given 'such a small emotional palette to work with'. Although she and her female friends often speak about their emotions together, she told the interviewer, men seemed to be different:

> I think they have a very hard time still naming what
> it is to be scared or vulnerable or afraid, and it's not
> just that they can't talk about it – it's that they can't
> sometimes even identify what they're feeling … When
> I hear sometimes my male friends talking about these
> manifestations of what, to me, is clearly fear, or clearly
> shame, they really can't even express the word itself.

It's interesting that Yanagihara's catalogue of emotions includes no positive ones: I shall return to this later.

The novel, then, looks as if it's going to be a masculine version of *The Group*: a study of a closed society, its language and rituals and secret codes. It's a theme in which Yanagihara has shown interest before. In her first book, *The People in the Trees* (2013), a rather heavy-handed parable of colonial exploitation unpersuasively entwined with a lurid tale of child abuse, the main character, a physician who's investigating a Micronesian tribe whose members achieve spectacular longevity, is struck 'by the smallness of the society, by what it must be like to live a life in which everyone you knew or had ever seen might be counted on your fingers'. The strongest parts of that book reflected the anthropological impulse behind the doctor's wistful observation: the descriptions of the tribe's habitat, rituals, and mythologies were imaginative and genuinely engaging, unlike the clankingly symbolic paedophiliac subplot. (The search by Western doctors for the source of the natives' astonishingly long life spans inevitably invites exploitation and ruin; like the island children whom the doctor later adopts and abuses, the island and its tribal culture are 'raped' by white men.)

Yanagihara's new book would seem, at first glance, to have satisfied her wish for a 'tribe' she could devote an entire novel to: it focuses on a tiny group that is circumscribed to the point of being hermetic. Indeed, *A Little Life* keeps its four principals and their lives in such tight close-up that they do feel 'little' – not because their concerns are small (they aren't) but because, as other critics have noted, the novel provides so little historical, cultural, or political detail that it's often difficult to say precisely in what era the characters' intense emotional dramas take place. The only world here is the world of the four principals.

Yet *A Little Life*, like its predecessor, gets hopelessly sidetracked by a secondary narrative – one in which, strikingly, homosexual paedophilia is once again the salient element. For Jude, we learn, was serially abused as a child and young adult by the priests and counsellors who raised him. This is the dark secret that explains his tormented present: self-cutting and masochistic relationships and, eventually, suicide. (The latter plot point isn't anything the experienced reader won't have guessed after fifty pages.) Yanagihara's real subject, it turns out, is abjection. What begins as a novel that looks as if it's going to be retro – a cross between Mary McCarthy and a Stendhalian tale of young talent triumphing in a great metropolis – soon reveals itself as a very twenty-first-century tale indeed: abuse, victimization, self-loathing.

This sleight-of-hand is slyly hinted at in the book's striking cover image, a photograph by the late San Francisco photographer Peter Hujar of a man grimacing in what appears to be agony. The joke, of which Yanagihara and her publishers were aware, is that the portrait belongs to a series of images that Hujar, who was gay, made of men in the throes of orgasm. In the case of Yanagihara's novel, however, the 'real' feeling – not only what the book is about but, I suspect, what its admirers crave – is pain rather than pleasure.

*

This is a shame, because Yanagihara is good at providing the pleasures that go with a certain kind of fictional anthropology. The accounts of her characters' early days in New York and their gradual rises to success and celebrity are tangy with vivid aperçus: 'There were times when the pressure to achieve happiness felt almost oppressive,' she writes at one point; or, 'New York was populated by the ambitious. It was often the only thing that everyone here had in common.'

By far the most fully achieved of the four characters is the actor, Willem, and its most persuasive narrative trajectory the story of his rise from actor-waiter to Hollywood stardom, punctuated by flashbacks to his rural childhood. (A touchingly described relationship with a crippled brother suggests why he's so good at both the empathy and self-effacement necessary to his work – and, eventually, to his relationship with the hapless Jude.) A passage that comes about two thirds into the novel, in which he realizes he's 'famous', demonstrates Yanagihara's considerable strengths at evoking a particular milieu – clever, creative downtown types who socialize with one another perhaps too much – and that particular stage of success in which one emerges from the local into the greater world:

> There had been a day, about a month after he turned thirty-eight, when Willem realized he was famous. Initially, this had fazed him less than he would have imagined, in part because he had always considered himself sort of famous – he and JB, that is. He'd be out downtown with someone, Jude or someone else, and somebody would come over to say hello to Jude, and Jude would introduce him: 'Aaron, do you know Willem?' And Aaron would say, 'Of course, Willem Ragnarsson. Everyone knows Willem,' but it wouldn't

be because of his work – it would be because Aaron's
former roommate's sister had dated him at Yale, or he
had two years ago done a reading for Aaron's friend's
brother's friend who was a playwright, or because
Aaron, who was an artist, had once been in a group
show with JB and Asian Henry Young, and he'd met
Willem at the after-party. New York City, for much of
his adulthood, had simply been an extension of college
… the entire infrastructure of which sometimes seemed
to have been lifted out of Boston and plunked down
within a few blocks' radius in lower Manhattan and
outer Brooklyn.

But now, Willem realizes, the release of a certain film 'had created
a certain moment that even he recognized would transform his
career'. When he gets up from his table at a restaurant to go to the
loo, he notices 'something different about the quality of [the other
diners'] attention, its intensity and hush …' This is just right.

It's telling that Yanagihara's greatest success is a secondary character: once again, it's as if she doesn't know her own strengths. For
as *A Little Life* progresses, the author seems to lose interest in
everyone but the tragic victim, Jude. Malcolm the biracial architect, in particular, is never more than a cipher, all too obviously
present to fill the biracial slot; and after a brief episode in which
JB's struggle with drug addiction is quite effectively chronicled,
that character, too, fades away, reappearing occasionally as the
years pass, the grand gay artist with a younger boyfriend on his
arm. Overshadowing them all are the dark hints about Jude's past
that accumulate ominously – and all too coyly. 'Traditionally,
men – adult men, which he didn't yet consider himself among –
had been interested in him for one reason, and so he had learned
to be frightened of them.'

The awkwardness of 'which he didn't yet consider himself among' is, I should say, pervasive. The writing in this book is often atrocious, oscillating between the incoherently ungrammatical – 'his mother … had earned her doctorate in education, teaching all the while at the public school near their house that she had deemed JB better than' – and painfully strained attempts at 'lyrical' effects: 'His silence, so black and total that it was almost gaseous …' You wonder why the former, at least, wasn't edited out – and why the striking weakness of the prose has gone unremarked by critics and prize juries.

Inasmuch as there's a structure here, it's that of a striptease: gradually, in a series of flashbacks, the secrets about Jude's past are uncovered until at last we get to witness the pivotal moment of abuse, a scene in which one of his many sexual tormentors, a sadistic doctor, deliberately runs him over, leaving him as much a physical cripple as an emotional one. But the wounds inflicted on Jude by the paedophile priests in the orphanage where he grew up, by the truckers and drifters to whom he is pimped out by the priest he runs away with, by the counsellors and the young inmates at the youth facility where he ends up after the wicked priest is apprehended, by the evil doctor in whose torture chamber he ends up after escaping from the unhappy youth facility, are nothing compared to those inflicted by Yanagihara herself. As the foregoing catalogue suggests, Jude might better have been called 'Job', abandoned by his cruel creator. (Was there not one priest who noticed something, who wanted to help? Not one counsellor?)

The sufferings recalled in the flashbacks are echoed in the endless array of humiliations the character is forced to endure in the present-day narrative: the accounts of these form the backbone of the novel. His lameness is mocked by JB – a particularly unbelievable plot point – with whom he subsequently breaks; he compulsively cuts himself with razor blades, an addiction that lands him in the hospital more than once; he rejects the loving attentions of a kindly law professor who adopts him; he takes up with a sadistic male lover who beats him repeatedly and throws him and his wheelchair down a flight of stairs (!); his leg wounds, in time, get to the point where the limbs have to be amputated. And when Yanagihara seems to grant her protagonist a reprieve by giving him at last a loving partner – late in the novel, Willem conveniently emends his sexuality and falls in love with his friend – it's merely so that she can crush him by killing Willem in a car crash, the tragedy that eventually leads Jude to take his own life.

You suspect that Yanagihara wanted Jude to be one of those doomed golden children around whose disintegrations certain beloved novels revolve – Sebastian Flyte, say, in *Brideshead Revisited*. But the problem with Jude is that, from the start, he's a pill: you never care enough about him to get emotionally involved in the first place, let alone affected by his demise. Sometimes I wondered whether even Yanagihara liked him. There is something punitive in the contrived and unredeemed quality of Jude's endless sufferings; it often feels as if the author, who is an editor at the *New York Times'* Styles magazine, is working off a private emotion of her own.

Yanagihara must have known that the sheer quantity of degradation in her story was likely to alienate readers: 'This is just too hard for anybody to take,' Gerald Howard, the executive editor at Doubleday, told her, according to the *Kirkus* interview. 'You have made this point quite adequately, and I don't think you need to do it again.' But somehow, the second-time novelist managed to prevail over one of the most respected senior editors in the business. ('Not many passages that were up for cutting were cut,' *Kirkus* laconically observed.)

It's worth speculating as to why Yanagihara persisted. In *The People in the Trees*, the doctor studying the island culture recalls wishing as a child that he'd had a more traumatic childhood – one in which, indeed, the presence of a crippled brother might bring the family together. 'How I yearned for such motivation!' he cries to himself as he recalls his early years. As Yanagihara recognizes in this passage, which is meant to condemn the character, there is a deep and unadult sentimentality lurking behind that yearning; and yet she herself falls victim to it. In *A little Life*, as we know, she concocted the crippled brother, produced the traumatic motivation. In the end, the novel is little more than a machine designed to produce negative emotions for the reader to wallow in – unsurprisingly, the very emotions that, in her *Kirkus Reviews* interview, she listed as the ones she was interested in, the ones she felt men were incapable of expressing: fear, shame, vulnerability. Both the tediousness of *A Little Life* and, you imagine, the guilty pleasures it holds for some readers are those of a teenaged rap session, that adolescent social ritual par excellence, in which the same crises and hurts are constantly rehearsed.

We know, alas, that the victims of abuse often end up unhappily imprisoned in cycles of (self-) abuse. But to keep showing this unhappy dynamic at work is not the same as creating a meaningful narrative about it. For all its bulk, Yanagihara's book is, essentially, a pamphlet.

Interestingly, it is because of, rather than despite, this failing that *A Little Life* has struck a nerve among critics and readers. Jon Michaud, in *The New Yorker*, praised its 'subversive' treatment of abuse and suffering, which, he asserts, lies in the book's refusal to offer 'any possibility of redemption and deliverance'. Michaud singled out for notice a passage that describes Jude's love of pure mathematics, in which discipline he pursues a master's degree at one point – another in the preposterous list of his improbable accomplishments. (Here again, her editor balked – 'Howard also thought Jude was too unbelievably talented,' the author conceded in the *Kirkus* article – but was again overruled.) For Jude, Michaud interestingly observes, maths takes the place of religion in an unredeemable world:

> Not everyone liked the axiom of equality … but he had always appreciated how elusive it was, how the beauty of the equation itself would always be frustrated by the attempts to prove it. It was the kind of axiom that could drive you mad, that could consume you, that could easily become an entire life.

The citation allows him to conclude his review by declaring that 'Yanagihara's novel can also drive you mad, consume you …'

Michaud's is a kind of metacritique: the novel is to be admired not for what it does, but for what it doesn't do, for the way it bleakly defies conventional – and, by implication, sentimental – expectations of closure. But all 'closure' isn't necessarily mawkish: it's precisely what can give stories an aesthetic and ethical significance. The passage that struck me as significant, by contrast, was one in which the nice law professor expounds one day in class on the difference between 'what is fair and what is just, and, as important, between what is fair and what is necessary'. For a novel in the realistic tradition to be effective, it must obey some kind of aesthetic necessity – not least, that of even a faint verisimilitude. The abuse that Yanagihara heaps on her protagonist is neither just from a human point of view nor necessary from an artistic one.

In a related vein, Garth Greenwell in *The Atlantic* praised *A Little Life* as 'the great gay novel' not because of any traditionally gay subject matter – Greenwell acknowledges that almost none of the characters or love affairs in the book are recognizably gay; it's noteworthy that when Willem discusses his affair with Jude, he declares that 'I'm not in a relationship with a man … I'm in a relationship with Jude,' a statement that in an earlier era would have been tagged as 'denial' – but because of its technical or stylistic gestures. Yanagihara's book is, in fact, curiously reticent about the accoutrements of erotic life that many if not most urban gay men are familiar with, for better or worse – the pleasures of sex, the anxieties of HIV (which is barely mentioned), the omnipresence of Grindr and porn, of freewheeling erotic energy expressed in any number of ways and available on any numbers of platforms. (When Jude tries to spice up his and Willem's sex life and orders three 'manuals', some readers might wonder not in what era but on what *planet* he's supposed to be living.) But for Greenwell, *A Little Life* is distinguished by the way it

> engages with aesthetic modes long coded as queer:
> melodrama, sentimental fiction, grand opera …
> By violating the canons of current literary taste, by
> embracing melodrama and exaggeration and sentiment,
> it can access emotional truths denied more modest
> means of expression.

Greenwell cites as examples the 'elaborate metaphor' to which Yanagihara is given – as, for instance, in the phrase 'the snake-and centipede-squirming muck of Jude's past'.

But not everything that's excessive or exaggerated is, *ipso facto*, 'operatic'. The mad hyperbole you find in grand opera gives great pleasure, not least because the over-the-top emotions come in beautiful packages; the excess is exalting, not depressing. It is hard to see where the compensatory beauties of *A Little Life* reside. Certainly not in Yanagihara's language, which is strained and ungainly rather than artfully baroque. As for melodrama, there isn't even drama here, let alone anything more heightened. The structure of her story is not the satisfying arc we associate with drama, one in whose shapeliness meaning is implied, but a monotonous series of assaults. It's hard to see what's so 'gay' or 'queer' in this dreariness.

There is an odd sentimentality lurking behind accolades like Greenwell's. You wonder whether a novel written by a straight white man, one in which urban gay culture is at best sketchily described, in which male homosexuality is for the second time in that author's work deeply entwined with paedophiliac abuse, in which the only traditional male–male relationship is relegated to a tertiary and semi-comic stratum of the narrative, would be celebrated as 'the great gay novel' and nominated for the Lambda Literary Award, America's premier literary honour for LGBQT literature. If anything, you could argue that this female writer's vision of male bonding revives a pre-Stonewall plot type in which gay characters are de-sexed, miserable, and eventually punished for finding happiness – a story that looks less like the expression of 'queer' aesthetics than like the projection of a regressive and repressive cultural fantasy from the middle of the last century.

It may be that the literary columns of the better general-interest magazines are the wrong place to be looking for explanations of why this maudlin work has struck a nerve among readers and critics both. Recently, a colleague of mine at Bard College – one of the models, according to *Newsweek* magazine, for the unnamed school that the four main characters in *A Little Life* attended – drew my attention to an article from *Psychology Today* about a phenomenon that has been bemusing us and other professors we know, something the article's author refers to as 'declining student resilience: a serious problem for colleges'. A symptom of this phenomenon, which has also been the subject of essays in *The Chronicle of Higher Education* and elsewhere, is the striking increase in recent years in student requests for counselling in connection with the 'problems of everyday life'. The author cites, among other cases, those of a student 'who felt traumatized because her roommate had called her a "bitch" and two students who had sought counselling because they'd seen a mouse in their off-campus apartment'.

As comical as those particular instances may be, they remind you that many readers today have reached adulthood in educational institutions where a generalized sense of helplessness and acute anxiety have become the norm. In these institutions, young people are increasingly encouraged to see themselves not as agents in life but as potential victims: of their dates, their roommates, their professors, of institutions and of history in general. In a culture where victimhood has become a claim to status, how could Yanagihara's book – with its unending parade of aesthetically gratuitous scenes of punitive and humiliating violence – not provide a kind of comfort? To such readers, the ugliness of this author's subject must bring a kind of pleasure, confirming their pre-existing view of the world as a site of victimization – and little else.

This is a very 'little' view of life. Like Jude and his abusive lover, this book and its champions seem 'bound to each other by their mutual disgust and discomfort'. Like the deceptive image on its cover, Yanagihara's novel has duped many into confusing anguish and ecstasy, pleasure and pain.

The American Boy

One spring day in 1976, when I was fifteen years old and couldn't keep my secret any longer, I went into the bedroom I shared with my older brother, sat down at the little oak desk we did our homework on, and began an anguished letter to a total stranger who lived on the other side of the world. We lived on Long Island, in one of twelve identical 'splanches' – split-ranch houses – that lined a street in a suburb that had, until relatively recently, been a potato farm. It was very flat. The stranger to whom I wrote that day lived in South Africa, a fact that I had gleaned from the brief bio under the author photograph on her book jackets, which showed a middle-aged woman with a pleasant face and tightly coiled grey hair, her eyes narrowed and crinkling at the corners: perhaps humorously, perhaps simply against the sun. I had got her street address from the *Who's Who* in our school library, where I often spent recess, bent over an encyclopedia entry that I particularly liked, about the Parthenon. Over a grainy black-and-white photo of the ruin as it appears today you could flip a colour transparency of how the building had looked in ancient times, gaudy with red and blue paint and gilding. I would sit there, day after day, contentedly toggling between the drab present and the richly hued past.

For the letter I wrote that day, I used the 'good' onionskin paper, anxiously feeding each sheet between the rollers of a black cast-iron Underwood typewriter that had been salvaged from my grandfather's braid-and-trimmings factory in the city. I used it to type up school reports and term papers and, when nobody was around, short stories and poems and novels that I never showed to anyone – single-spaced pages so shaming to me that even when I hid them in the secret compartment under a drawer in the oak cabinet across from my bed (where I also hid certain other things: a real ancient Egyptian amulet I'd got as a bar-mitzvah gift from a shrewd godparent, a half-completed sketch I'd made of a boy who sat in front of me in English class) I imagined that they gave off some kind of radiation, a telltale glow that might betray the nature of the feelings I was writing about.

Now I was putting those feelings onto these translucent sheets, which protested with a faint crackle every time I advanced the carriage. When I was finished, I put the letter into the lightweight airmail envelope on which I'd typed the address: Delos, Glen Beach, Camps Bay, Cape 8001 South Africa. I didn't make a copy of what I wrote that day, but I must have confided a fear that my correspondent would reply to my effusions with a form letter, because when her answer came, a few weeks later, typed on a pale-blue aerogram – the first of many that would find me over the next eight years – it began, 'I wonder whoever told you I'd send you a "form letter" if you wrote to me. Are there really writers who do that?'

It was a question I didn't know how to answer, since she was the only writer I'd ever tried to contact. Who else would I write to? In those days, I had two obsessions – ancient Greece and other boys – and she was, I felt, responsible for both.

*

The author to whom I wrote that day, Mary Renault, had two discrete and enthusiastic audiences; although I didn't know it at the time, they neatly mirrored my twin obsessions. The first, and larger, consisted of admirers of her historical fiction. The second consisted of gay men.

Between 1956 and 1981, Renault published a number of critically acclaimed and bestselling fictional evocations of Greek antiquity. Like the works of Marguerite Yourcenar (*Memoirs of Hadrian*) and Robert Graves (*I, Claudius*), authors to whom she was compared, Renault's novels were often cast as first-person narratives of real or invented figures from myth and history – a technique that efficiently drew modern readers into exotic ancient milieus. The best known and most commercially successful were *The Last of the Wine* (1956), which takes the form of a memoir by a young member of Socrates' circle, through whose eyes we witness the decline of Athens in the last part of the Peloponnesian War; *The King Must Die* (1958), a novelization of the early life of Theseus, the legendary Athenian king who defeated the Minotaur; and a trilogy of novels about Alexander the Great – *Fire from Heaven* (1969), *The Persian Boy* (1972), and *Funeral Games* (1981).

Renault, who was born in London in 1905 – she emigrated to South Africa after the Second World War – had published a number of crisply intelligent contemporary love stories between the late thirties and the early fifties; to her meticulously researched recreations of the past in the later, Greek-themed books she was able to bring the emotional insight and moral seriousness you expect from any good novelist. Many reviewers appreciated the way she reanimated both myth and history by means of ingenious psychological touches. (She once said that the Theseus book didn't gel until she had the idea of making the mythical overachiever diminutive in stature: he's a legendary hero, but also just a boy with something to prove.) Patrick O'Brian, the author of

Master and Commander, was an admirer; he dedicated the fourth Aubrey-Maturin book to her, with the inscription 'An owl to Athens' – the ancient Greek version of 'coals to Newcastle'. Academic classicists were also enthusiastic. One eminent Oxford don told an eager amateur that to get a sense of what ancient Greece was really like one had only to read Renault – 'Renault every time.' ('That really bucks me up,' she exclaimed, when this remark was reported to her during her final illness.) The combination of historical precision, literary texture, and epic sweep won Renault a large public, particularly in the United States; her books, which have been translated into some twenty languages, have sold millions of copies in English alone.

One of those copies was a thick Eagle Books paperback of *Fire from Heaven* that was stuffed into a bookcase in our downstairs playroom, next to the black leather recliner. I read it when I was twelve, and I was hooked. Alexander the Great was my first serious crush.

It was my father who put the book in my hands. A mathematician who worked for an aerospace corporation, he had been a Latin whiz in high school and sometimes enjoyed thinking of himself as a lapsed classicist. When he gave me the paperback, I looked at the cover and frowned. The illustration, of a blond young Greek holding a shield aloft, wasn't very convincing; I thought he looked a lot like the boy who lived across the street, who had once taken a bunch of us waterskiing for his birthday. My dad said, 'I think you should give this a try,' averting his eyes slightly, in the way he had. Forty years later, I wonder how much he'd already guessed, and just what he was trying to accomplish.

Fire from Heaven traces Alexander's childhood and youth, ending with his accession to the throne, at the age of twenty. I finished it in a couple of days. The next weekend, I went to the public library and checked out the sequel, *The Persian Boy*, which had just been published. It views Alexander's conquest of Persia and his nascent dream of forming a vast Eurasian empire from an unexpected angle: the book is narrated by a historical figure called Bagoas, a beautiful eunuch who had been the pleasure boy of the defeated Persian emperor Darius and who later became Alexander's lover, too. I read *The Persian Boy* in a day and a half. Then I reread both books. Then, after taking my dad's copy of *Fire from Heaven* upstairs and placing it inside the oak cabinet, I got my mother to take me to the B. Daltons bookstore in the Walt Whitman Mall, in Huntington, where, for a dollar ninety-five, I bought my own Bantam paperback of *The Persian Boy*. Its cover featured, in miniature, the haunting image that appeared on the hardback edition from the library: a Michelangelo drawing, in dusty-red chalk, of an epicene Oriental youth in three-quarter profile, wearing a headdress and earrings. Whenever someone mentions '1973', or 'junior high school', this small, delicate, reddish face is what I see in my mind's eye.

My fascination with these books had little to do with their canny evocations of Greek history, the persuasiveness of which I couldn't appreciate until years later. An important narrative thread in each novel is a story of awakening young love – homosexual love. In *Fire from Heaven*, Renault sympathetically imagines the awkward beginnings of the relationship between Alexander and Hephaistion, a Macedonian of high birth who, the evidence strongly suggests, was his lover. In *The Persian Boy*, Bagoas, sold into slavery at ten, already world-weary at sixteen, finds himself drawn to Alexander, who has suddenly become his master as well as the master of the known world. In both novels, arduously achieved seductions give the narratives a sexy charge: Renault makes Alexander the aloof object of the longings of the other, more highly sexed characters, Hephaistion and Bagoas, who must figure out how to seduce him.

Most seductive of all to me was the young characters' yearning to love and be loved totally. 'Say that you love me best,' Bagoas dreams in *The Persian Boy*; 'I love you ... You mean more to me than anything,' Hephaistion exclaims in *Fire from Heaven*; 'Do you love me best?' Alexander asks in the latter novel's opening scene. (These expressions of deep emotional need run like a refrain through Renault's contemporary novels as well.) As it happens, 'longing' – in Greek, *pothos* – has, since ancient times, been a key word in the Alexander narrative. In a history of Alexander's campaigns written by the second-century-AD historian Arrian, *pothos* recurs to describe the inchoate craving that drove Alexander – far more insistently than any mere lust for conquest or renown. Renault clearly felt the pull of all this longing, too: in addition to the three Alexander novels, she wrote a psychologically oriented biography, *The Nature of Alexander*.

Reading Renault's books, I felt a shock of recognition. The silent watching of other boys, the endless strategizing about how to get their attention, the fantasies of finding a boy to love, and be loved by, 'best': all this was agonizingly familiar. I knew something about *pothos*, and thought of the humiliating lengths to which it could drive me – the memorizing of certain boys' class schedules or bus routes, the covert shuffling of locker assignments. I was astonished, halfway through *Fire from Heaven*, to find that this kind of thing had always been happening. Until that moment, I had never seen my secret feelings reflected anywhere. Pop music meant nothing to me, since all the songs were about boys wanting girls or girls wanting boys; neither did the YA novels I'd read, for the same reason. Television was a desert. (*Will & Grace* was twenty-five years in the future.) Now, in a novel about people from another place and time, it was as if I had found a picture of myself.

There's a scene in *The Persian Boy* in which Bagoas realizes that he's in love with Alexander; in the slightly high style Renault developed as a vehicle to convey Bagoas' Oriental provenance, she describes this moment as (I now realize) a kind of internal coming out – a moment when, for the first time, a young person understands the nature of his own feelings:

> The living chick in the shell has known no other world. Through the wall comes a whiteness, but he does not know it is light. Yet he taps at the white wall, not knowing why. Lightning strikes his heart; the shell breaks open.

Reading *Fire from Heaven* and *The Persian Boy* was such a moment for me. Lightning had struck, the shell lay broken open. I had begun to understand what I was and what I wanted; and I knew that I wasn't alone.

'IT'S NOT WHO YOU ARE, IT'S WHAT YOU DO WITH IT'

Renault was herself a lesbian, the elder daughter of a doctor and a primly conventional housewife. It was not a happy home. Both the contemporary and the Greek novels feature unsettling depictions of bad marriages and, particularly, of nightmarishly passive-aggressive wives and mothers. Renault's mother had clearly hoped for a 'nice' girl instead of the unruly tomboy she got, and preferred Mary's younger sister. (Decades after I first encountered Renault's books, it occurred to me that all this could well be the source of the 'love me best' motif that recurs so often in her work.) In later life, the author made no bones about having wished she'd been born a boy. Her first-person narrators are always men.

Indeed, it's possible to see in her lifelong fascination with dashing male heroes – Alexander the Great above all – an unusually intense authorial projection. In a letter to a friend, Renault recalled admiring the head of a statue of the Macedonian conqueror, which had given her an 'almost physical sense of the presence of Alexander like a blazing sun below the horizon, not yet quenching the stars but already paling them … His face has haunted me for years.' David Sweetman, in his *Mary Renault: A Biography* (1993), referred to *Fire from Heaven* as 'a love letter to the boy hero'. It's no accident that her very first book, written when she was eight, was a cowboy novel. From the start, she seems to have been searching for an ideal boy protagonist, a fictional reflection of an inner identity. In all her work, boyishness is an unequivocally positive quality – even, or perhaps especially, in women.

Although Renault was entranced by the Greeks from an early age – by the time she finished high school, she had devoured all of Plato – at St Hugh's, a women's college at Oxford, she studied English. After taking her degree, she decided against teaching, one conventional route for unmarried, educated middle-class women, and instead trained as a nurse; her first three novels, published during the war years, were written during her off-hours from clinics and hospitals. In 1934, she met Julie Mullard, a vivacious young nurse who would be her life partner for nearly fifty years, until Renault's death. In a 1982 BBC documentary, the two come off as unpretentious and suspicious of self-dramatizing fuss.

The couple stayed in England during the war, but after Renault won the hundred-and-fifty-thousand-dollar MGM prize for *Return to Night*, a 1947 novel about a woman doctor in love with a handsome, troubled, much younger actor, she became financially independent. ('You're the best of all ... I love you. Better than anyone,' the doctor tells her lover in the novel's final pages.) They emigrated to South Africa almost on a whim, after reading travel advertisements following a particularly grim post-war winter. It was in Africa that Renault wrote the last of her contemporary novels. Soon after, she turned to the Greeks.

As she later told the story, the decision to start setting her novels in ancient Greece began with a question rooted in her early reading of Plato. During a pleasure cruise that she and Mullard took up the east coast of Africa, Renault recalled, she got to thinking about the Greek historian Xenophon – a stolid, less intellectually adventurous fellow-student of Plato's in Socrates' circle, who later became famous for the military exploits he recounted in his *Anabasis* – and began to wonder what the members of that circle might actually have been like, as people. The product of her inspiration was *The Last of the Wine*.

Toward the end of her life, Renault wrote that the novel was 'the best thing I had ever done'. It's not hard to see why she thought so. A shrewdly unsentimental historical portrait of Athens at the beginning of its moral and political decline, it is enlivened by a love story between two of Socrates' students and deepened by a surprisingly vivid recreation of Socrates' philosophical dialogues as, well, dialogue. There are rich and nuanced cameos of historical characters (not least, Socrates himself) and grand set pieces, all rendered with exacting fidelity to the original sources. Renault fans like to cite her stirring description of the great Athenian fleet's departure for its invasion of Sicily – a misguided campaign that ended in disaster.

And, perhaps better than any other of the Greek novels, *The Last of the Wine* demonstrates how Renault used subtle but telling touches to persuade you of the Greekness of her characters and settings. Classical Greek tends to be loaded with participles and relative clauses; Renault reproduced these tics. ('He, hearing that a youth called Philon, with whom he was in love, had been taken sick, went at once to him; meeting, I have been told, not only the slaves but the boy's own sister, running the other way.') She also used 'k' rather than the more usual Latin 'c' in her transliterations of proper names – Kleopatra, Sokrates – which gives her pages just the right, spiky Greek look. As a result of this minute attention to stylistic detail, the novels can give the impression of having been translated from some lost Greek original.

It's possible to see Renault's shift from the present to the past as motivated by something other than intellectual curiosity. Setting a novel in fifth-century-BC Athens allowed her to write about homosexuality as natural. In *The Last of the Wine*, the narrator muses on the abnormality of Xenophon's apparently exclusive heterosexuality: 'Sometimes indeed I asked myself whether he lacked the capacity for loving men at all; but I liked him too well to offend him by such a question.'

The hinge that connects her earlier works, love stories in which intelligent people – doctors, nurses, writers, actors – struggle with various emotional conundrums, and the later, historical fiction, in which the fact of love between men, at least, is no conundrum at all, is a novel called *The Charioteer*. Published in 1953, it is set, despite its classical-sounding title, during the Second World War, and wrestles with the issue of 'Greek love'. Older gay men can recall that, in the fifties and sixties, to walk into a bar with a copy of this book was a way of signalling that you were gay. Today, the book is referred to as a 'gay classic'.

I finished reading *The Charioteer* for the first time on 28 December 1974, when I was fourteen. I know the date because I recorded it in my diary. The man who placed it in my hands was a music teacher, around my parents' age, whom we knew to be gay: he had a 'roommate' with whom he shared a house in a nearby suburb. My mother and father were open-minded, and they saw nothing wrong in letting their four sons hang out with this civilized man, who took us to concerts and restaurants, and who let me sing with the church choir he directed.

What my parents didn't know was that the music teacher sometimes left copies of *Playgirl* lying around when I visited his house. I was both curious and embarrassed. Curious because of course I wanted to look at pictures of naked men, having spent hours pretending to be interested in the *Playboy* centrefolds the kids on my block would steal out of a neighbour's garage; and embarrassed because I perceived that it wasn't appropriate for this middle-aged man to be making porn available to a fourteen-year-old. Curiosity prevailed. Two years had passed since I'd read the Alexander books – paperback copies of which were now stacked, along with Renault's other books, into a neat little ziggurat in my bedroom cabinet – and there were things I wondered about, specific things, that weren't described in the Mary Renault books. I would wait for my teacher to go into another room, to start dinner or put on a recording of Thomas Tallis, and would snatch the magazine up and look at the photographs, which both titil-lated and repelled me. It was exciting to see the nude male bodies, however patently silly the cowboy boots or policeman hats might be; but it was hard to connect those images to the ideas of love that I had taken away from *Fire from Heaven* and *The Persian Boy*.

I remember the day that this teacher handed me the jacketless hardback of *The Charioteer*, with its dark-grey buckram boards. We were downstairs in his den, and he'd been playing me a rare LP of ancient Greek music. I was feeling very grown-up and was trying to impress him with my passion for all things Greek – a subject that led me, soon enough, to Renault's novels. He said, 'If you like Mary Renault, there's another one I think you'll be interested in.' He motioned me to follow him upstairs to his bedroom. He searched in a bookcase for a moment until he found what he was looking for. I took it home and started reading it. At first, the Second World War setting disappointed me; I had no interest in modern history.

The title of *The Charioteer* alludes to Renault's beloved Plato. In the dialogue called 'Phaedrus', the soul is likened to a charioteer who must reconcile two horses, one white and well behaved (the rational and moral impulses), the other scruffy and ill-bred (the passions). Renault's book recasts the Platonic conflict as a human drama. Laurie Odell, a wounded young soldier who is recovering at a rural hospital – his given name is Laurence, but Renault pointedly used ambiguous names and nicknames whenever she could – finds himself torn between a secret love for an idealistic Quaker youth, Andrew (who seems drawn to Laurie in an innocent, nonsexual way), and a more complex, physical relationship with a slightly older naval officer, Ralph. The plot pushes Laurie toward a culminating choice between the two men. That choice implies another: whether to remain a loner or to enjoy the solidarity afforded by the local gay set, whose members Renault paints in campy colours: they're named Bunny and Binky and Bim, and wear Cartier bracelets. Laurie, by contrast, is a kind of holy fool: 'His loneliness had preserved in him a good deal of inadvertent innocence; there was much of life for which he had no formula.'

I, too, was an innocent. By a kind of literary osmosis that is possible only when you're young, I absorbed without question Renault's idealization of severe, undemonstrative men; I wasn't yet able to recognize, in the author's clichés of gay effeminacy, certain unexamined prejudices of her own. Nor did it occur to me to question a central element of the text: the rather dated assumption that it would be better for Andrew never to be made aware of his sexuality. (It 'would scatter his whole capital of belief in himself,' Laurie thinks. 'He must never know.')

Now, of course, I can read the book as it ought to be read, as a coming-of-age story: Laurie abandons the inchoate but potent ideals of adolescence, symbolized by the pure and curiously sexless Andrew, in favour of an adult relationship, one that is physical as well as emotional, with complicated and compromised Ralph, who, like Laurie, bears physical as well as emotional scars. But, because I was so young when I read the novel for the first time, I saw the arc from the ideal to the real, from youth to maturity, as a tragic one. To me, Andrew and Ralph were figures in a vast allegorical conflict. Under the white banner of Andrew there was Renault, and true love, and the ancient Greeks, with their lofty rhetoric and marmoreal beauty; under the black banner of Ralph there was *Playgirl*, and sex, and thoughts about naked men – the messy and confusing present.

Although there was much of life for which I had no 'formula', either, I thought I knew enough to decide that, if being gay meant marching under the black banner – aligning myself with my music teacher, or the few characters you saw on TV who, you somehow knew, were gay: the limp-wrists and the effete, the spineless Dr Smith on *Lost in Space* and the queeny Paul Lynde character on *Bewitched* – then it would be better to remain alone.

Unlike Renault's Greek novels, which portrayed desire beneath the scrim of a historical setting, *The Charioteer*, whose characters used words like 'queer', allowed for no evasions. 'I know what I am,' I wrote in my diary the day I finished reading it for the first time. By then, I was obsessively in love with a yellow-haired swimmer who put up with my dogged stalking for three years before he turned around one day early in our senior year and, planting himself in front of his locker, which I had gone to some lengths to ensure was next to mine, told me quite calmly that he didn't want to talk to me anymore, and didn't. But I had never thought of my feelings for him as 'gay' or 'queer': it simply was how I felt. 'I know what I am,' I wrote. 'Now I must think what to do with it.'

'What you are … what to do with it' is a paraphrase of a line from *The Charioteer*. Someone utters it during a climactic scene at a birthday party that's being given for a young gay doctor. At the party, the characters start arguing about what would now be called identity politics: about whether the thing that sets you apart ought, in some fundamental way, to define you. As lonely as he is, Laurie finds himself resisting the temptation of joining this group – of 'making a career' of his 'limitations', as he puts it to himself. It's in response to this debate about identity that Ralph articulates the liberating formula: 'It's not what one is, it's what one does with it.'

Renault grew up in an era in which it was difficult to think of homosexuality as anything but a limitation; to her credit, she was independent-minded enough to try to resist that prejudice. Later in the book, the doctor rejects the premises that make blackmail possible:

> I don't admit that I'm a social menace … I'm not
> prepared to accept a standard which puts the whole of
> my emotional life on the plane of immorality. I've never
> involved a normal person or a minor or anyone who
> wasn't in a position to exercise free choice … Criminals
> are blackmailed. I'm not a criminal. I'm prepared to go
> to some degree of trouble, if necessary, to make that
> point.

Renault later wrote that this passage of dialogue 'gave the start-ing-point to my first historical novel' – *The Last of the Wine*, in other words, the novel in which homosexuality wasn't considered a limitation.

When I was fourteen, the characterization of homosexuality as a 'limitation' seemed reasonable enough. How could it not be a handicap, when it left you with freakish feelings that no one else you knew seemed to share, apart from middle-aged men who left dirty magazines around for you to pick up, feelings that you knew, more instinctually than consciously, you had to hide? What I did with it, after a few anxious months of trying and failing to picture the vast, nearly featureless landscape of the future, one in which the only road sign now, brand-new, freshly painted, bore the word 'queer', was to try to be good – to try to be like Laurie Odell. 'I must make some good resolutions for the new year,' I had written in my diary. 'I will try to do better next year.'

The next year, I turned fifteen, and still didn't really know what 'better' might mean. Finally, I decided to write to Mary Renault and ask her.

'GETTING THE SOIL IN YOUR GARDEN RIGHT'

In my first letter to Renault, I poured out my story – ancient Greece, discovering her books, discovering that I was gay through her books. In her reply, which arrived in mid-April, just after my sixteenth birthday, she deftly deflected my adolescent effusions while putting to rest my anxieties about form letters:

> Are there really writers who do that? I knew film stars
> do. You can't blame them, really; apart from the fact
> that about half the people who write to them must
> be morons who think they really are Cleopatra or

whoever, they get such thousands that if they attempted
answering themselves they'd never get to the set.

Writers, though, write to communicate; and when
someone to whom one has got through takes the
trouble to write and tell one so, it would be pretty
ungrateful to respond with something off a duplicator.
I think so, anyway.

This, as she had intended, pleased me. And yet of my fervent
confessions there was only the briefest acknowledgment, which
segued immediately and harmlessly into a charming compliment
and a gentle dismissal:

I am truly glad the books have meant all this to you;
especially as you write very good English yourself ...
Greek history, or something, has certainly given you a
clean and simple style. I wish you the very best of luck
with your work, and a happy fulfilled career.

I read and reread the letter. I was a gay adolescent; I was accustomed to overinterpreting. Just as I wasn't what I pretended to be,
so everyone and everything else, I thought, concealed secret
meanings, communicated in hidden codes. (I had to think a
moment before I realized that 'a duplicator' was a copying
machine.) But there was nothing else, apart from the scrawled
signature and, below it, printed instructions about how to fold
the aerogram. 'Verseël Eers Die Twee Syklappe, Dan Hierdie Een
– Seal The Two Side Flaps First, Then This One.'

'Meant all this to you'? Maybe I hadn't been clear enough. I sat
down and started another letter.

This time, I enclosed a few pages of one of the short stories I
had secretly written. Like nearly everything I wrote then, it was

about an intense friendship between two fourteen-year-old boys, one of whom was, inevitably, serious and dark-haired and creative, while the other was, just as inevitably, carefree and blond and athletic. This story, which was more ambitious than the others – it had a prologue set in a kind of classical limbo – was, like the others, a slavish pastiche of Renault: her diction, with its faint aura of pre-war England ('Phaedo, whatever do you want?'), her settings ('Under the ancient olive tree, the two young men were talking'), her characters ('Speaking of Sokrates, have you seen him lately?'), even her punctuation. Renault, according to her biographer, had a particular fondness for the semicolon. I still remember the thrill I felt when one of my college professors wrote, in the margin of an undergraduate essay, 'You have semicolonitis!'

I was convinced that this lofty effort would persuade her that I would be a worthy correspondent. Feeling very much the author, I was emboldened to ask her whether she, too, had a kind of compulsion to write – although I secretly doubted whether hers had the same source as mine. For me, writing was a kind of sympathetic magic, a way of conjuring the swimmer boy and keeping him close.

She wrote back within a couple of weeks, at the end of April. I know she must have read the story because of her tactful allusion to it:

> Your nice letter came this morning. Something tells
> me you are going to have a future as a writer. Keep
> at it; very few people get published at 16 or even 20,
> but don't worry … There is only one way to learn to
> write and that is by reading. Don't read for duty, try
> all the good stuff though, sample it, then devour what
> stimulates and enriches you. This will seep in to your

own work, which may be derivative at first but this
does not matter. Your own style will develop later.

Now that I am a writer who has received mail from young readers, I appreciate the patience and gentleness of this paragraph. I
doubt that, at the time, I registered the implications of 'which
may be derivative'; it was enough that she thought I had a future
as a writer. This show of confidence dulled the disappointing
force of her equally graceful but firm leave-taking:

> Yes, you are right, I do have a compulsion to write
> and am very frustrated and unhappy if I am kept from
> doing it … And this is the reason I can't go on writing
> to you. Not that it is too much trouble; writing a book
> is very much more trouble; but if I wrote more than
> one thank-you letter to all the people who are kind
> enough to write to me, I would never write another
> novel again. Or I would have to take to those 'form
> letters' – rather than which I wouldn't answer at all.
>   So this really is goodbye – but the very best of luck
> to you all the same.

This time, I felt no great disappointment. Over the next months,
as my stalking of the blond swimmer became more abject, as
more and more meals ended with me bursting into tears and
locking myself in my room as my parents clumped helplessly
down the hallway after me, the sentence 'Something tells me you
are going to have a future as a writer' served as a charm. I knew I
had no right to expect anything else from her.

Then, that December, she sent me a Christmas card.

I will never know why she changed her mind and wrote again,
eight months after she said that she couldn't go on corresponding;

at the time, I was so excited by her overture that I didn't dare ask. But I can speculate now. When I read Sweetman's biography, ten years after Renault's death, I learned that the mid-1970s had been a particularly trying period for her. In the autumn of 1974, she fell and injured her leg, necessitating an irritatingly lengthy recovery. Soon afterward, Mullard, who was high-strung, suffered a minor breakdown and had to be briefly institutionalized. At just about the time that Renault and I exchanged our first letters, she had decided to put her affairs in order and make provisions for her estate. Perhaps she thought that a letter from an American teenager every now and then might provide some distraction, despite (or perhaps because of) the adolescent turmoil it contained.

Something else has occurred to me. Like all writers, Renault spent much of her time alone; a good many of her friends, as I also learned later, were gay men, often ballet dancers and actors and theatre people. What she did not have in her life, as far as I know, was children – or students. I wonder whether she wished for some. (In *The Charioteer*, Laurie is described as someone who 'usually got on with strong-minded old maids'; was that how she saw herself?) Shrewdly drawn scenes of apprenticeships, of actors or princes or poets learning their craft, figure in a number of the novels. In *The Last of the Wine*, Socrates, faced with an earnest, if pretentious, student, resorts to 'teasing him out of his pomposities' – as canny a characterization of what it's like to teach freshmen as any I know of.

Renault's special feeling for the relationship between a teacher and a student imbues the poignant finale of *The Mask of Apollo*, her 1966 novel about an Athenian actor who gets mixed up in Plato's disastrous scheme, in the 360s BC, to turn a corrupt Sicilian tyrant into a philosopher-king. Years after the fiasco, the actor meets the teenaged Alexander, already charismatic and alive with curiosity about the world, and realizes, wrenchingly, that this youth would have been the ideal student for Plato, now dead:

> All tragedies deal with fated meetings; how else could
> there be a play? Fate deals its stroke; sorrow is purged,
> or turned to rejoicing; there is death, or triumph; there
> has been a meeting, and a change. No one will ever
> make a tragedy – and that is as well, for one could not
> bear it – whose grief is that the principals never met.

I wonder whether something like this was in Mary Renault's mind that day in December when she decided to write back to me after all. Maybe she liked the thought of having a student – someone to tease out of his pomposities. Maybe, with all that grief around her just then, she thought she could at least avoid the grief that comes of never making contact.

We corresponded for the next eight years. I always addressed her as 'Miss Renault' or 'Mary Renault'; I still can't think of her as 'Mary'. She only ever addressed me as 'Daniel Mendelsohn' and, once I was in college, 'Mr Mendelsohn'. During that time, I finished high school, went to college, graduated, got my first job. She published her biography of Alexander and two more novels. We didn't write often – a few exchanges a year – but knowing that she was out there, interested in my progress, was like a secret talisman.

During the first few years, when I was still in high school, I tried not to be too familiar or too earnest – the mistake that I had made in my first couple of letters. (Recalling a lesbian novel she disliked, Renault wrote of its 'impermissible allowance of self-pity' and 'earnest humourlessness'.) Instead, I would tell her about what I was reading, some of which, of course, was chosen with an eye to pleasing her. 'I am delighted you've been reading the Phaedrus,' she wrote to me early in 1978, when I was a senior in high school. 'It's good furniture for any mind.' Sometimes she would make suggestions. 'Have you ever tried Malory's *Morte D'Arthur*? It is very beautiful. On no account read a version pulped down into modern English, it ruins the flavour.' A year earlier, I and the other eleventh graders had been made to memorize the opening lines of *The Canterbury Tales* in the original Middle English, an exercise that we both feared and derided; reading her letter, I began to wonder, as I hadn't done before, what it might mean for language to have 'flavour'.

Occasionally there would be an item about her or one of her books in the news; it gave me a thrilling sense of privilege to be able to write to the author herself to learn more. When I was a junior in high school, the teacher who had given me *The Charioteer* showed me an issue of a magazine called *After Dark*, which I only later realized was a gay magazine. It featured an ambitious photo spread about the upcoming movie adaptation of *The Persian Boy*, and referred to young dancers and actors who were hoping to be cast as Bagoas. Excited, I wrote to Renault asking for details. 'I certainly wish they had not raised the hopes of so many actors in this way,' she replied, explaining that the movie rights hadn't even been sold yet, 'and I wish too that so many actors didn't imagine that the book author has any say in the casting! They could as fruitfully approach the office cleaner.' (Sweetman, in his biography, relates how a young actor had written to her, offering to have 'the operation' if it meant getting the part. 'That,' she wrote back to him, 'would be gelding the lily.')

I continued to send her the stories I was writing. As I reached the end of high school, these were getting darker: the beginning of my senior year, in the fall of 1977, had been scarred by the confrontation with the blond swimmer. Later that day, I ran out of my house and walked around the blandly identical neighbourhoods for hours. At one point, I climbed to the top of an overpass and looked down – not serious, but serious enough. Then I burst out laughing, amused by my own theatrics. It was a beautiful autumn afternoon, and in a year I'd be in college, where I'd be able to study Greek and Latin and find new, like-minded friends; where, I secretly hoped, there might be a Laurie Odell for me. I wrote about this incident to Mary Renault, aware, as I did so, of wanting her to perceive that I was learning from her – that I wasn't giving in to adolescent foolishness. I was, after all, someone who had a future as a writer.

She read these later stories, too. By this point, one (or sometimes both) of the two inseparable friends who were always at the centre of my fiction, the brunet and the blond, the writer and the athlete, would die of a rare disease, or meet with a terrible accident. As she had done before, and would do again, Mary Renault ignored the impermissible self-pity and the earnest humourlessness, and simply encouraged me:

> Just carry on enjoying yourself with writing. Love what you are doing and do it as well as you can, and the tree will grow. Nobody ever did their best work at 17 except people who died at 18! You are now just getting the soil in your garden right – except that unlike a garden, even at this stage your work is producing flowers, very likely not yet ready for the flower-show, but giving you a lot of joy.

The stories did not, in fact, give me much joy. But knowing that she had read them did.

'WAS IT SOMEONE YOU KNEW?'

I wrote to Renault less frequently once I went off to the University of Virginia. (The swimmer had grown up in Virginia; I thought there might be someone else like him there.) I started learning Greek during my first semester, and found a kind of happiness in grammar, which insisted on a level of precision not available in English: the nouns, often familiar-looking (*anthrōpos*, *historia*, *klimax*), each one of which has five different forms, depending on how it's used in a sentence; the vast spiderweb of the verb system. For me, as for many beginning classics students, learning Greek and Latin unlocked the secrets of my own language. With delight I learned that 'ephebe' consists of *epi*, 'upon', and *hēbē*, 'youth': an ephebe is a male at the acme of his youth. And you learn, too, to sniff out a fake. The word 'homosexual', for instance, is a solecism, a hybrid of Greek (*homos*, 'alike') and Latin (*sexualis*, 'sexual'). A *homo*-word with a purer pedigree, as I learned when I started reading Homer in Greek, was *homophrosyne*, 'like-mindedness', which is the word Odysseus uses, in the *Odyssey*, to describe the ideal union of two spouses – the kind of union that he's trying to return home to.

My own quest for *homophrosyne* was proving unsuccessful. No Laurie Odell had materialized. How did you make contact? There was, I knew, a gay student union that met regularly in one of the many red-brick-and-white-stucco neoclassical buildings on campus, undistinguished knockoffs of Jeffersonian originals. But I was dismayed to see that the building was right in the middle of the campus; I was terrified that someone I knew would see me going in. So I would walk past the posters for the meetings, my eyes briefly alighting, as tentative as a fly on a peach, on the word 'gay', as I made my way each morning to Greek class, during my first year, or, the next year, to Greek 201 ('Plato's *Apology*'), or, the year after, to the course in which, for the first time, I read Sophocles in Greek. The text, I remember, was *Philoctetes*, a play about a crippled hero who has been abandoned on a desert island for so long that it's no longer clear whether he can rejoin society.

Beneath my fear of being found out, a larger anxiety lurked. I was starting to worry that, even if I were to 'make contact', the ideal I'd found in *The Charioteer* didn't exist. There was a boy in one of my English classes, a tall, dark-haired prep with a beaked nose and a Tidewater accent, who, I now realize, was trying to make contact with *me*. He'd stop me after lectures and ask if he could borrow my notes; once, after mentioning that he was in one of the choral groups, he called to invite me to come to his dorm room to listen to his new LP of Purcell's *Come Ye Sons of Art*. But I never called him back. After a while, he started asking some other kid for notes at the end of lectures.

I studied hard and absorbed my grammars and didn't confide any of this to Mary Renault. She had brought me to the Greeks, and had shown me what I was, and it was somehow shaming to let on that I was having a hard time finding anyone like the characters in her novels. Somewhere in *The Persian Boy*, when the young Bagoas is being schooled at Susa in the arts of the courtesan, the kindly master who is preparing him for service to the King reminds him of a crucial rule of life at court: 'Never be importunate, never, never.' I was no longer sixteen, and I was determined never to importune her.

She must have noticed, at any rate, that I was no longer enclosing short stories with my letters. That's because I wasn't writing anymore. How silly those stories had been! I was twenty-one; I was going to be a scholar, not a writer. I was comforted by the incantatory rhythms of grammatical paradigms; by syntax, which was soothingly indifferent to emotion. During my senior year, *Funeral Games* was published. I went to the local bookstore every day to see if it had come in yet and, when it did, bought it and read it right away. The novel begins as Alexander is dying and proceeds to describe in grimly unsentimental detail the story of the internecine power struggles that resulted from his premature death. I was struck by the starkness of the narrative. Gone were the exalted adolescent yearnings of *Fire from Heaven*, gone the plush erotic Orientalisms of *The Persian Boy*. It was as if all feeling had been stripped away. I read it with a kind of sour enjoyment; it matched my mood. I wrote her to tell her how much I'd liked it. 'Your letter gave me very great pleasure,' she began her reply:

> Besides its generous appreciation of what the book is about, this is actually the first letter about it from an ordinary reader – meaning of course one who had no professional or personal reason to read the book. I am so glad that you liked it.

I knew what she meant, but I was a little hurt. I, at any rate, thought that I had a 'personal' reason to read it.

My letters to Renault were even less frequent after I graduated from college. I was too embarrassed. For one thing, I had decided not to go on to do a graduate degree in classics, which she had once urged me to do, on the ground that it was always good to have 'solid' knowledge of a subject, even if one wanted to be a writer rather than an academic. I wrote that I was forgoing graduate school because I 'hoped to gather knowledge of the world' – probably because I had read somewhere that she had become a nurse in order to gain real-life experience to write about.

I moved to New York City and found a job as an assistant to a small-time opera impresario whose obscene tirades against disloyal conductors and greedy sopranos would seep, like his cigar smoke, beneath the smoked-glass door of his inner office in the tiny 'suite' he rented, in the Steinway Building, on West Fifty-seventh Street, into the area where I was stationed. Sitting at my desk while he shrieked into the phone, I was too timid even to quit. But in my letters to Renault I swaggered and lied and pretended to be using my classical learning to gain insight into the real world. In the spring of 1983, I wrote her a letter that I ostentatiously typed on our company stationery (DANIEL MENDELSOHN, ASSOCIATE): 'I've found that reading Plato while one isn't actually studying intensively gives one an entirely new perspective – like being a Christian on weekdays.' (That last phrase is an almost verbatim citation from *The Charioteer*.) I went on grandiosely, 'After all, it wasn't meant to be read and discussed at cocktail parties, but lived, in a way; or so I think.'

The fact is that I wasn't spending much time on Plato. Mostly, I was going out to bars: Boy Bar, down on St Marks Place, where young men, self-consciously 'over' the disco aesthetic just then, lounged in khaki shorts and Topsiders and played pool at a table under a giant stuffed fish; the Pyramid, where you'd go afterward, once your standards had started to erode; the Works, on the Upper West Side, with its aloof actor-waiters in their too-carefully pressed polo shirts, lined up neatly against the black walls like empty bottles; bars that didn't last long enough for me to remember their names, while I tried, as I continued to put it to myself, to 'make contact'.

Sex rarely appears in Renault's books. It's either omitted altogether or suggested with such elegant circumlocution that, when I first read them, I sometimes didn't realize that certain passages were sex scenes. This was partly because of the author's own idealized exaltation of platonic love, and partly for reasons that she identified as writerly ones. 'If characters have come to life,' she once wrote, 'one should know how they will make love; if not it doesn't matter. Inch-by-inch physical descriptions are the ketchup of the literary cuisine, only required by the insipid dish or by the diner without a palate.' As I reread her books in high school, I looked in vain for signs of what lovemaking might actually be like; what (for instance) 'a trick I learned at Susa' (as Bagoas recalls of an attempt to liven things up in bed with the Persian emperor) might be, or what 'the sufficient evidence of his senses' (the hint that Laurie and Ralph have finally slept together, in *The Charioteer*) might allude to. But in college I had finally, if fleetingly, discovered sex, and in New York it was everywhere, if you wanted it. It seemed perfectly reasonable to have sex if you couldn't find love. Occasionally, I'd bring someone home, or go to his place, and often it would be pleasurable and sometimes it would be someone I liked. But always in the back of my mind was a certain image of what I wanted, and since nobody I met quite matched it, I held back. I had come to feel that getting involved with real people was, somehow, a betrayal.

Sometimes I comforted myself with this thought: hadn't Laurie Odell also been a loner? The first summer I lived in New York, a friend told me about a gay therapist who 'did group' on the East Side, and suggested that I join; it was a great place to meet nice guys, he said. I went for about five sessions. Some of the men were in relationships with each other: one couple consisted of a tall, extraordinarily handsome young man of about my age and his 'lover', a short, quite ugly man in his forties with a gigantic nose. I thought it surprising that they would be together. Never having had a lover, and embarrassed by my lack of experience and, even more, by the secret ideal that was keeping me from experience, I rarely said anything during the sessions. Finally, one day, the others turned to me all at once and asked me to talk about myself. At some point, inevitably, I mentioned the Mary Renault books and what their vision of love meant to me. 'Oh, *Mary*,' the big-nosed lover of the beautiful ephebe said, and only after a moment did I realize that he was not referring to the author but addressing me, 'join the *real* world!' I never went back to 'group'. I recorded this incident in my journal. The entry ends with the sentence 'I ought to write Mary Renault soon.' But I didn't.

In April, 1983, I wrote my last letter to her. In it, I lied and concealed and sprinkled the pages with allusions to Plato. I enclosed, as I sometimes liked to do, a cartoon from this magazine having to do with the ancient world. In it, a corpulent king is getting the lowdown from his vizier on a visiting delegation: 'The Athenians are here, Sire, with an offer to back us with ships, money, arms, and men – and, of course, their usual lectures about democracy.' In early May, she replied. She began by thanking me for the *New Yorker* cartoon. ('I don't know if it would have amused Thukydides; he didn't amuse easily, he had seen it all; but I bet it would have given a good laugh to Philip of Macedon, when that arch democrat Demosthenes made a pact with the Great King of Persia.') Then she went on to tease me. 'I'm glad you're enjoying Plato. Of course he meant his ideas to be lived ... But he certainly felt happy at having them discussed at drinking parties. Look at the Symposium!' I was too mortified to reply. I thought she must be appalled by me.

That summer, I decided that I wasn't cut out for 'the real world', and began to make plans to apply to graduate school in classics. Early in September of 1983, I walked out of the Steinway Building just as a handsome man, blond and square-jawed, pedalled past on a bike; he grinned and rang his little bell at me. We dated for a while, but, as before, I wasn't quite sure what to *do*, now that I had a 'relationship'. Later that month, I wrote in my journal, worrying that, whereas the characters in books seemed to have so much forward momentum, I didn't. I still wasn't sure how you got to be the author of your own life. The journal ends there. The only additional item is a clipping from the *Times*, dated Wednesday, 14 December 1983.

I had been thinking about sending Renault a Christmas card but hadn't got around to doing it. Then, that Wednesday morning, I walked into the Steinway Building, went through the lobby past the display of grand pianos, got into the elevator, scanned the front page of the *Times*, and suddenly said, loudly, 'Oh, *no!*' I slumped against the back of the elevator and started crying. The only other person in the elevator was old Mr Koretz, the Holocaust survivor who rented the office next to ours.

'What happened?' he asked, stooping a little and bringing his large face close to mine, his eyes gigantically magnified by his glasses. He was tall, often wore a raincoat, and his slightly phlegmy Middle European consonants were comforting. 'Did someone die?'

I shoved the *Times* in his direction and pointed. Down below the fold, next to the contents, under the heading 'Inside', was the item that had caught my eye: 'Mary Renault Dies. The historical novelist Mary Renault, who based many of her best-selling books on the legends of ancient Greece, died in Cape Town. Page B5.'

Mr Koretz gave me a noncommittal look. 'It was someone you knew?'

'Yes.' I nodded; then I shook my head. 'No.' He gave me a look. 'It's hard to explain,' I said.

After work, I hurried home to write a condolence letter to a person whose existence I couldn't know of until I turned to page B5 and saw there, at last, the discreet proof of a suspicion I had long entertained but never dared ask about ('the writer's companion of the last 50 years, Julie Mullard'). 'Dear Miss Mullard,' I began; and then, not for the first time, poured out my heart to a stranger in South Africa.

A month later, a card arrived. On the front, the words 'IN MEMORIAM MARY RENAULT 1905–1983' were printed in black. To my surprise, the handwritten note inside suggested that this companion knew who I was. ('She was never aware of any generation gap. People were people to her.') Had Mary Renault discussed me with her companion? What else had they talked about? At that moment, I wasn't so much afraid that my confidences had been shared as I was startled to realize that Renault had existed for other people: that she wasn't only 'Mary Renault', who wrote novels and sometimes wrote to me, but was also 'Mary', which was how Mullard kept referring to her, a woman who might have casually discussed this and that with her companion – for instance, the letters she had been receiving over the past decade from a young American – the way my parents discussed this and that: work, *New Yorker* cartoons, things that had come in the mail.

I put Mullard's card in a large manila envelope that, years earlier, my mother had provided for this correspondence, labelling it, as she liked to do when she organized my things, with my initials, in blue Magic Marker. ('Mary Renault: DA.') I'm pretty sure that, as I did so, I told myself that this was the last letter I'd ever be receiving from Camps Bay, Cape Town, South Africa.

For the next twenty-five years, this was true. Then, one morning in December, 2008, the letters started coming again.

'THE AMERICAN BOY'

It was because of a review of a book of mine, a collection that contained an essay I'd written about Oliver Stone's film *Alexander*. I had ended the piece by mentioning how Renault's Alexander novels had inspired me to become a classicist and, eventually, a writer. The reviewer mentioned the Renault connection. Three weeks later, a handwritten letter with colourful South African stamps was forwarded to me. 'Dear Daniel Mendelsohn,' it began, and went on:

> GW Bowersock's NYRB review of your *How Beautiful* … reveals that the Daniel Mendelsohn of whom I am an avid reader is no other than 'the American boy' of whom Mary Renault used to speak with enjoyment many years ago!

My correspondent identified herself as Nancy Gordon. The handwriting was firm and clear, although she was quite elderly. ('I am 87. Old. Old. Old.') She told me that her late husband, Gerald, a lawyer and writer, had been a member of PEN South Africa when Mary was president, and that the two couples – Nancy and Gerald and Mary and Julie – had spent a good deal of time together. Nancy was the sole survivor of the little group. 'Mary, Julie and Gerald are all gone, but I feel somehow called,' she wrote, 'as humble messenger from Mary, to salute you. She would have been so chuffed!' At the end of the letter were her signature and e-mail address.

Then, in a P.S., she asked, 'Do you still feel for Mary?'

It was a complicated question. Of course I felt for 'Mary'. In every sense, she has accompanied me through my life. The ziggurat of books has been disassembled and reconstituted in various apartments and graduate-student lodgings over the years, but it is still there. The Eagle Books *Fire from Heaven* and the Bantam *Persian Boy* are now so fragile, the pages so brown and brittle with age, the covers so mummified in Scotch tape that long ago lost its adhesive, that you can't really read them. They're sitting on a shelf in my bedroom, as wizened and unrecognizable as relics.

And yet, as the years passed, I wondered whether I would have been recognizable to her. When Sweetman's biography of Renault came out, I read it right away; in one passage he writes about Renault's distaste for 'the worst aspects of the [gay] sub-culture … the constant search for sexual gratification without affection, the impermanence of most relationships'. Well. I'd never found a Laurie; although I'd been with some good men, the one-night stands vastly outnumbered the affectionate encounters and long-term relationships. In graduate school, I had been a leader of the Gay Alliance and been involved in a good deal of campus activism. I debated, as I did so, whether this constituted 'making a career of one's limitations', and decided that it didn't.

So yes: I still felt for Mary. But what had she felt for *me*? I knew, of course, that she had read my letters carefully – and not only because of her thoughtful replies to them. In 1978, when I was in my first year at Virginia, her penultimate novel, *The Praise Singer*, about the great lyric poet Simonides, was published. On page 44 there's a scene in which Simonides, who was famously ugly, recalls how, as a youth, he had resolved to kill himself: having climbed to the parapet of a temple, he looks up at the bright sky and realizes he's being foolish. In real life, he went on to have a happy and fulfilled career. She had indeed paid attention.

But had there been anything else? Until I got Nancy's letter, I thought I would never know. This is why I said 'yes' when, after a year of writing to Nancy – a correspondence that has grown far larger, by now, than the one I shared with Renault – she invited me to come to Cape Town, to see Delos, the bungalow down by Camps Bay, the beach where Renault and Mullard had lived, where Renault had received my letters and written hers to me, and to meet some of Renault's friends, who had also wondered what had become of 'the American boy'.

*

We spent four days in Cape Town. 'We', because I took my father: I owed him this. We stayed in a hotel overlooking Camps Bay. It was odd, as we drove there from the airport, to see the words Camps Bay on road signs. I'd been writing the name for years, and had never thought of it as a real place.

The climax of our visit was a dinner party at which Nancy Gordon gathered a few of Mary Renault's old friends. Nancy is small and vivid; she greeted me and my father wearing a floor-length, brightly patterned cotton dress, with horn and wooden bangles going up both arms. In the distance, we could see Table Mountain's strange flat top, the mist pouring over it like dry ice off of a stage. Before the others arrived, she pointed to a chair in the corner of her living room: 'Mary used to like to sit in that chair. She'd sometimes come over to our place for a drink looking out at the beach and I remember she would suddenly get up and say, "I must go write to my American boy."'

My American boy. When we had checked into our hotel, we found an envelope from Nancy containing a few handwritten sheets labelled 'Remembering Her'. One of the memories she'd jotted down was of the family who lived in the bungalow next to Renault's, 'with lots of kids, all very blond'. The boys, Nancy wrote, had all been excellent surfers, and Mary had loved watching them. Now, as we stood there in Nancy's living room next to the chair, looking out the large plate-glass windows at the surf where the neighbour boys had played, I thought: Mary Renault had turned away from the blond boys to write to me.

The other friends arrived. To each man or couple, Nancy would exclaim that I was 'the American boy' to whom Mary used to write, all those years ago. Over dinner, they all traded what were, clearly, favourite anecdotes. There were stories about Mary and her love of sports cars, stories about how Mary had found out that her gardener was growing marijuana and spent the night flushing it down the toilet, the story of how Mary and Julie insisted that the fig leaf on a bronze statue of Mercury they'd bought be replaced by an anatomically correct male member. 'As nurses,' Renault had told the workman, 'we *certainly* know what penises look like.' At one point, I mentioned that she had made me read Malory's *Le Morte D'Arthur*, and everyone laughed. 'She made *everyone* read Malory,' someone cried out. 'All of us had to!'

I sat and listened, waiting to hear something that would give me a clue to what she'd have felt about me and my writing. What would she have made of my first book, with its matter-of-fact descriptions of the way that I and so many of the gay men I know have lived – the endless talk of wanting boyfriends, of finding a 'real' relationship, and the late nights spent hooking up online? At some point, I asked Owen Murray – a former ballet dancer to whom Renault, he told me with a sly grin, had once said, 'I wish I'd been born with your body and face' – whether she knew about what really went on between men. I had visited the house he shares with his partner, which is filled with small mementos of Renault: Venetian glass paperweights that had sat on her desk and windowsill, the statue with its add-on penis. Taped to the refrigerator were photographs of Murray, shirtless, still muscular, smiling broadly, at gay parades, on gay cruises, at gay clubs; I figured that he would know what I meant when I said 'what really went on between men'. But it was hard for me to fathom his response. 'Mary wanted her men friends to live up to the Greek ideal,' he said. I was a classicist, and I knew that the ideal of 'Greek love' was itself a fantasy of Victorian 'inverts' who, as Renault had done, projected their *pothos* for an accepting society onto the distant past. The 'Greek ideal': what could this mean in real life? When I pressed Murray on this point, he said, 'She liked her friends to be coupled.' I shut up and listened to the stories.

Toward the end of the evening, the conversation turned to the many correspondents Renault had had. 'People used to write her *all* the time,' Owen said. 'Married men who were secretly gay, closeted men – there were *thousands* of letters when she died.' Someone else mentioned a prominent American politician who had come out to Renault in a letter, as I had done all those years ago; the others nodded knowingly, enjoying the expression on my face when I heard the famous name. I asked where all these letters were and what had become of them. Owen said that they had been destroyed after Mary's death, in part to protect the men who had written them. I thought of my onionskin pages, blackening and curling in the flames.

During the next couple of days, I visited some of the men who had been at Nancy's dinner. Each showed me some precious relic, and each offered me a keepsake. Owen gave me an address book, with alphabetical tabs, in which Renault had scrawled notes on various works in progress. (Under 'I' there's a page on which she wrote the word 'Ideas', and then a few lines with a sketch for a scene that ended up in *The Mask of Apollo*.) There were some copies of manuscripts ('Notes on Oedipus', 'Notes on the King Must Die'), given me by Roy Sargeant, a theatre director who was making plans to stage a play he'd commissioned, in which the shades of Renault and Alexander meet in the Underworld. Nancy gave me the dainty porcelain cup Renault drank from as she worked.

I took them all. Then my father and I flew home. At some point, I turned to him and shared a thought I often have as I sit awake on a long-haul flight: I think, I told him, about the bags of mail in the cargo hold below, what fervour they contain, what lives they might alter.

Eventually, my father fell asleep. I remained awake, replaying in my mind the events and conversations of the previous few days. In particular, I was thinking of something that Owen had said at Nancy's house. Although I had been enjoying the anecdotes and reminiscences, I was feeling unsatisfied; there was no way of knowing, finally, what Mary Renault would have thought of the man that the American boy had become. Then, toward the end of the evening – during the conversation about all the people who wrote letters to Mary Renault – Owen, who'd been watching me react to the surfeit of new personal details about her, spoke up. He talked slowly and loudly, as if addressing the others, but I knew that he was talking to me. 'Mary used to say to people who wrote wanting to know her that they should just read her *books*.' He paused and then gave me the tiniest smile. 'But she understood why they wrote her personal letters.'

At that moment, sitting at a table eight thousand miles from home, I saw that I'd come to South Africa chasing a chimera. I had already found the Mary Renault I needed, years earlier. I thought again of the yellowing books on my shelf; I thought, too, of the relationships that had never quite worked out, edged aside by a phantom out of a novel. She had shown me a picture of what I was, when I needed to see it, and had given me a myth that justified my fears and limitations. The writers we absorb when we're young bind us to them, sometimes lightly, sometimes with iron. In time, the bonds fall away, but if you look very closely you can sometimes make out the pale white groove of a faded scar, or the telltale chalky red of old rust.

That was last year. As I write this, I'm sitting in my office. Hanging on the wall opposite my desk is a signed photograph of Mary Renault. When Nancy Gordon first wrote to me, she mentioned that she had it, and that she had been wondering to whom she might give it. ('I can't give it to just anyone.') So she sent it to me, and I framed it. It's clearly from the same sitting as the one that appeared on Renault's dust jackets, the one in which she's crinkling her eyes against the sun. On the bottom she had scrawled, 'With love from Mary'; but there's nothing at the top, no dedication. I suppose it was for Nancy and Gerald. Then again, when you're a writer, you never know who will end up reading you, or how. I never pretend, when visitors ask me about it, that it was meant for me. But she is up there, watching me as I write.

– The New Yorker, 7 January 2013

Acknowledgements

Nearly all of the pieces collected here were originally written for *The New York Review of Books* and *The New Yorker*, and my first debt of thanks is due above all to my editors at those publications: the late Robert B. Silvers, a great mentor and beloved friend whose guidance and inspiration I sorely miss, and Leo Carey, on whose taste, humour, good sense, and erudition I rely so greatly. Tremendous gratitude is also due to two great friends who have been my unofficial editors for a long time now, and without whom I would be lost: Bob Gottlieb and Chip McGrath. I am also deeply grateful to my heroic editors at William Collins for getting this 'American boy' into English hands at last.

As for the dedicatees: in 1988 I had the great good luck to be part of a graduate seminar on Plato given by (as she was then called) Mary Margaret Mackenzie: with her, if not with the *Parmenides*, there was a great *coup de foudre*, and the ensuing thirty years of friendship with MM – and, in time, her family: Martin, Kate and Mark and the kids, Poppy, and the amazing Sarah, whom I still think about often – have been an adventure at once intellectually dazzling and dizzyingly fun. That the 'cousin in America' whom MM often spoke about should have turned out to be Patrick McGrath, my fellow New York writer and (along with the divine Maria) a wonderful friend, was clearly what my mother calls a *bashert*: a coincidence so right that it was just meant to be. My subsequent absorption into the extended McGrath clan has been a source of endless pleasure, and I am absolutely delighted to be able to dedicate this UK publication to them all.